A
PILGRIMAGE
to ETERNITY

A
PILGRIMAGE
to ETERNITY

* * *

FROM CANTERBURY TO ROME
IN SEARCH OF A FAITH

TIMOTHY EGAN

VIKING

VIKING
An imprint of Penguin Random House LLC
penguinrandomhouse.com

Maps by Jeffrey L. Ward

LIBRARY OF CONGRESS CATALOGING-IN-PUBLICATION DATA
Names: Egan, Timothy, author.
Title: A pilgrimage to eternity : from Canterbury to Rome in search of a faith / Timothy Egan.
Description: New York City : Viking, 2019. | Includes bibliographical references and index. |
Identifiers: LCCN 2019015599 (print) | LCCN 2019021460 (ebook) |
ISBN 9780735225237 (hardcover) | ISBN 9780735225244 (ebook)
Subjects: LCSH: Christian pilgrims and pilgrimages—Europe.
Classification: LCC BV5067 .E33 2019 (print) | LCC BV5067 (ebook) |
DDC 263/.04245632—dc23
LC record available at https://lccn.loc.gov/2019015599

Printed in the United States of America
1 3 5 7 9 10 8 6 4 2

BOOK DESIGN BY LUCIA BERNARD

To my siblings:
Maureen, Kevin, Mary Ann, Colleen, Kelly, Dan.
You can go home again.

CONTENTS

A
PILGRIMAGE
to ETERNITY

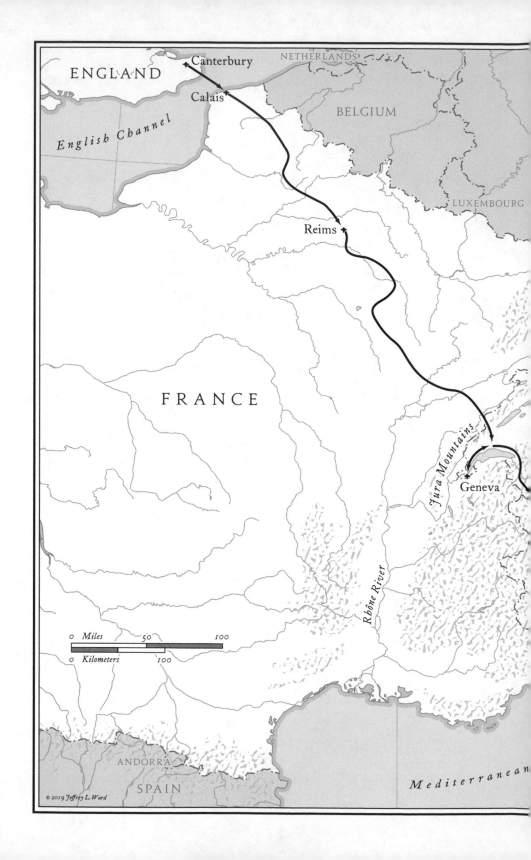

ENGLAND

Canterbury

Calais

English Channel

NETHERLANDS

BELGIUM

LUXEMBOURG

Reims

FRANCE

Jura Mountains

Geneva

Rhône River

Miles
0   50   100

Kilometers
0   100

ANDORRA

SPAIN

Mediterranean

© 2019 Jeffrey L. Ward

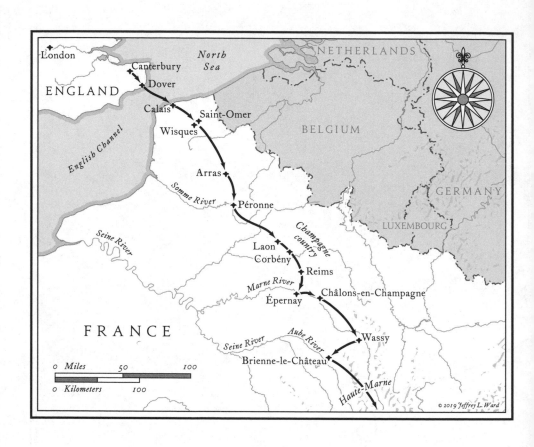

I

QUEST

LAND OF KINGS AND ATHEISTS

LONDON FALLING

The passage to eternity begins on the Piccadilly Line to Cockfosters. Contain the snickering, you tell yourself during the gentle forward rocking through London's Tube. By now, you should be purged of the trivial and juvenile. You should be in pilgrim mode. You've prepared for a journey of more than a thousand miles by walking hills and stairs, by breaking in shoes and building calf muscles, by shedding weight and inconvenient thoughts. You've tried to knead doubt into a lump of manageable anxiety. Getting in spiritual shape was much harder. You tidied up your affairs, made a donation to charity. Atoned. You ended a thirty-year feud with a man you've known since college. Although, when you told him all was forgiven, he responded with a quizzical look and said, "Were we in a feud?" You hope the soul has not gone dark. You've given it a scrub, cleaned out the grime from long-held grievances, petty jealousies, and spells of intolerance. The goal is to be fresh, open to possibility.

At Heathrow earlier today, after a nine-hour flight from my home in Seattle, I felt inexplicably cheerful in the grim fluorescence of an international customs barrier, ready to roam.

"Are you alone?" the British officer asked. I wanted to say, "Aren't we all," but a sign warned that this was a gate of utter seriousness; it was a crime to joke.

"Why are you alone?"

I explained that I was starting a pilgrimage from Canterbury to Rome, the Via Francigena.

"The what?"

Well, surely you've heard of the Camino de Santiago in Spain, I told him. More than a quarter million people walk some part of that dusty path to the tomb of the Apostle Saint James every year. I will follow a less-known trail, once the major medieval route from Canterbury to Rome, the Via Francigena. The name means, roughly, the Way Through France, and is pronounced frahn-*chee*-jeh-na. More of a braid than a single road, it traces a course described by Sigeric the Serious, archbishop of Canterbury, when he walked through Europe to see the pope in the year 990. My plan is to travel the entire route of the Via, about twelve hundred miles on foot, on two wheels, four wheels, or train—so long as I stay on the ground. The Via Francigena crosses the English Channel to Calais, wends through dark towns still shadowed by King Clovis, Napoleon, and war, to hilltop cathedrals said to hold calcified scraps of saints and proof of miracles. It leaves the cold interiors of northern France for the revitalizing air of the mountains and the Reformation, deep into Switzerland. Up, up, up into the Alps after that. Down, down, down through the *Sound of Music* hamlets of the Val d'Aosta. Then south into the radiance of Tuscan villages first inhabited in the Etruscan era twenty-five hundred years ago. In the end, it's a straight line to St. Peter's Square over the fabled Roman road, in hopes of meeting a pope with one working lung who is struggling to hold together the world's 1.3 billion Roman Catholics through the worst crisis in half a millennium.

Now HERE IS my first stop, St. Pancras station in central London. It's another curious name, sounding like an homage to an internal organ.

The tourist information booth has nothing on the origin. "Some kind of saint." Pancras, it turns out, was a teenage martyr, killed by the Romans in AD 304 for refusing to worship one of their gods. The boy was beheaded. He has a special place in England because some of his relics—body parts and the like—were carried to these shores in the first systematic attempt to bring Christianity to the island, in the sixth century.

The morning is lovely, May sunlight pouring through the big glass walls of the station. I pick up a couple of papers and magazines, happy to be in a city where print journalism is alive and shouting. It's tempting to overstate things in the daily grind of events, but the news of the day seems monumental on all fronts. Britain is cracking up—an existential fight. Having shaped so much history for so many centuries, a fractious former imperial power struggles to find its place in the world, and with how much of that world to open its doors to. No nation is an island—even one that is an island—entire of itself. A shared national narrative, difficult in the best of times, is far out of reach for "this precious stone set in the silver sea," in Shakespeare's perfect tribute.

And something else is running through the national disquiet: the kingdom is fast losing its belief in God. For the first time, more than half of all British say they have no religion at all. Some are looking for answers in the five-thousand-year-old Neolithic mystery of Newgrange in Ireland, a circular mound of tomb passages older than the Great Pyramids at Giza—a fascination of the neo-pagans. Others are dogmatically atheistic, if that isn't oxymoronic. In between are people who haven't given up on the Big Questions, but are checking out of organized religion in droves. The collapse has hit the Church of England hard, with just 15 percent of UK residents now calling themselves Anglican, the faith founded by Henry VIII. To this day, the head of the church, ninety-three-year-old Queen Elizabeth II, is also head of state. For centuries, in order to hold office or even attend college, you had to take an oath of supremacy, swearing to the monarch's absolute power at the top of this nation's established church.

One story predicts the end of British Christianity within fifty years, when the religion brought here with the bones of Saint Pancras will become "statistically invisible." Across the pond, a much slower-moving but similar trend is taking hold in America. There, the fastest-growing segment of belief is no particular belief—the Nones, as they're called. Nearly seven in ten Americans are still Christian. But if White Anglo-Saxon Protestants were indeed the rootstock of the United States, then the mother ground is nearly barren. What's happening is a mass exodus, particularly among the young: 71 percent of people aged eighteen to twenty-four say they have no religion. Since 1980, the Church of England has shuttered a thousand places of worship—great stone heaps, finely masoned and arched to high purpose, now demolished, sold at auction and repurposed, or left to rot.

This news sharpens my purpose. At times, we have trouble seeing history as it slow pivots. But here now is a moment that's been building for a century. Britain—and much of Europe, the theological cradle of Christianity—has never been so removed from belief in God. It's likely that a higher percentage of people once worshipped Odin or Jupiter than those who now regularly pray to the carpenter's son from Nazareth. Elsewhere, the world is becoming *more* religious, and Christianity is growing, robustly so in China and Africa. With 2.2 billion followers, the faith that began as a small Jewish sect is by far the planet's most popular and diverse religion. But in Europe, where the rules of the spiritual here and hereafter were shaped over centuries of bloodshed, it's all a shrug.

One reason I want to follow the Via Francigena is to experience layers of time on consecrated ground. There's barely a village along the way that has not played host to some life-changing event, a cathedral stairway that has not been trod by martyrs, madmen, or monarchs. Would there come a day when all those shrines and reliquaries would be nothing but Michelin-starred curiosities—left behind, like the great rock faces of Easter Island or Stonehenge? What was *that* all about, we may ask, looking at haloed humans fronting an oversized edifice in marble. In that sense, this adventure is an attempt to find God in Europe before God is gone.

But I have another motive to get moving over this sanctified pathway. For the enfeebled Church of England, the figure of Jesus is almost an afterthought; he is "sometimes compelling," as the Anglican bishop of Buckingham recently put it. I'm looking for something stronger: a stiff shot of no-bullshit spirituality. I have no idea what that is. I've never been "saved" or visited by an apparition or even had a prayer answered, that I know of. I'm a skeptic by profession, an Irish Catholic by baptism, culture, and upbringing—lapsed but listening, like half of all Americans of my family's faith. I'm no longer comfortable in the squishy middle; it's too easy. I've come to believe that an agnostic, as the Catholic comedian Stephen Colbert put it, "is just an atheist without balls." It's time to force the issue, to decide what I believe or admit what I don't.

I'm clearly not a theologian. Others can fight over doctrine, as they have for centuries. Others can see grave peril in something as simple as allowing a divorced Catholic to receive communion. The dancing-angel-counting on that head of a pin will continue until end times, preferably far out of sight. But if there are a small number of hardened truths to be found on this trail, let the path reveal itself. I feel driven by something I read from Saint Augustine during my prep work: "Men go abroad to admire the heights of mountains, the mighty waves of the sea, the broad tide of rivers, the vast compass of the ocean, the circular motion of the stars, and yet they pass over the mystery of themselves without a thought." We are spiritual beings. But for many of us, malnutrition of the soul is a plague of modern life.

One member of my family was nearly destroyed by religion. The men of faith in our diocese committed a monstrous crime. Another sibling was made whole by religion, after losing a son to murder and finding that no one but God could salve her wounds. There are no clean lines in our clan, only a muddle—rage mixed with redemption. I'm still haunted by the last hours of my mom's life. She was a well-read, progressive Catholic, a mother of seven. "I'm not feeling it, Timmy," she said, the color fading from her face, the strangling tendrils of her brain cancer closing in, that lethal glioblastoma. "I'm not sure anymore. I don't know what to believe or what's ahead. I don't . . . know."

I arrived on a Boeing 747 that is nearly twice as long as the Wright brothers' first flight. I begin my passage with all the world's known knowledge in the palm of my hand. And yet, I feel that so much is still unknown—the unquantifiable, my mother's doubts on her deathbed. At the depth of this year's dreary winter, I went to a "Search for Meaning" festival at Seattle University. I assumed it would be just a handful of the usual search-for-meaning suspects lamenting the meaninglessness of it all. But the major events were sold out, demand much greater than supply. At the same time, I started looking at pictures of the enchanting Via Francigena, this magnificent curiosity through the heart of secular Europe. The tug—and yes, the light, particularly in Italy—was irresistible. Here was a chance to consider two thousand years of theological thinking, refined by some of the best minds and tortured souls, all the opinionated ghosts of the Via Francigena.

Rome, by plane, is less than three hours away. My camino will take months, depending on dogs encountered, feet blistered, bad water ingested, and the wondrous distractions in between. Sigeric's route gained prominence at the height of the medieval era, when upward of two million people journeyed south along this way every year. They took to the road to escape miserable lives, to look for plunder, to find a miracle cure for the everyday diseases that killed adults in their prime. And many thousands slogged through forests and bogs, past dens of thieves, renegade knights, and redoubts of rabid dogs, in searing heat and mortal cold, as a way to cinch a place in heaven. During a papal jubilee—a holy year—the church offered this pact: make an epic journey to Rome and receive a plenary indulgence in return, the slate of sin wiped clean. And no doubt, thousands more went out of a genuine desire to connect to God. It's the same feeling today that motivates the 200 million people worldwide who make some form of spiritual pilgrimage every year. But among the 40,000 who stride over part of the modern V.F., most are not on a religious journey. They are seeking space to think, to reflect, to "learn how to waste time," as the European keepers of the trail reported in their most recent analysis.

IN CANTERBURY, I walk from the train station to the cathedral, with one task ahead of me before I do anything else. I find my way to an office inside the medieval compound of the church and present my blank credential, the official record of anyone who attempts the Via Francigena. This is a personal record more than anything else, though the Catholic Church requires that certain stages be completed in order to receive the Vatican seal of the Testimonium at the end. I get my first stamp, the emblem of a cross on a shield, imprinted on a square of the page, marking a beginning. I start as a father, a husband, an American deeply troubled by the empty drift of our country. And for the next thousand miles or so, I will try to be a pilgrim.

TWO

A CANTERBURY TALE

The altar where Archbishop Thomas Becket was hacked to death by a quartet of knights on a December evening in 1170 was always a reason to come to Canterbury. You would want to kneel on the cold floor where the most powerful man of God in the kingdom fell. You might be lucky enough to get a drop of his diluted blood, the most precious commodity of the most visited site in a cathedral so crowded with history it is called England in Stone. You would, at the least, start a proper pilgrimage to Rome by leaving something of value behind at the place where church and state clashed with the shattering of a skull. And so today you study the bronze sculpture of two swords in the cathedral, and wonder why an 850-year-old crime scene is still one of the most sacred sites in all Christendom. It's the first question a pilgrim confronts on the Via Francigena.

"Who will rid me of this meddlesome priest?" The exact phrase of King Henry II may be less Shakespearean. He might have said "turbulent" priest. Or some other variant. No matter: the intent was the same. And so on December 29, nearly six centuries after the first archbishop of

Canterbury had built a palace of worship on this ground, Henry's knights butchered Thomas Becket. That should have been the end of it. But to still the heart of a nation's highest-ranking ambassador of Christ, at a time when the church held sway over nearly every aspect of life and death in Europe, was not just a shocking affront; it was a declaration of war against the world order, undertaken to change the balance of power.

Almost instantly, the church proclaimed Thomas a martyr and a saint. Miracles occurred at his tomb in the church. The blind could see. The deaf could hear. The lame could walk. Word spread of the magic of his mortal remains. To touch any part of him was to be cured. Pilgrims started coming, a trickle at first, then a flood, finally an industry. In ten years' time, more than seven hundred miracles were attributed to Becket. Of course, as an alternative to common medieval medical practices like drilling a hole in the skull of the sick—the practice known as trepanning—the concentrated mental power of belief had a chance at success. A pilgrimage was one of the primary ways to cure smallpox, leprosy, or the skin-disfiguring malady of St. Anthony's fire. The cathedral and its bloodstained floor became England's premier shrine. Canterbury flourished. Its inns and pubs filled with travelers and holy fools. English literature was birthed by the fictional stories of these pilgrims in these inns, stories crafted by Geoffrey Chaucer in the late fourteenth century. His tales were ribald, witty, with characters who sounded like real people. In the end, there was always a twist.

Cowering at the reaction of the faithful, King Henry II was disgraced. He said the murder was a terrible mistake. He built a monastery and pilgrim hospice as repentance. He donned a sackcloth, scratchy and filthy, and walked barefoot on a cold night through the streets of Canterbury, flogged by eighty monks. When he reached the cathedral, the king showed everyone his bleeding back, then crawled inside to spend the night next to the crypt of the man who would become the most famous saint in England.

To this day, Thomas Becket continues to haunt the mother church of the global Anglican faith. "When I'm in Canterbury I go through a door leading me to the steps on which the blood of Thomas Becket fell in 1170." So began a recent sermon by the Most Reverend Justin Welby, the 105th archbishop of Canterbury. "It's a slightly odd feeling." Welby is a sad-faced, late-middle-aged cleric who is so self-effacing you want to slap him—*Snap out of it, man, your predecessors made kings crawl and popes tremble!* He is one of only three people on earth allowed to touch the Crown; the monarch and the royal jeweler are the others. A new king or queen is anointed with holy oils administered by his hand, sealing the sovereign to God. And yet, Welby feels emasculated every time he sees the list of the 104 prior archbishops on a wall in the cathedral, all the way back to Augustine, the first man to hold the title (not the philosopher, but an Italian evangelist).

In his way, Welby is like many of his fellow British, ritually apologizing for this or that. He is sorry for colonies. He is sorry for homophobia. He is sorry about pedophiles among clerical ranks. He is sorry that Christians can sound "holier than thou." He laments "secular stagnation" and "the long years of winter in the church." Civility is gone, and in its place "we have seen an upwelling of poison and hatred that I cannot remember in this country for very many years." All of this begging-of-pardon and whimpering prompted a fellow Anglican, writing in the *Daily Mail*, to ask, "What is the point of the archbishop of Canterbury?" It's a fair question.

The strength of this archbishop is his story. As the son of two alcoholic parents, his childhood was miserable. He was "the shyest, most-unhappy-looking boy you could imagine," one classmate recalled. Faith was an afterthought. "I vaguely assumed there was a God, but I didn't believe," said Welby in a profile in the British press. "I wasn't interested at all." After school at Eton and Trinity College, he married, started a family, and rose to become a petroleum executive. But his first child, a girl who had yet to see her first birthday, was killed in a car accident in Paris. The grief and search for healing sent him into the ministry. Somewhat awkwardly of late, Welby has tried to explain his outward melancholy. He suffers from what he calls "the black dog of depression"—no small thing in a country where suicide is the leading cause of death for men under the age of forty-five. It takes him down into a place that is "beyond description, hopeless." He seems very lonely as well, another national scourge. Britain just named its first minister for loneliness to deal with what the prime minister calls "the sad reality of modern life."

Just before he was enthroned by the queen in 2013, he found out that his father, Gavin Welby, a bootlegger with a rakish reputation, was Jewish. This history had long been hidden from him. Imagine that: a half-Jew leading a state church that had done so much to further hatred of Jews. It was English clerics who spread the blood libel—the toxic notion that Jews killed Christian children in order to use their blood for ritual purposes—as a way to dodge mounting financial debts. Jews were expelled from England in 1290, in part because of the reach of this mortal lie and other falsehoods planted by Christians. Back then, the archbishop's father would have been an outcast, forced to flee for his life, his home and savings seized. Welby has yet to find a way to use his unusual story, even though he understands the power of narrative to move lives. He did make a plea in another sermon to the legions of atheists, the snarky press, the collapsed and no longer listening. "It is impossible to understand the world today," he said, "without understanding religion."

MY GUIDE FOR A TOUR of the cathedral is a cheeky fellow, quick-witted and well attuned to the slightest slip in the attention of our small group. So, while he dutifully notes that there has been a Christian church on the cathedral grounds since the first stone was stacked in the year 597, he is eager to point out the naughty secrets of this English Vatican. *Up here* in a ceiling of the former monks' cloister, look closely: there is the image of a mermaid of some sort, or the early Starbucks logo, openly displaying what looks like her genitalia. *Oh, those monks*, toiling away in the darkness of winter on thin gruel, their fingers worn to sandpaper—such pranksters! And *over there* in one large stained-glass window: observe the parable in the colored panels. It tells the story of a felon who was blinded for his crimes, then had his sight restored during his pilgrimage to Canterbury. But his family never gave money to the church for this miracle, so they lost a child. The moral: donate or die.

And finally, on our way out, we marvel at Christ Church Gate, the superbly ornamented outdoor entrance wall to the cathedral compound. The guide directs our attention to one small carving in particular, just beneath a Tudor rose. It appears to be a naked woman, full-breasted, but wait!—is that a penis? Indeed, the figure is a hermaphrodite, he tells us, probably the joke of a bored craftsman. Curious, though, when I try to buy a copy of *The Canterbury Tales* at the Anglican bookstore, the clerk tells me no, no, no, waving his finger. They can't sell *The Canterbury Tales* here at Canterbury Cathedral—just a pamphlet-sized edition with the introduction. The book is too bawdy, full of sexual innuendo. No place in a church for such a thing.

Answering the call of bells pealing for evensong, I dash away in time to get a place deep in the heart of a cathedral that was twenty-three generations in the making. I'm seated in a high-backed pew carved with exquisite designs, the wood aged to dark chocolate. The acoustics are superb. And when the multiracial and multigenerational weave of voices—all angelic in white—comes together, the sound wafts upward to the vaults and carries me away with it. I'm not sure if this is prayer, homage, or performance, but it's a transcendent few moments for the soul. By the time I go for a run at sunset atop the twenty-foot-high walls first built by the Romans, Canterbury has made its way into my heart. It's a garden city, soft and green, veined by a river split into two, with Tudor homes and thick-waisted fruit trees and international students in plaid uniforms who know a Chaucer verse by heart. What the Romans created, the Nazis nearly destroyed. Almost a third of the town was hit by German bombing. The explosives unearthed bedrock of the lost urban design: relics of a pagan heritage to go with Canterbury's pilgrim lineage. Worshippers of Woden, who got around on a horse with eight legs, and Thunor, the Anglo-Saxon god of bad weather, were given a fresh appraisal.

ONE BENEFIT of the disgustingly unhealthy full English breakfast— eggs and thick bacon, black pudding and sausage, baked beans, buttered toast, and a grilled tomato—is the incentive to trot off and canter, a word that owes its origin to this city. I have another day here before I start the Via Francigena, with a few pilgrim tasks still ahead. One is to visit the natal home of English Christianity. When the Romans left Britain more than four centuries after Julius Caesar first landed in 55 BC, the island dissolved into clans and tribal kingdoms—Christian Celts in the west and north, the more recently arrived Germanic Angles and Saxons in the east and here in Kent. The barbarians from the Continent gave their name to their new island home—*Angland.* More than a century earlier, Ireland, never conquered by Rome, had fused its Druidic traditions into a lively form of indigenous Christianity, largely due to the persuasion of a tireless former slave, the man known as Saint Patrick. The Irish wove this religion, and their art, monastic settlements, and written and oral traditions, into other parts of the British Isles, and eventually the European mainland. This came at a time when a fledgling faith born among unlearned Galilean fishermen had passed from its persecution phase, through embrace by the Roman Empire, to efforts by bands of missionaries to seed the pagan pockets of Europe.

But the south of Angland stuck with the old gods. The story has it that Pope Gregory sent Augustine north "to a barbarous, fierce and unbelieving nation whose language they did not understand," as one early historian put it. Lucky for him, Queen Bertha, the wife of local pagan King Ethelbert of Kent, was Christian by way of her French background, and she welcomed the men from Rome in 597. The other alternative, more typical, would be to throw the foul-smelling strangers into the sea, anchored to stones. With Bertha's prodding, the king eventually abandoned his own deities and welcomed the religion of a foreign people into his realm.

Christians from afar had no power or leverage in these strange lands of many gods. A century before, they had converted much of present-day France and Germany—as they did Ireland—without state violence or coercion. Their message was optimistic, born of hope, salvation for men and women, no matter their standing among the class-bound clans. They were charitable toward the poor, and affectionate to each other. "How these Christians love one another!" said a pagan among the new arrivals. They promoted a Christ who said he had been "anointed to bring good news" (the god-spel in Old English) to the downtrodden. Nor was the conversion in southern England aided by military victory—a prayer answered in battle, proof of the value of upgrading from one deity to another, as these things often were. The king's wife, Bertha, simply won him over with the passion for her faith. A large monastery eventually rose on land given to the Catholics by Ethelbert.

But what's this? The foundational footprint of British Christianity, the former monastery and burial grounds of Ethelbert, Bertha, and Augustine, is rubble: a vast ruin behind a fence in the heart of the Canterbury World Heritage site. It looks like a portent of things to come. I walk over a hushed field of ankle-high grass, between scatterings of stone from a Middle Age complex that once closed off the sky overhead. I see a two-story, crumbling brick arch, the floor of a former cathedral nave, a few pillars holding nothing. Who would destroy a place so crucial to England's sense of self? Nazis, I presume. *The bastards.* No, it was fellow English who did it. First by neglect, and then by deliberation—tied to the shifting loyalties of the Crown.

Beware the marriage of church and state, for the divorce is always violent. Six hundred years after that crew of humble missionaries stumbled ashore, Becket had pushed the boundary of ecclesiastical control, putting Catholics in cassocks beyond the reach of civil institutions. "The clergy," he insisted, "should be ruled by their own law." This change, shielding priests and monks from nonreligious courts for crimes like rape or murder, infuriated the king. But the killing of Becket only strengthened the grip of the clerical class. It would be 360 years before another monarch in England dared to defy a pope. That came in the 1530s, when Henry VIII broke with Rome over his marital desires and declared himself Supreme Head of the Church of England. Emboldened by his unlimited new spiritual powers, Henry VIII set about destroying the old Christian establishment. Thomas Becket's ghost was the first to go. The saint's shrine was demolished in the cathedral, and those miracle-inducing body parts were dispersed. He was declared a rebel and traitor by royal proclamation. Other saints were downgraded as well, and stained-glass depictions of their lives were smashed. In 1538, the king closed the abbey that stood where I now stand, ending nine centuries of monastic life. All over the kingdom, monks were forced into the street, their treasures confiscated by the Crown. Thousands of books were destroyed, leaving Oxford University, among others, without a library collection for almost seventy years.

Pilgrimages were outlawed, shutting off the flow to the south for English Christians. Henry VIII was excommunicated. A religious war followed. After Henry's death, one of his children, Mary, a Catholic, used state violence to restore the Roman faith; she sent nearly three hundred people to die in various human bonfires. You can still find her dour countenance all over Canterbury. It came as a surprise to look up from a pint in a pub and see Bloody Mary staring back at me from a frame on the wall. Another daughter of Henry's, Elizabeth I, attacked Catholics during her long reign. Mass was forbidden, bishops were executed. For a time, clerics hid in "priest holes," brick shelters, and were fed through tubes in the masonry.

No matter who was in power, the medieval Becket trade remained highly competitive. The cult that had developed around every conceivable body part—hair, teeth, a piece of a finger—spread far and wide after he was martyred a second time by Henry VIII. Any church of standing needed a saintly relic, if not from Becket, then from a certified entrant to heaven. The reason was simple: relics could produce miracles, crucial to conversions. Relics had supernatural power. They gave off energy. And relics could generate a small fortune from people who paid to view them, and were rewarded in return with a specific reduction in years spent in that foggy lounge of purgatory.

Although Henry VIII had tried to erase every trace of Becket from Canterbury, his long-dead nemesis got the last word. Today, the newer shrine that I saw, with the shadowed swords, draws throngs of people. In 1982, John Paul II, the first pope to visit Canterbury Cathedral, knelt in silent prayer at the spot where Thomas was killed, the marble floor worn by the knees of millions of pilgrims. In 2016, a bone fragment of the saint was brought to England from Hungary and given a tour worthy of a Rod Stewart revival. "Becket's Elbow to Return to Site of His Murder" was the headline in *The Guardian*. It makes sense that a king's murder of a Catholic archbishop would still have so much resonance. For what is the story of Christianity but another state execution—the killing of a seditious Jew by a Roman governor?

I was told I could find the saint's relics at the comparatively small Catholic church of Saint Thomas of Canterbury. The sacred scraps are behind glass, above the altar in the Martyrs' Chapel. One object is a piece of cloth from his clerical vestment. The other is a bone chip, wrapped in jewels, though there is no explanation of what part of Becket's frame this came from. The skeletal nugget could be anyone's, and the cloth could be a fraud as well. In this dark and lonely chapel in Canterbury's old town, you have to accept on faith that the two holiest items did indeed belong to Thomas Becket. I sit and take in what aura there is, the years and hopes imbued in these average-looking objects. I think of all the people with tumorous bellies or sightless eyes, pleading. Sadly, I'm not feeling any-thing. But then, I didn't ask for anything. Not just yet.

THE NEXT MORNING, Sunday, brings me to the oldest church in the English-speaking world—Saint Martin's. It may be the oldest active community in the English-speaking world, as some in Canterbury assert. Saint Martin's is a modest clump of brick and rock, off the street in a nest of ancient yews and gravestones that have settled into ashen-colored per-manence. Set next to a prison, Saint Martin's is both a cemetery and a church, all of it exuding decay—not the best enticement for young people to join a faith on the brink of extinction in Britain. The chapel was first built in Roman times for a sect of local Christians. The Saxons, the Nor-mans, the Tudors, and Anglicans all added on to it, so that the structure is a compact tutorial in English history—not unlike the self-evident geol-ogy lesson in the tiers of the Grand Canyon. It was here that Queen Ber-tha took Augustine and his forty monks when they arrived at Canterbury in 597.

On the way to the church, I saw my first sign to the Via Francigena: a yellow cartoon pilgrim in a loose-fitting tunic, with a wooden staff and a bindle of his possessions over his shoulder. What a thrill! Follow this elfin wayfarer for a thousand miles and you'll never get lost. Either that or you'll recover from a lifetime of being lost. I was encouraged by the sight of a pair of young pilgrims, two women briskly striding out of Canter-bury. Just behind them was a covey of middle-aged trail walkers, with heavy, high-end backpacks and lightweight hiking sticks. Heading out to see the world along Pilgrims Way, they were excitedly chattering like sol-diers going off to war. I felt the same way. There is nothing like a begin-ning, when the slate is clean, the road open, the tank full of optimism.

Outside Saint Martin's is a small welcoming sign: "We do not have all the answers. We are on a spiritual journey. We look to Scripture, reason and tradition to help us on our way. Whoever you are, we offer you a space to draw nearer to God and walk with us." I'm impressed. Since when does the oldest church in the English-speaking world—or any church, for that matter—not have all the answers? The words appeal to my awakened pilgrim spirit.

Inside, I'm shocked. There are no more than twenty people at mid-morning Sunday service. Most are elderly, save for a child playing in the back. Christianity "has perhaps proved more influential in shaping human destiny than any other institutional philosophy," wrote the historian Paul Johnson. If so, is this the end of the line of that influence, the whimper? A woman seizes me immediately, sensing a fresh soul.

"Oh, good morning!" she exclaims. "Welcome, welcome, welcome!" She takes me forcefully by the arm and guides me to a tray of baked goods.

"Would you like a cookie?"

No cookie, thanks all the same. But perhaps some juice, I mumble.

"Yes, juice. Of course! Is apple cider all right? The local cider is quite good."

"Well then—"

"But this is not local, and nor are you. Do tell me your name and where you come from. We're so excited you decided to join us."

Things have gotten stickier than I want them to be. *No religion for me, please, I'm pretending to be British.* Where is Anglo reserve when you need it? I had hoped to slip in quietly, find a place in the back, and observe a solemn service in an iconic setting. I thought I might reflect on the Romans who knelt here, on Augustine's Italian monks newly cast into the gloom of an English November, on Becket's road to defiance of his king, on the truths that have held Christianity together through the years. Instead, I feel like the blood donor in a roomful of hemophiliacs.

"Oh, please, you must at least *try* the cookies."

The church is museum quality. But it has a pulse—and a humane one at that. There's a little side table where pilgrims can get their passports stamped, and a collection box for donations to the Muslim refugees huddling in filthy camps just across the Channel. After juice and cookies, the service gets under way with a few songs and readings. It's very moving. The same message from the outside is repeated in the *Pilgrim Post*, the stapled monthly journal of the parish. "We do not have all the answers. We are on a spiritual journey." The newsletter promotes an upcoming talk: "The Bible: Can it still be read as the unique truth about God?"

A parishioner recounts a recent trip to Auschwitz, ending with a moral paradox that has long troubled people of faith: "Where was God in the Holocaust?" Where, indeed? Is there any plausible explanation for why a just God would allow the murder of six million Jews, and six million other innocents—the disabled, gays, Soviet and Polish civilians, Roma? Or even a single random killing of a single fine person? The answer provided here is the hardy and frustrating perennial: God gave humans free will. It's our choice. We blew it, we screwed up, and in the twentieth century we committed the most heinous crime of all time. The parishioner doesn't quite phrase it that way, but close. "Maybe the question is not so much why did God allow the Holocaust to happen, but why did we?"

Saint Martin's is without a vicar on this Sunday. A part-time substitute, the Reverend Jo Richards, cannot be here either, but she has sent along one of her sermons to be read. Women make up the majority of new Anglican ministers. The faith has come full circle. Just as a woman, Bertha, was responsible for Christianity taking hold in a big part of England, it now looks like women will have to save it. Jo explains that in the Greek New Testament there are two words for time. *Chronos* refers to that which can be measured in seconds, hours, and days, the time by which most of us live our lives. *Kairos* tracks the quality moments "where time seems to stand still and there is awe and wonder all around."

Afterward, I'm surrounded again and peppered with questions. How did I like the service? Would I care to attend midweek prayer? And one last plea on behalf of the uneaten cookies. *So dreadfully sorry*, I say, trying my best at a British apology. I'm on *chronos* time, with miles ahead of me, though hoping to encounter *kairos* time along the way.

A snow-haired man, perhaps sensing my unease, guides me to the front of the church, the original Roman-built section. He introduces himself as a lay minister, longtime parishioner, and amateur historian. I ask this gentleman about the archbishop of Canterbury: what he thinks of the Jewish heritage of the leader of the Church of England.

"Oh, but he's not Jewish. Haven't you heard?"

No, I hadn't heard. I should have had the AOC on my Google news alert, otherwise I wouldn't have missed the major twist in the Very Reverend Welby's story.

"He's a bastard."

It turns out his father is *not* Gavin Welby, the bootlegger of Jewish descent, who married Lady Williams of Elvel and had a son nine months after they were betrothed. His biological father is Sir Anthony Montague Browne, deceased, a former Royal Air Force officer who was the last private secretary to Prime Minister Winston Churchill. When first informed of this preposterous claim, the archbishop went out and had a DNA test taken to disprove it, using hair samples from a brush kept by Sir Anthony's widow. But the test confirmed the story: Archbishop Welby was indeed this other man's child—*illegitimate,* in the official parlance of church and legal disrepute. Welby was stunned.

Dogged by the predatory press—"Archbishop Conceived During Mum's Drunken Romp with Churchill Secretary"—his mother issued a statement explaining the turn of events. Just days before her wedding, she had slept with Browne. "Although my recollection of events is patchy, I now recognize that during the days leading up to my very sudden marriage, and fueled by a large amount of alcohol on both sides, I went to bed with Anthony Montague Browne. It appeared that the precautions taken at the time didn't work and my wonderful son was conceived as a result of this liaison."

I leave the time-dented little church trying to put the twist in this Canterbury tale in perspective. Not so long ago, Welby would have been forced to resign, shamed on the way out the door, through no fault of his own. Once a bastard, always a bastard—that was the authoritative view.

It wasn't until 1969 that the Church of England ended a nearly four-hundred-year-old ban on anyone born illegitimate from becoming archbishop of Canterbury. Burke's Peerage, the keeper of titles held by inbred earls and viscounts, didn't include illegitimate children until 2009. The whole notion of "illegitimacy" is a horrid concept, damning a child at birth with a special kind of original sin. Welby has tried to make peace with this latest revelation. Don't laugh or feel sorry for him, he says—his life story is a redemptive one. "To find that one's father is other than imagined is not unusual," he said in a statement. "I know that I find who I am in Jesus Christ, not in genetics."

In the face of collapse, doom, and ridicule, I can't help but think that a church that confesses to not having all the answers, guided by a man who once would have been shunned as mentally ill for his depression, persecuted for being a Jew, or scorned as a bastard, has a future in this messy world. The things Welby discovered about himself would have condemned him at any other time in the two millennia of Christianity. This is progress, though it may have come too late to matter.

THREE

AT THE CLIFF OF THE KINGDOM

It is so much easier to leave Britain than to enter it. But standing atop the White Cliffs of Dover, I wonder: Why leave? A sun-fused mist lies over the Channel, enough haze to obscure the Continent just twenty-three miles away. On the other side are thousands of people from some of the most wretched places on earth, all hoping to cross over to this chunk of chalk. The spot where England falls to the sea was the envy of Napoleon and Hitler, though neither was able to breach the briny barrier, and Julius Caesar and William the Conqueror, who did. Here is a Roman lighthouse as well as a castle crowning the bluff, built for pilgrims by Henry II when he was still doing penance for the death of Thomas Becket. And in my own expansive mode, I'm trying to forgive the English for what they did to the Irish through eight hundred years of institutionalized cruelty. That same Henry invaded Waterford a year after his knights split Becket's skull. For my ancestors, it was all misery from then on. Most of the horrors were committed in the name of religion, Christian on Christian. Oh *that*, the English say whenever I bring up the tangle of our tormented heritage. *Let it go.*

Why leave, when your feet are swollen and you already miss your family not even one week into an uncertain journey? Why leave, when those closest to you think you're daft; most of them don't even believe in God. "This old guy with a beard in the clouds—what a fairy tale," said a longtime friend, having made a gradual life transition from annoying born-again to annoying atheist. I've got *The Confessions of St. Augustine* on my Kindle. But I'm also traveling with Christopher Hitchens, the great, late polemicist. He's a combustible companion for days when I might go wobbly, as I just did at Saint Martin's in Canterbury. "To us atheists, no spot on earth is or could be 'holier' than another," he writes. I won't argue with him for now. I'll let him state his case from a book subtitled *How Religion Poisons Everything*. As for my expedition, Hitchens is not encouraging. "To the ostentatious absurdity of the pilgrimage," he writes, "we can counterpose a leisurely or urgent walk from one side of the library or gallery to another."

Well then, why ever leave the British Library—largest in the world by items catalogued? I find one answer in the blog of a pilgrim who just left, trundling down the Via Francigena to Rome a few days ahead of me. Carlo Laurenzi, London-born to Italian-immigrant parents, buttoned up his home, strapped on an overly stuffed backpack, and started hoofing it south from Canterbury. Laurenzi is sixty-three, and his trip may be nothing more than a break from "the sad reality of modern life," as his prime minister put it. But he's also trying to resolve a spiritual quandary. He is unable to explain a couple of events in his life—occasions when he should have been killed in freak accidents. It made him think he was spared for a reason, that perhaps a greater power intervened. He won't call it miraculous, just something he's unable to square with his atheism. Deep walking, a term modern pilgrims throw around, is a way to resolve his inner conflicts.

"I cannot slot in those anecdotes and experiences into my intellectual framework," he wrote of his motive for taking to the Via Francigena. "Am I going insane? I hope not, but I'm surprised to be having to revisit something that I thought I'd left behind for good."

Laurenzi, a nonbeliever, must feel encouraged by recent words from Pope Francis. One might be better off as an atheist, he suggested, than a bad Christian. By that, he meant a Christian who exploits other people. He also warned against excessive rigidity, saying that those who tell us "it's this or nothing" are not Catholics, but heretics. These kinds of statements leave me rubber-faced in cartoonish astonishment. *He said . . . what?* The pope made this bad-Christian observation after a visit to Sweden, the center of European neo-heathenism, where eight out of ten people are atheists or have no belief in any religion. It's easier to come out as gay in Sweden, as a story on that secular stronghold noted, than to be an out Christian.

I'm trying to write a letter to this pope, after mulling it over for weeks, working up the nerve. Yeah, O.K., I might as well be writing to Santa Claus. I want a pony, and an interview with the Vicar of Christ on Earth. I could try the journalistic route, using my *New York Times* credential. But after checking with colleagues in Rome and Manhattan who are far better connected and knowledgeable about Vatican affairs than a spiritual stray from the American West, I'm discouraged. Francis moves in mysterious ways, dialing people out of the blue, no pattern to his access. He would probably think I expect him to answer for all the centuries of ecclesiastical malpractice—the execution of heretics, fostering of wars, suppression of science and sexuality, not to mention the modern criminal clergy. That's not what I'm after.

Francis is the first pope from the Jesuits, a nearly five-hundred-year-old religious order known to produce many a brilliant thinker among the ranks of its educators. So . . . what if I try to play the Jesuit card, with the help of a priest I know? Father Stephen Sundborg, S.J., now a much-loved university president and theologian, was a teacher of mine in high school, a fresh-faced novitiate at the time. He was one of the few Jesuits who didn't send me down to the office of the chain-smoking, radish-nosed, 250-pound vice principal to drop my pants and get my adolescent butt whacked with a perforated hardwood paddle. Father Steve is a friend, a highly evolved human, and he just returned from his own audience with Il Papa. Here goes:

To the Holy Father:

One of the oldest forms of discovery, affirmation, and search
for enlightenment is the pilgrimage. And one of the oldest
of pilgrimages is the Via Francigena, from Canterbury
to Rome.
  "Go, pilgrim, and take your place in the sun and your
share in the dust—heart awakened, forget the ephemeral."
  I'm trying to follow this advice from the Liturgy of Hours,
traveling a thousand miles on the Via Francigena for a look
at time and terrain.

Does that sound too pretentious? Or maybe it's condescending. Sure, the pope knows about the purpose of the V.F.—why state the obvious? He sees the church as a "people of pilgrims," as he has said. Every day, a fresh river of those pilgrims pours into St. Peter's Square for a wave and a smile from the Bishop of Rome. All right then: maybe a bit of sincere flattery:

I am intrigued by the Pope's advice on how "voracious
consumerism" can kill the soul. I'm moved by his treatment
of refugees. I'm fascinated by how he uses the echoes of
history—from the 500th anniversary of Martin Luther's
Reformation, or in his outreach to Anglicans—to forge a
fresh way.

Should I continue to use the third person in referring to Francis, as people do in the presence of a monarch—*And how is Her Majesty's toast this morning?* Or make a direct appeal? I stay in the remove, and try for a sweep of purpose to entice him.

> *As I wander from the shrines of European Christianity, with many of the great cathedrals empty, I'm interested in the Big Questions. How do we live in an increasingly secular age? What is our duty to our fellow humans—the refugees of war and sectarian strife—in a time of rising nationalism and tribalism? And what can the Gospel say to someone who thinks he can get all the world's knowledge from the internet?*

I close with a reference to the Jesuits in general, a prominent mention of Father Steve, and an acknowledgment that my request is a long shot. And this would have to mark my point of no return, moving out of the security of spiritual complacency and into the unknown. It feels more like a plunge from Dover's cliff than a gentle first step. Faith is groping at air during the fall, hoping to find something to grab on to.

THE WALK FROM CANTERBURY was eighteen miles, with little to slow a reasonably fit person trying to make three miles an hour, so long as you pack a big lunch, bring at least two liters of water, and take several long breaks. Out Monastery Street, down Pilgrims Way, past the villages of Patrixbourne and Womenswold, through cemeteries and farms, a stop at the inn at Shepherdswell, daydreaming through the tidy forest of Pidders Wood. There was an abandoned church, which another pilgrim, a graduate student named Julia Peters, had alerted me to after I contacted her following her own trip to Rome. Built in the twelfth century, this place served Christians from Becket's day until the Beatles broke up. It's now classified as "redundant," the euphemism of Anglican euthanasia.

Dover is slump-shouldered and sullen, still sulking after losing much of its European traffic to the Channel Tunnel in 1994. At a sidewalk kiosk on a pedestrianized street, I pick up a dog-eared book, *The Last Thousand Days of the British Empire.* Leafing through it, I realize that many Brits have never known anything but decline their entire lives. Some resent the descendants of those once ruled by colonial masters, now shaping the UK of tomorrow. The response of people who mourn the demise of *Rule, Britannia* is to go small, to close the doors, to feel put upon. Yet the island is not at war or mired in economic depression. The crisis in Britain is somewhat psychological, maybe self-induced, with a hint of hypochondria. Perhaps it's tied to the uncertainties of the kingdom's newfound spiritual independence. Say what you will about faith, but it anchored a nation for centuries. "There's never been a better time to be alive, yet we feel so glum," said Ian Goldin, an Oxford professor, speaking before the assembled elites at Davos. "So many people feel anxious. So many people feel this is one of the most dangerous times."

Dover Castle looks good for its age. Guardian of the sea below, it's part of a sprawling site run by English Heritage, the official custodian of more than four hundred places dear to the national story. Inside Henry's Great Tower are people dressed in medieval clothes, performing medieval tasks, but they do not have medieval teeth. I ask a serf who's grinding grain into flour about the miserable medieval diet. I assume, as the Thomas Hobbes line has it, that life in those days was nasty, brutish, and short. A simple cut on the finger might inflame to an infection, which could become gangrenous, and fatal. Plagues like the Black Death swept through the cities, wiping out two-thirds of England's population between 1348 and 1350, and a third of France's. Half the people in Europe died of disease before their thirtieth birthday. Anyone taller than five-foot-ten was a giant. Leeches were part of a medicinal kit that included a hot balm of pigeon turds for treating kidney stones. Soap was a lump of boiled mutton fat and wood ash. Men wore underpants. Women did not. And subsisting on leathered beef, in the pre-dentistry era, must have produced a surfeit of people with jack-o'-lantern smiles.

"Actually, most of them had pretty decent teeth," says the costumed guide in the castle. That is, until great quantities of sugar were brought to Europe from the New World. Sugar changed everything. A sweet tooth could quickly lead to no teeth. But distant-past Brits didn't just gnaw on gristle and slurp gruel while farting around the fire, he explains. (Or, if they were lucky, listening to Roland the Farter, a twelfth-century flatulist.) They boiled up big cauldrons of soups and stews, which were highly nutritious, and baked fat loaves of bread from what we would now call ancient grains.

They ate with their hands. Forks didn't become common until well after Henry VIII had died, though I doubt if modern cutlery would have reduced his portion sizes. At harvesttime, tables were heavy with fresh produce—fresh, that is, up until supper. Vegetables were always cooked to excess, or brined and pickled for storage. To eat a raw plant was considered a bad thing. The food was washed down by mead—a fermented honey concoction—ale, or wine from France. "The English drink no water," one medieval chronicler observed, "unless at certain times upon religious score." The bristled end of a reed served as a toothbrush.

Wandering upstairs, I duck under short entrances and explore the quarters for pilgrims from eight hundred years ago. Like me, they would have had a hesitant moment before leaving their tight little world for a Via Francigena of rumor, danger, and uncertainty. They would have questioned their motives: Could walking toward a distant city really bring a person closer to God? And what about all the feral thoughts arising after prayer went unanswered? Some may have left Dover as believers, only to arrive in Rome as atheists. A medieval pilgrimage was a rough test of faith, the most unpredictable and independent thing a person could do in a short life.

In the castle, the larger rooms were dormitories for the masses walking to Rome, where people slept on the floor, assured of protection inside this heavily insulated fortress. Other rooms, for the elites, are high-ceilinged, the floors polished. The bed boards on display are at a distinct angle at the head, which I imagine would make it difficult to slip into a decent slumber. It was common to sleep somewhat upright, another heritage docent explains, as a way to keep evil spirits from entering the body at night. To lie flat was similar to a dead body in repose—inviting the devil to enter.

Outside, the mist has lifted. The view is stunning. From a perch above the castle walls, I take in the gentle chop of the Channel, leading away to the near beyond, where the tribes of Europe have long assembled for conquest. After crossing, the Romans built a landing named Dubris, and connected it by road and bridge over the River Thames, to another establishment, Londinium. Napoleon thought he could follow in their footsteps. "We have six centuries of insults to avenge," he said. But his Grande Armée, unlike the javelin-bearing Romans who landed fifteen miles north of Dover, or the papal-sanctioned Normans who beached to the south, never made it across the water. It was another time in May when the bedraggled scraps of French and British forces were cornered for slaughter by the Nazi war machine in 1940, at the beach in Dunkirk. Would England fall, the Swastika soon to fly over the Palace of Westminster? Home, as the soldiers who queued up in the sand while the Germans strafed them, was almost close enough to touch—home, these white cliffs below me. You're followed out of the castle compound by a renewed sense of debt to the last members of a dying generation. If you look away, you can see those shivering boys at water's edge, ordinary people who saved the world.

IT'S TIME TO PUT my doubts in a pocket, and the UK behind me. I'm ready to see the Via, the Pas-de-Calais, the Champagne country, a village built on miracles, the city that Joan of Arc liberated, Napoleon's boarding school, the Alps, and the most glorious Italian hill towns. Now that I've written my letter, Pope Francis is an even stronger pull—that goofy smile of his, the lightness of being, a surprise a day. He jolted the world from his first hour on the stage, when the immigrant's son Jorge Mario Bergoglio took the name of a half-starved mystic from Assisi, the saint who didn't own money, property, or shoes. The twelfth-century Francis was known as Il Poverello, the Little Poor Man. The twenty-first-century Francis, the first non-European pope in a thousand years, started his papacy as the most popular person on earth, gracing the covers of *National Geographic*, *Time*, and *Rolling Stone*. Of late, he's been overwhelmed by fresh reports of cover-ups of sexual abuse of children. The tragic stories repeat themselves, from every corner of Catholicism, and reach deep into the institutional keepers of the faith. It makes you wonder if there is some fatal flaw, some poison in the water of the so-called One True Church. This paradox—how a belief founded on a gospel of love could cause so much pain—is a big reason why people are leaving the pews in droves. And it's no small part of my struggle as I step into the pilgrim realm.

Still, it's hard not to like a pope who is honest about his imperfections, a long way from infallible, a pope who withdraws his hand when people try to kiss his ring. His life experiences go well beyond the cloister. He was a bouncer at a nightclub. He fell in love with a woman before he entered the priesthood. He worked in a chemistry lab, a budding scientist. As pope, he washes the feet of prisoners and the poor, shares meals with the homeless and refugees. He dials up complete strangers on the phone, just to say hello. He hasn't watched television since 1990. When reminded that his church has long considered homosexuality "an objective disorder," Francis shrugged it off with the most memorable line by a pope in a century: "Who am I to judge?" No longer would the church be known mainly by what it's against, but what it's for.

A schoolgirl from Sweden said that none of her friends believed in God. What was her obligation to them? "It's not that you have to convince them of your faith," he told her. He said a similar thing not long after the whiff of white smoke rose from the chimney above the Sistine Chapel, announcing the Francis era in 2013. "Proselytism is solemn nonsense, it makes no sense," he said. "I believe in God, not in a Catholic God. There is no Catholic God. There is God and I believe in Jesus Christ, his incarnation."

Think of all the centuries when the message was convert or be killed. Think of the people who were put to death because they believed in science over dogma. Think of all the murders committed in the name of Christian orthodoxy. Think of the edict of Pope Boniface VIII in the year 1300: "We declare, state, define and pronounce that it is altogether necessary to the salvation of every human creature to be subject to the Roman pontiff." Or the decree of Pope Alexander VI, father of ten through multiple mistresses: he divided the New World between Portugal and Spain in 1494, natives be damned (they were). Think of the Inquisition, initiated by a later pope who said he would gather the wood to burn his own father. Think of the nineteenth-century invention of papal infallibility, of papal condemnation of freedom of speech and freedom of worship. Think of the twentieth-century pope Pius XII, who sent Hitler a friendly letter in 1939 and was silent on the Holocaust.

Think of that history, and you come to the conclusion that there's only one thing wrong with Pope Francis: too bad he isn't twenty years younger. He rises at four-thirty every morning and powers through a brutal schedule driven by the urgency of his dwindling time left on earth. But he has trouble breathing, with just that one good lung, and a heart condition as well. After he turned eighty, he thought he might last only a few more years. "At my age we are preparing to go," he told an audience at World Youth Day. When the kids gasped, he tried to reassure them. "Who can guarantee life? No one."

Off I go then, hoping to find at the end of the trail a vigorous old man with the free-spirited joy of a young man. But first, I pluck a small stone from the beach and put it in my pack—a little chip of England for the road. When the pope was asked about his secret to happiness, he said: Slow down. Take time off. Live and let live. Work for peace. Don't keep negative feelings bottled up. Enjoy art. Enjoy books. Play. And one more suggestion, another reason to join the queue of travelers getting ready to leave Britain in the harbor at Dover: "Please don't see life from afar."

FOUR

BESIEGED AT CALAIS

The canals of Calais enclose an island made by man, in a city flattened because of a madman, in a part of the country where no one can say with certainty what it is to be French anymore. I bob along in a small stream of pilgrims fanning out from the harbor, blinking into a late-afternoon sun that seems stuck in the sky. It's too hot for May. And too bright and shiny for all the misery that presents itself around one of the busiest ferry ports in the world. I immediately bump into Charles de Gaulle and his wife, Yvonne, holding hands on a stroll through the town where they were married in 1921. The statue of the first couple of the Resistance is a personal touch in a drab square just off the waterfront, the Place d'Armes, in the old town. Old being a relative term. Calais has been razed and rebuilt with regularity, as conquerors come and go. I pass a pair of bomb-sniffing dogs leashed to a pair of assault-rifle-toting gendarmes. The police wear bulletproof vests and talk grimly into their shoulders. Here comes another pair, and another, and a fourth. This is occupied Calais.

My fellow pilgrims are trying to find religion. The authorities pay no attention to us. Silly walkers with their floppy hats and overpocketed cargo pants. Which way to the Monty Python skit? But thousands of others are trying to *flee* religion. The police are all over them. For a time, the refugees lived in the Jungle, forty acres of squalor on a wind-scraped sandlot at the edge of Calais, until it was bulldozed under orders of the government. They were asylum seekers, these foreigners, a fifth of them children without adults, some from Aleppo and Mosul—towns dating to the biblical era, now gutted because of the latest iteration of a fight over the legitimate successor to the Prophet Muhammad, who died in 632. In this case, ISIS was formed as a Sunni reaction to Shiite overreaching in Iraq. In Syria, what began as a rebellion against a murderous dictator turned into a sectarian bloodbath between the two major branches of Islam, with regional and global powers taking sides. Calais is living with the consequences.

The goal of the refugees is to latch on to a truck bound for Britain through the nearby Channel Tunnel, or to hide in the hold of a train or ferry. Although most of the former Jungle residents were supposed to be relocated around France, many scattered to the shadows of Calais. They sleep in the woods. They hunker down in parks or abandoned warehouses. Some have drowned or been hit by trains or run over by cars. Some have been teargassed, beaten with clubs. Others will continue to walk until they drop, or get arrested, or smuggle aboard a skiff, or catch that lorry to the magical godless kingdom across the Channel.

I'M HAPPY TO BE on the mainland, odd as it is to be a wanderer of privilege among wanderers of sorrow. Just being in France is a mood changer. Asking for something basic, say, *Où sont les toilettes*, makes you feel more sophisticated. When Oscar Wilde was released from prison in 1897, having served two years of hard labor for the crime of being gay, he fled to France on his own road to Rome. A broken man, legally deprived of the right to see his children, denied a visit from his dying mother—his spirits lifted the moment his feet touched French soil. I was thinking of Wilde because he had just been pardoned. The British government announced that thousands of men, living and dead, would have their gay criminal past purged under a new law named for Alan Turing, the World War II code breaker who was convicted of homosexuality in 1952. Wilde, the greatest wit and brightest playwright of the late Victorian age, was a pauper when released, and sickly. He described himself as "ruined, disgraced—a leper, a pariah to men." He would never put his old life back together, not even close; he would seldom even laugh again. "All pity, or the sense of its beauty, seems to me dead," he wrote. But being so low, so humiliated, brought him closer to something bigger than himself. He would spend the next three years of his life, up until his death at the age of forty-six, trying to answer the rumblings in his soul—a side he seldom showed in his plays or many witticisms. In prison, he noted, "I found myself in the company of the same sort of people Christ liked, outcasts and beggars."

The best-known monument in Calais depicts other kinds of beggars, the ones who nearly starved to death in their homes. In Calais, geography has always been destiny. As the closest landing point in France, it was much coveted by the English. They laid siege to it in 1346, early in the Hundred Years War, which actually lasted longer than a century. Calais had canals, which formed a moat around the old town, and walls inside that. The English had patience and food. Facing death by starvation after a year, a few of the trapped inhabitants emerged. Among them were six leading citizens, who offered to give up their lives if King Edward III would spare the remaining residents. Rodin's sculpture *The Burghers of Calais* depicts the moment when the shackled and emaciated six came forth to face the English king. I'd seen a cast of the figures at Stanford University, where they lack context in a palm-shaded and flip-flop-trodden courtyard.

Here, Rodin's masterpiece fronts the Flemish Renaissance–style town hall, the *hôtel de ville*. The burghers' bones poke through their skin, and sackcloth clings to their skeletal frames. The faces are full of dread, as they await executions. The king's wife took pity on them and persuaded her husband to let them live. Still, they could not stay in their homes. Edward proceeded to ethnically cleanse Calais of its own people, who lost everything, and replace them with those from the other side of the Channel. The English stayed for more than two hundred years, their last toehold in France, until they were driven out by a siege against them. Many of the people who repopulated the city were French Protestants, on the run from Catholic persecution in other parts of their country. And then the Germans invaded in the last century.

That's the Calais story, a very moving civic narrative of defiance and dispossession. But it doesn't apply to the latest refugees from religion. Calais has been down on its luck for some time. Population is falling, and the lace factories that spun wedding garments and gloves for the world have dwindled to a few. One in five adults is without a job. In this part of France, economic despair has left many people looking for scapegoats. And in Calais, they don't have to look far.

"We don't want them!" a man shouted outside the refugee-processing center. Protesters hissed when mention of Aleppo and Mosul came up. Allowing exiles from those ruined cities into France is seen as treason to a culture, a threat to the Christian heritage. The migrants are paying for the crimes of a few, while fleeing the larger crimes of the many. The day I arrived, a terrorist in Manchester set off a bomb at a concert, killing twenty-two people, including children as young as eight.

It would be wrong to expect the residents of Calais to remember ancient times. But history does boomerang. In the twelfth century, Saint Bernard of Clairvaux barnstormed around France, working Christians into a fever over the infidels who held Aleppo and Mosul. It was the duty of every follower of Jesus in France to reverse the journey taken by today's migrants—to purge those biblical cities of their Muslim overlords. "Cursed be he who does not stain his sword with blood!" said Brother Bernard. This powerful monk, an adviser to popes and kings, almost single-handedly started the Second Crusade, a grisly and pointless expedition in the two centuries of war between Christians and Muslims.

"We're not racist," a man at the refugee center explained in a television report. "We're here to support French identity."

French identity—do tell where I can find it. I'm meandering about in search of the embodiment of that identity, the church of Notre-Dame, where de Gaulle was married. It is the oldest monument in Calais, dating to the thirteenth century; it holds a place in this city as the Notre-Dame of Paris does for all of France—"the epicenter of our lives," as President Macron said after fire gutted the roof of the iconic cathedral. I'm coiled and ready to spring my pathetic French on an unsuspecting public, but no targets appear. It's after four o'clock, the sun is still merciless, and I'm starting to crave the cool interior of an ancient holy space. In a neighborhood that is ghostly at this hour, I behold *l'église Notre-Dame*. Windborne weeds grow out of the sides of the upper reaches of the church, like untrimmed hair in the ears of an old man. If nothing else, I'm hoping to get my pilgrim passport stamped. The main entrance door is locked, which is strange. And today, May 22, is de Gaulle's birthday, so you'd think there would be somebody here to note the occasion. I walk around the side, knocking on different doors.

Disappointed, I head toward the heavily guarded train station. I have a couple of options for the first continental leg of the Via Francigena. I'd heard that the French do a terrible job of signing this route. What I heard is correct. The V.F. was designated a European Cultural Itinerary in 1994, recognizing it as a vital vein in the long history of these Christian nations, and also as an effort to lure tourists to less-traveled regions. But I see more signs for the nearest McDonald's, an imperial interloper.

I can strictly follow Sigeric, whose next stopping place was tiny Guînes, seven miles away on a route that promises to be boring, hot, and flat. Another slightly more distant destination, Amettes, is the intriguing birthplace of Saint Benoît Labre, known as the Vagabond of God. He was homeless for the entirety of his adult life, living on the streets of eighteenth-century Europe, clothed in rags, his skin covered with scabs and bug bites. His last years were spent in the ruins of Rome's Colosseum. This life of pure vagrancy made him a saint after his death at the age of thirty-five. That, and more than 130 miracle cures attributed to him. His hometown holds a big festival in his honor, and thousands of people come to see the little house where he lived with fourteen siblings, the straw mattress where he slept, and a few of his body parts in the church. Today, they would cashier this repulsive bum out of Calais.

Or I can divert by train twenty-three miles inland to Saint-Omer, one of the overlooked marvels of medieval Europe. Saint-Omer is near a monastery where I want to stay, just off the Via. I'm told there's a library holding books that are thirteen hundred years old.

Full disclosure: I'm not impressed by Sigeric the Serious. Aside from the fact that he was mirthless by reputation, his record of the Via is minimalist and unmemorable. It's basically a listing of all his stops, without comment. But as the first person to write up a specific pilgrim route connecting Canterbury to Rome, he gained geographic immortality. It's as if we knew about the Lewis and Clark trail from the notes of the company clerk. As an asterisk in history, Sigeric is also remembered for giving lousy advice to King Ethelred the Unready, who took the throne in 978 after plotting the murder of his half brother Edward the Martyr. (Like some Native American names, these old English monikers will often tell you everything you need to know about a person.) Sigeric, as archbishop of Canterbury, urged the king to pay off the Vikings to keep them from sacking Kent. The Norsemen took the protection money, ten thousand pounds of silver, but invaded anyway a few years later. Saint-Omer it is, then, off to see some of the oldest books in the world.

On my way to the station, I step away from a swoosh of police cars, racing somewhere in a heaving wail of Euro sirens. The somewhere is not far, just a few blocks from the church. The commotion is outside the office of Secours Catholique, which distributes food and clothes to refugees—all without proselytizing, mind you. Earlier this spring, police fired tear gas at volunteers who were attempting to give breakfast to thirty people. Countless children have been abandoned and are hungry, the charity pleaded. Didn't Christ say we have an obligation to help "the least of these brothers of mine"? Sorry: it would only encourage them to stay, the authorities say. So, French police are trying a modern variant on the Calais siege: starve the migrants into leaving.

The fight today is over showers. Secours Catholique brought in two portable trailers with water tanks—a chance for some of the wanderers to clean up. This infuriated the mayor, who had a dumpster dropped at the entrance to prevent access. Somebody has called in a shower violation this afternoon, bringing the enforcers. A priest vows that he won't surrender until a few hungry children have been taken care of.

So here is another boomerang: a religion whose leaders once called on followers to wage savage war against faraway cities held by people of a different religion now fights to feed and protect forsaken members of that same faith from those same faraway cities. It's heartening, a selfless act. The handful of people who still work every day to keep Christian tradition alive in France—those who *should* be most threatened by loss of identity from outsiders of another religion—are practicing the core tenets of what they preach. On this day in May, the great centuries-old sanctuary of Notre-Dame may be unwelcoming and lifeless, but don't let it be said that the Catholic Church has given up on Calais.

FIVE

THE LOST CITY OF SAINT-OMER

One way to God in the Middle Ages was to write from first light till dusk in a scriptorium stuffed with silent monks. Your fingers ached and seized up. Your lower back was a nag of pain. Your eyes blurred. Your legs went numb. Your stomach growled. Your mind wandered, making you miss a word, which could lead to a misinterpretation by a high-ranking reader, who then committed heresy by repeating the error, ending with his head on a spike. Your home and place of work was a factory of recluses who were not allowed to talk while they put goose quills to parchment, copying sacred text. In this way, for more than a thousand years, books were produced and the spiritual and intellectual life of the Western world was preserved and passed on. These monks were machines in service to advancing Christianity and culture. It could take four men working two years to create a single large and lavishly colored manuscript. Some of the scribes couldn't read. Others were nearly blind.

The tattoos of knowledge were pressed between the skins of animals. I'm holding one now, dating to the twelfth century, with a cover of cattle hide so thick I can run my hand over the bristled hairs. Inside, the colors pop—brilliant reds, blues, and greens, applied to the parchment with egg white. Turning the stiff pages with my white-gloved hands, I notice little notes on the side. The imposition of silence didn't keep the word slaves from making personal remarks in the margins:

"I am very cold."

"Thank God, it will soon be dark."

"Writing is drudgery."

"The parchment is hairy."

"I am exhausted."

It sounds dreadful, this life. But the daily grind of writing was also a form of prayer, and so, another passage to eternity. "Monasteries had power, they produced these books for people in power," says Rémy Cordonnier, the head of ancient collections at the library of Saint-Omer. "The writing was also a way to know yourself, a way to communicate with God, and a way to get into heaven." Cordonnier is blue-eyed and bearded, sockless today with a dress shirt and jeans. He has a doctorate in art history, which served him well when he made one of the most extraordinary discoveries in the book world: a First Folio of the collected works of William Shakespeare, hiding in musty anonymity just a few feet from Latin treatises on indecipherable topics. He has opened the inner sanctum of the library to me, on very short notice, because he loves what these books mean, and he seldom passes up a chance to let the long-dead voices in the volumes speak again.

I found this great vault of literary treasures on an unremarkable side street, next to a school. Saint-Omer was once a magical and lively place, a scholastic center, a trade exchange for wool, wine, and wisdom. A Burgundy-born bishop, Omer, working the low country of a pagan corner of Europe, sent monks forth to found a monastery on the banks of the River Aa in the year 638. It was a buggy marsh with a couple of hillocks, sparsely populated by people living hard, stunted lives—a tribe of Germanic Franks. A town sprang up around the abbey. The brothers diverted the river for agriculture, a web of water still put to use by a handful of farmers today. The social order—laws and rules to live by, a community of commerce, a shared sense of purpose—had largely collapsed with the fall of the Western Roman Empire more than a century earlier. To these barbarians, as they were long called, Christians brought illuminated books, advanced carpentry, refinements in how to grind grain using the power of water through a mill. The church "stood for everything that was progressive, enlightened and humane in Europe," wrote Johnson in his history of a faith.

Christians came not to conquer. What animated them was the story they told, the same one passed on by the Celtic monastics from Ireland: a son of God who was also a man, a Jew born in Galilee who lived a short life preaching around Judea, was killed in Jerusalem by a Roman prefect, and then defied death itself. Many dozens of people saw the risen Christ; some chose death rather than recant. This Son of God spoke in the idiom of the people, using parables to make his points. If his message was easy to understand, it was even easier to embrace. Love is intoxicating. Hate is poison. Above all, take care of the least among you. Revere creation. He preached tolerance rather than condemnation, and liberation from rigid societal norms of class and religion. He was a charismatic rebel—defiant in the prime of his life, passive at his execution. He was called Christ from the Greek word *Kristos*, anointed one.

Over the centuries, the abbey grew upward and outward, with cathedral-high arches and fine-chiseled stone throughout. And it grew inward, as generations of tonsured monks labored over hundreds of manuscripts. It is said that Irish ascetics saved civilization, harboring the Western world's written knowledge while Europe fell under plunder to illiterate hordes. But more broadly, in the early Middle Ages, Christian ascetics *created* a civilization that grew into the Europe that would determine much of the world's fate. With books tied to their waists, the wandering evangelists founded nearly 150 monasteries between 575 and 725. By 1300, Saint-Omer was one of the biggest cities on the northern mainland. The pattern that took hold here was matched elsewhere: from monastery in a marsh or forest, to town, to thriving regional community, to literacy and laws, to institutions of learning and prayer, to a semblance of modern life. It certainly wasn't democratic. And women had very little standing. But what is still called the Dark Ages was anything but.

Now Saint-Omer is a shell of forgotten Christianity, fossilizing by the day. I feel some sadness for this place because it is so intriguing yet doesn't quite know what to do with its endowment from the ages. That's my initial impression. Its standing monuments are impossibly oversized for a town of 14,000. I turn one corner and come upon the vast remains of the Abbey of Saint Bertin, an open-air ruin of the original Christian footprint. It was rhapsodized by Victor Hugo for its ghostly grandeur. The floor is grass. The roof is sky. The arched Gothic entrances are intact, in places, with headless saints of stone mounted on pedestals. "Such places are truly holy," Hugo wrote, "man has meditated and communed with himself therein." I cross over a canal, walk down a row of immaculate seventeenth-century town houses, and stumble upon a stoop from which Thomas Becket preached during his exile here, while in his less deadly first feud with Henry II. I leave a sleepy square after a life-affirming breakfast of *café au lait* and almond-crusted *pain au chocolat* to find the Bibliothèque de Saint-Omer.

From the street, the building is a blank wall of don't-look-twice, about as nondescript as a medieval department of motor vehicles. After the doors open, I walk up one flight of steps and enter a wood-paneled salon of thirty-five thousand rare books. So many stories. So many opinions. So many prayers. And most of them incomprehensible to the average reader. As my blue-collar dad used to ask, in appreciative and near-drunken wonder while listening to blind Italian tenor Andrea Bocelli, "What's he trying to say?" Almost a third of the volumes were rescued from the destroyed Abbey of Saint Bertin. Others were saved from Henry VIII's rampage against the monasteries in England and smuggled across the Channel. The spines were built to last, with bulging leather vertebrae. Consider that the Book of Kells, the illuminated manuscript of the four Gospels, is Ireland's greatest national treasure, finished about the year

800. People line up in the rain of Dublin to view the monks' calligraphy on display inside Trinity College. But Saint-Omer's library has hundreds of minor masterpieces from the same period onward. None are as impressive as the Book of Kells, but each in its way is a work of art—just as ancient, just as intricate, just as compelling.

A single book in this room is worth more than the real estate on the block: a Gutenberg Bible. It's one of only four in France, and one of fewer than two dozen or so intact originals left on the planet. Writing was slow to evolve. The earliest expressive forms were scrawls on flat clay tablets— cuneiforms. What they wrote about was utilitarian. This changed with the Greeks. Among other things, they had a sense of humor, evident in lighthearted poetry on wine jugs. The Romans wrote on scrolls of dried papyrus; smaller ones, tucked in the pockets of centurions, were portable, like paperbacks. History, philosophy, epic poems—all found their way into the transcribed concerns of the scrolls spread by the Empire. Then, for a thousand years, from the fall of Rome in the fifth century to the dawn of the printing press with Gutenberg's Bible, books were made by unknown toilers in places like Saint-Omer.

But there was a limit to how much knowledge one person could acquire. Medieval scholars believed that each human could store only a finite amount of information. God set the range. And how did people know when they'd reached the point where not another nugget of new thought could be taken in? We can only wonder, for the scribes did not leave behind a tool for measuring full mental capacity.

I ask Cordonnier whether I can see the oldest surviving printed book in the world, his Gutenberg. It would be a disservice to my calling if I didn't try. Cordonnier laughs at my request; he wonders if I'm being ironic. *Ce n'est pas possible,* says the librarian. The Gutenberg is far too valuable, worth a hundred million dollars or more. Under lock and key and heavy guard. As a consolation, Cordonnier guides me to the Shakespeare. It is visible through a thick glass case, opened to *The Tragedie of Romeo and Juliet.* Published in 1623, seven years after his death, the First Folio contains the bulk of Shakespeare's output. It is luminous. Not a flat or dead thing. It was Cordonnier who made the discovery in 2014. He was sifting through the collection of English-language literature when a very thick and heavy book caught his eye. The title page was torn off. But once Cordonnier more closely examined it, he realized that he had come upon the find of a life-time. For a lover of ancient texts, it was an emotional moment.

The digital age has done nothing to dim the popularity of Shake-speare. But what about the Bard's book-mates stacked on shelves of an-tique wood here in Saint-Omer? Who still listens to voices from the European literary cradle, slowly fading away in this nursing home of ge-riatric books? Who reads Latin calligraphy, or Old English? Who has any sense of what these books *are trying to say*? At one time, nearly every word in this library was dictated truth, passed on in the copying of scribes. Gutenberg's printing press made a mockery of that monopoly. Anyone's word could be dictated truth, and so it was, with new versions of the Bible customized for various sects. In our time, the chaos of the internet re-duced truth to a near-worthless commodity. But surely all that medieval meditation on God has some place in an era of disposable thought.

"I can see a day when people won't have any idea what the religion in these books means," says Cordonnier. "It is already happening. The stu-dents next door, they don't know what this is. They feel they don't have to know. But look around France. Our holidays are still tied to religion. The names of our cities, our streets, come from religion."

Cordonnier was raised Catholic, but now—he's a weddings and fu-nerals kind of churchgoer. In that, he is typical of the French. Although 53 percent consider themselves Catholic, only 5 percent of the faithful attend Mass on a regular basis—which means that practicing Catholics make up less than 3 percent of the population of France. "I'm not very reli-gious," says Cordonnier, "but I think religion has been good overall. A civ-ilizing force. Now, we can do good without religion, so people don't feel they need it anymore." And how about himself? The man who spends his days among the words of those who saw penmanship as prayer—does he still need it? "I will tell you this," he says, after giving my question some thought. "Devotion is one of the only things that you don't see in other species."

A FEW BLOCKS from the library, construction crews are working to spiff up Saint-Omer's cathedral, Our Lady of Miracles. It got its start not long after the abbey rose on the riverbank in the seventh century. I duck into the church in search of its Rubens painting, *Descent from the Cross*. There's also an astronomical clock and an enormous Gothic organ. All are spectacular. But none are as intriguing as a rough stone tomb off to one side, dating to 723. This scratched-up rock bed holds the remains of Erkembode—the Saint Who Walks. The legend of Erkembode is that he was a selfless man who traveled throughout Flanders on foot looking for land that nobles might give to the poor. His legs eventually gave out, leaving him crippled. Atop the tomb today are dozens of tiny shoes. They are pink and green, spotted and flowered, plastic and leather, Velcro and laced. None would fit the feet of anyone older than five. Children who cannot walk make a pilgrimage to Saint-Omer to leave their shoes atop the tomb of the Saint Who Walks, in hopes of—well, something.

The shoes of little disabled children are overpowering, and almost move me to tears. Christopher Hitchens would be scornful. Miracles were cheap magicians' ploys used early on to get people to believe in Christianity—"the tawdriness of the miraculous," he called it. That age is long gone. Now, what passes for supernatural events are hallucinations—of statues weeping and bleeding—and unworthy of a god with power, he wrote. I take his first point, for miracles were indeed a recruiting tool, wielded first by Jesus, who famously changed water into wine to keep a wedding party going at Cana. (Note to Mormons.) But it's hard to look at this thirteen-hundred-year-old tomb and be entirely dismissive. Every few days or so, the shoes are cleared away. And every few days after that, the tomb is covered again. The church does not promote it. It happens on its own. Do children walk because of it? Probably not. But Erkembode's tomb tells them they are not alone; they can join a community of hope.

Nearby, a hive of construction blocks the main entrance to the Jesuit chapel of the old college, which shoulders the great library where I spent most of the day. When Catholics in England were banned from educating children in their faith, the Jesuits built an expansive college here in 1593. The school was filled with young English elites and produced a signer of the American Declaration of Independence and a coauthor of the Constitution—members of the Carroll family. Another graduate, after the college was forced to move, was Thomas Francis Meagher, the Irish revolutionary, American Civil War general, and governor of Montana Territory. Then it was largely abandoned and fell into disrepair. Now, masons, cement mixers, and stone polishers labor on different parts of the five-story façade and marble-floored interior. The massive old Catholic school is undergoing a top-to-bottom restoration, "where heritage plays a major role," as a sign explains.

So, my first impression of Saint-Omer was wrong. The town on the banks of the River Aa has figured out what to do with its endowment from the ages. The great books, the college where generations of Catholics were educated, the eighth-century tomb, and the tiny shoes in the cathedral. Saint-Omer realizes that it cannot escape its past. The Lost City has embraced all that nearly fell away. The ossified shell of ancient Christianity will be polished, highlighted, sold to tourists, though its overall meaning may be more elusive with each passing day.

I wonder how many visitors will agree with Victor Hugo's observation on the ruins of Christian France, from the centuries when religion advanced with books instead of armies. "What they contained of truth has remained and become greater." If that sounds like the romantic casting of a man of faith, think again. Late in life, Hugo was asked by a census taker if he was a Catholic. "No," he replied, "freethinker."

SIX

A NIGHT AT THE MONASTERY

The walk to the Abbey of Saint Paul in Wisques should take no more than three hours—a pleasant urban stroll, then an empty country-side. That's what my guidebook says. This will give me just enough time to unspool the twine cluttering my mind after a long breakfast at the splendid eighteenth-century home where I spent the night. My room was on the third floor, with large double windows overlooking a garden of fruit trees, climbing roses, and late-blooming lilacs. Last night, with twi-light lingering well past ten o'clock, I filled the claw tub in the bathroom, opened the shutters to get a waft of flowery fragrance, and fell asleep. When I woke, the water was lukewarm, the sky had darkened, and I felt both renewed and ready for bed. My hosts had stuffed me with dark ale and sausages for dinner, and homemade jam on fresh bread with a fruit plate for breakfast. All of it—the huge room (with a marble fireplace), two meals, and a family that tolerated my high school French—was 55 euros. A pilgrim doesn't have to suffer.

My breakfast-mate was a troubled man from a troubled part of France who was working as a delivery driver, part-time, to get him through a retirement that was anything but leisurely. He told me his country had failed him. The elites in Paris, the Eurocrats in Brussels—they cut their deals, traded away the factories of northern France, and left behind hollowed-out villages of desperation. He had a chronic cough and was very pale, and he smoked. I asked him if he'd been inside the Cathedral of Miracles here in Saint-Omer—not because I thought he might find a cure, but just to move the conversation along. No, he shook his head. For most of his life, he was a Catholic, but he will never set foot in a church again. "Pedophiles," he said. He spit out the word. "What they did to all those little boys—it sickens me." I did not have the heart to tell a man betrayed by the two main institutions of his country that France—so far—had not failed me.

Because of the late start, I'm hiking in midday heat, temperatures in the upper 80s. This is crazy, and shows a lack of discipline on my part. A mix of sweat and sunscreen streaks my face and stings my eyes. I'm somewhat embarrassed to put on the floppy hat I got at REI, because it makes me look like one of those earnest German hikers you see all over Europe. Screw it—I need the protection. I had stuffed the guidebook deep inside my twenty-two-pound pack. I also forgot to charge my phone. Now I can't get out of Saint-Omer. I take the wrong way off a roundabout, get caught up in heavy traffic on a busy street with no sidewalk. I follow one road to a dead end, another that comes to a stop in the vast parking lot of a closed factory. All of that takes two hours, and still I'm only at the periphery of Saint-Omer. Dogs startle me and snarl. The straps of my pack are starting to cut into my shoulders. People honk and flip me off. Kids roll down their windows and shout. The French are no longer charming; they're assholes.

By the three-hour mark, I'm finally in the countryside. I can see the round towers of the monastery through the haze of a still day, another hour away, at least. There's no shoulder on this single-lane road. When a car comes at me I have to step aside into a drainage ditch. No one slows to wave or veers to give me room. So much for the meditative value of deep walking.

Wisques is a village of fewer than two hundred people, and nobody is stirring when I arrive in late afternoon. Not a soul. Not a car. Not a dog. It looks eerily prosperous, as if run by the affluent dead. There is no restaurant, no bakery, no small store, no place to fill water bottles. But here, for the first time since Canterbury, is a big detailed sign of the Via Francigena. It places me in the early stages of the pilgrimage, miles of flatland farms all around. *Vous êtes ici!* Good to know. The cartoon pilgrim here is a sly-looking fellow in pressed shorts with a requisite silly hat tilted to one side. At least he doesn't have a cigarette hanging out of his mouth. While studying the billboard, I hear voices and look up the road. I'm soon joined by a young couple from Wales. They also got lost, though they're taking it better than me. Their plan is to stay at the convent run by the sisters, up a steep hill. I had considered that, but, still haunted by memories of thick-knuckled nuns boxing my ears in grade school, I opted for the brothers at the monastery. "Every pilgrim has to walk their own camino," said the woman, as this pair bid me adieu.

Although I'm now on the Via-signed trail, I miss the turnoff. This costs me another hour. Not paying attention, I brush against a patch of nettles. The pain is low and constant, a junior-grade bee sting. When I arrive at the Abbey of Saint Paul after a gruesome march of perhaps twelve miles—most of it on pavement—I slow to take in this Benedictine refuge. It's still and sylvan, shadowed by its own forest. Round towers and spires rise from the gates of a closed-off, rectangular setting of brick, stone, and stucco. There are greenhouses, raised gardens, and plowed land; it looks like a good-sized working farm. Using hand tools, a couple of monks are tilling rows of vegetables. I announce myself, and mention the name of someone I'd spoken to on the phone. The man at the entrance looks askance at me, then disappears. When he returns after ten minutes, he tells me to wait in the cloister. He leads me down a long portico, locking two thick-oaked doors behind us as he goes. This is strange. But I'm fairly certain they'll put me up; the 53rd rule of Saint Benedict obliges monks to have a place for pilgrims.

The elderly abbot in charge of Saint Paul appears after another twenty minutes. He moves in closer and sniffs, sizing me up with what appears to be disgust. He looks crisp in his light cotton black cassock, short-cropped gray hair, rimless glasses. I'm sweaty, stinking, sunburned, my shirt stained, hair mussed, a patch of my leg inflamed with nettle burn. Without any niceties or small talk, without giving me his name or shaking my hand, he starts in with some questions.

"Are you a Christian?"

"*Je suis un pèlerin.*"

"We get lots of pilgrims here, but are you a Christian?" His English is better than my French, so that will be the language of this interrogation.

"I was raised Catholic."

"Yes?"

"And educated by Jesuits."

"Where?"

"High school, Gonzaga. In the Pacific Northwest. Spokane, Washington. Do you know where that is?"

"We have maps here at the monastery."

"I'm sure you do."

"Are you married?"

"Yes. Two kids—"

"Divorced?"

"Never."

"How are things in America?"

"Troubled."

"Why is that?"

"Trump."

"What's wrong with him?"

"Everything."

"I'll show you to your room."

"Is there Wi-Fi?" The abbot stops dead in his tracks and glares at me.

"I'm kidding."

In truth, I'm trying to go on a digital cleanse. One of my goals of this trip is to cut down on the amount of useless information I consume. Easy access to a world of tempting crap has clearly not been good for me. My attention span has shrunk. Sustained, deep reading and thinking are more difficult. I'm punch-drunk from the unrelenting present, the news alerts and flashes, all the chaos without context. I'm enslaved to a dopamine-induced loop, craving the brain chemical release that comes with every new text or tweet. I get lured into too much low-grade clickbait and tweets from somebody's dog. Do I have to respond to email instantly, lest some friend or colleague think me too distant, too high-and-mighty out here in an ancient slow lane? In that regard, the time difference—nine hours between Seattle and France—gives me a built-in cushion. While I wander about in spiritual befuddlement during the day, friends and family are asleep.

We walk down one more long corridor, up a flight of stairs to a second story.

The abbot opens an unlocked door. The room is no bigger than a prison cell, with a small single bed low to the ground, a sheet, a blanket, one pillow, a window overlooking the cloister. There's a thin towel barely larger than a handkerchief. He says I can use the bathroom down the hall to clean up. A shower? Kind of. There's water coming from a faucet in a stall. Sometimes it's hot. Sometimes not. The abbot is in a hurry to be done with me. I'm surprised, after our initial interview, that he doesn't seem the least bit interested in spreading the Word that Benedictines pray on all day, every day.

"There's no preaching here," he says. "That's not what we do. People come here to get away from things. You are on your own."

I try to talk a little politics, wondering how his fresh-faced president, Emmanuel Macron, the youngest head of state in France since Napoleon, will react to the latest terrorist attack. This startles the abbot.

"A terror attack?" He hadn't heard. "Where?" I tell him about the Manchester bombing—twenty-two people murdered by a fanatic in a worn-down part of England. He looks perplexed, then shakes his head. There is something reassuring in his insularity.

"I'll come get you for supper. You're free to look around, but don't disturb anyone."

I TAKE A BRISK SHOWER, change into fresh clothes, and slip down the stairway, as light-footed as a spirit. I want to see the layout. The monks tend beehives, vines, and greenhouses. Their vegetable rows look terrific—clean lines of beets, carrots, spinach, lettuce, rhubarb, potatoes. I wave to a man who is sweating through his ankle-length cassock while pushing a wheelbarrow. He doesn't acknowledge me; I assume he's deep in thought, or prayer, or contempt for strangers who wave to monks. There are no power tools that I can see, no motorized tractors. After leaving the empty ruins of Saint Bertin, it's great to see a *living* abbey, people who've given up all their possessions for a higher purpose. What did Pope Francis say when asked how to renew wonder? Live lean. "The more I have, the more I want," he said. "It kills the soul." Today's tableau at Saint Paul is truly timeless; it could be lifted from any of the fifteen hundred years since Benedict set down his rules, establishing the monastic order to which these brothers belong.

We know from the biblical Acts of the Apostles that early Christians lived spartan lives, taking the Gospel admonition of Christ to heart. "If you would be perfect, go, sell what you possess and give to the poor, and you will have treasure in heaven," he says in Matthew. They got rid of their worldly goods, cut family ties, and held everything in common. Later, the austerity could be unhealthy: flagellation, starvation diets, chaining oneself to a stone or column under a blistering sun. It took Benedict, a man of wealth from the Umbrian hill town of Norcia, to establish guidelines that would satisfy body and spirit—without the extremes. Born in 480, he moved to Rome to study. The church then was growing in two directions—one an organization intent on expanding its power, property, and control over the lives of Christians in a concentrated area around Rome and a few other Mediterranean cities; the other, individuals dedicated to spreading a simple gospel to largely illiterate people, pushing the frontier of faith. In the fourth century, a bishop named Ulfilas had moved among tribes north of the Danube in what is now Germany. The message of a glorious afterlife for the virtuous was a powerful selling point. As with the Irish monks, Ulfilas brought both religion and culture. He invented a Gothic alphabet that allowed people to read Scripture in their language, among other things. At the same time, a missionary named Martin founded one of the first monasteries in Gaul, a center for sharing the Christian word with peasants throughout today's France.

In Rome, the corruption, the accumulation of property, the political plays of an imperious church newly empowered by the rulers of a crumbling empire appalled Benedict. Taking refuge in the woods, he lived in a cave for three years. His asceticism was inspiring and drew followers to the monastery he founded at Montecassino in 529. By the time he died in 547—a year after Rome was sacked a second time—the Rule of Benedict proved to be a blueprint for how to live a healthy life of meaning, creating thriving communities while much of Europe fell into decay and plunder. It was built around humility, fraternity, and love.

The brothers cleared forests, worked elaborate farms, tanned leather, made wine, ale, cheese, and bread, and produced those majestic manuscripts I saw in Saint-Omer, storing much of society's knowledge and its sacred treasures inside cold, thick-walled compounds. They took vows of chastity, poverty, and obedience. Many lived contemplative lives, while others were prominent leaders of their communities. Cluny Abbey in Burgundy and Mont-Saint-Michel off the coast of Normandy were some of the most alluring of these homes for busy men. Though they were nominally without sex, silver, or free speech, the more powerful abbots eventually had servants and large bedrooms, and maintained close ties to royalty. They became more like the people Benedict had rebelled against. After a tour of monasteries in France, one church official found many a fornicating celibate, "living the life of Bacchanals." And while the labors of brothers who had taken holy orders brought prosperity to major abbeys and well-connected merchants, the average men of the faith did not share in the bounty. A daily ration could be a pound of bread and a pint of wine, no more. The able-bodied worked until they fell from exhaustion.

Individual monasteries had their peculiarities, bordering on pathologies. Monks slept on the ground or had separate beds of straw, except for younger ones, who were sometimes doubled up with older men. This raises several obvious questions. Silence for much of the day was a general rule. The idea was to clear the mind of distractions. A monk was not allowed to raise his eyebrows or roll his eyes. He was required to listen with his mouth open. He could not grin. "For us, bodily delights are nothing but dung!" said Bernard of Clairvaux. And yet, people who were free to go did not go. Life was simple and had meaning, so long as you followed the model of *ora et labora*—pray and work. Scripture was a living word, not a text. Divine Reading, *Lectio Divina*, was a four-step way to comprehend God's revelations. In the silence, in the community, in the shared sacrifices, the brothers found a measure of happiness.

Nordic invaders in the ninth and tenth centuries found something else: defenseless abbeys ripe for plunder. Raiders emptied monastic pantries of food, and cellars of precious goods. In response, some orders erected round towers—places to hide themselves and their treasures. The Norsemen used fire to smoke out the Christians, who were then put to the sword. But it's telling that in at least one place, the lonely rock isle of Skellig Michael off the Irish coast, a surprising transition took place—with the same selling point used to convert the Goths. In the year 993, Olaf Tryggvason set his sights on that raw, sharp-edged dollop of stone, rising to 714 feet from the turbulent chop of the Atlantic. There, monks lived on bird eggs and fish, climbing up and down the 670 steps to their beehive habitation in the most unlikely monastery in the world. Olaf was fresh off a successful coercion campaign that persuaded Ethelred the Unready to pay a fat bounty to avoid slaughter.

You can imagine the exchange at Skellig Michael: Gold crosses and silver chalices, *they're ours now.* Illuminated manuscripts, *give 'em over.* Dried fish, fermented drink, part of the Norse haul. And finally, from the invaders: *What else you got?* The monks offered eternal life. Intriguing. At a time when life expectancy was—what? Nearly a third of all people died before the age of five. Childbirth itself was often fatal for the mother. If you made it to your teens, you might see age forty-five. Olaf converted—according to Irish tradition—and he became the first Christian king of Norway.

By 1400, there were more than three thousand monasteries, with almost fifty thousand monks throughout western Europe. In the long sweep of this history, the Abbey of Saint Paul is a newcomer. But it has been through several near-death experiences. Within ten years of its founding in 1889, the monastery came up against the latest wave of anticlerical fever to sweep through France. The monks fled to the Netherlands rather than comply with laws that allowed state control over them. They returned in 1920, invited back after World War I. But fifty years later, they faced an existential crisis afflicting the greater church: the crash in religious vocations. Benedictines did no better at attracting new members to their ancient ways than other Catholic orders. By 2013, when Francis became pope, the average age here was seventy-five, and the monastery was prepared to close its doors. A few dying brothers would go down with the abbey. At the last minute, four monks from another monastery moved in, giving Saint Paul fresh life, such as it is.

These old men wake at five a.m. to the chime of a bell. After a splash of cold water on the face, they walk through the cloister to a chapel for matins, thanking God for bringing light to a dark world. At six-thirty, a piece of bread and jam is taken with a cup of coffee. This is followed by the second service of the day, lauds. Then, back to the cell for private prayer, the *Lectio Divina.* Mass in the traditional Latin is at ten o'clock. A fourth service comes just after noon, with a small meal following. It's off to work after that, in the farm, in the yard, in the laundry room, plastering walls, chopping wood, or pulling weeds. Afternoons allow for some socializing, taking care of personal things, writing. This leads up to vespers at six p.m., followed by dinner. A final service, compline, begins at 8:35. It's eat, pray, love, in the purest sense.

THE ABBOT SUMMONS ME shortly before seven. He seems reluctant to answer my questions. I'm trying to be minimally intrusive, just a couple of queries to quell my curiosity. I ask him about a recent earthquake in Norcia, the birthplace of Benedict, which destroyed the monastery and disturbed the soul of Italy. "We will rebuild," he says curtly. "We always do." He has questions of his own. I'm wary of giving up too much about myself, especially after reading the latest blog entry from Carlo Laurenzi, the British pilgrim who was here a few nights before me. As Carlo explained, the abbot "took my credenziale and gave me the third degree. He seemed more displeased about me being divorced. I didn't have the courage to add . . . twice!"

We descend a flight of stairs, walk down a long corridor, go up another rise. A monk holds a bowl of water outside the cavernous room where the main meal of the day is served. Another man dips a cloth into the bowl and insists on washing my hands—a very kind gesture. Now, inside the timbered, high-ceilinged dining hall, I gape at the soaring interior. It's very Harry Potter, drafty and vast, echoing with plates being set, chairs scraping, utensils clanking. The meal will be shared by a dozen monks, all looking at least seventy or older, save for one young man— young in comparison to the others. The abbot had warned me that dinner must be eaten in absolute silence. The only person who is allowed to speak is a designated talker who ascends to a lectern.

At my table are the two other pilgrims of the night, whom I met in the hallway. One is a highly educated man from Nepal, who is nearing the end of a reverse Via Francigena, going to Canterbury. His walk is dedicated to raising money for medical clinics at home. The other man is

French, about sixty years old, a father of two, with short, toothbrush-bristle hair, a squat nose on a square face. He looks like Shrek. He had told me before dinner that this was his fourth visit to the monastery. He's wealthy enough to give a large amount of money every year to the Bene-dictines to help them pay the bills, and he enjoys these retreats. We are seated with two monks at a wooden table.

The first course is pea soup, watery and flavorless, self-served from a large communal pot that is passed around. It's accompanied by dry bread, no butter. The silence brings out the slurps. As we finish up, the monk at the podium starts in with the evening's readings. He tells of the saints who will be commemorated tomorrow, outlines part of the Benedictine Rule, and then reads an essay from *L'Osservatore Romano*, the official newspaper of the Vatican. When I'm done with the soup, I try to catch the eye of the one youngish brother across the way, to no avail. He looks sad, and I imagine that he has come here for solace from some tragic life event. The next course—the main one—is cooked carrots. Two big serv-ing bowls are passed around. One of them has a piece of chicken in it, a leg. Shrek takes the wine and fills our glasses. After ten minutes or so, he fills them up again. It's an excellent red—a respectable *vin de pays*. But what did I expect? I'm in France, among an order of monastics who've been making wine for fifteen hundred years. Our table of five quickly consumes two bottles.

The chicken leg is never taken. The Frenchman motions with his eyes for me to have it. I motion for him to eat it. Then I shake my head in the direction of the monk to my left—*he* should take it. The brother waves his hand over his plate; he's had enough, thank you. In the end, I eat the drumstick in shame.

This austere meal among brothers of the cloth sends me back to my days at the Jesuit House of Gonzaga. The contrast could not be greater. The only way I could afford Catholic high school was to work off my tuition. My family had no money. Every day, after the last class and sports,

I'd hustle over to the large residence of the priests, where I was the main dishwasher in an industrial kitchen. The Jesuits, founded in the sixteenth century, were no recluses. They actively engaged with the world, and tried to influence it through politics and the reach of their educators. My toils in their kitchen came just before the big crash in vocations, coinciding with the final years of the Vietnam War, when young people became novitiates as a way to avoid the draft. The Jesuit House was packed with men in black. They began their evening with a raucous cocktail hour—Irish whiskey, mixed drinks, beer, and wine. Dinners were fantastic, particularly the Italian fare: lasagna, spaghetti and meatballs, cannelloni—and nobody scrimped on desserts. One priest, an ex-Marine who taught tenth-grade physics, had his own dietary restriction: he required a sixteen-ounce steak, well-done, with a pile of onions atop it, always served with his bottle of A.1. sauce. Every night, same thing. I never thought the Jesuits were hypocrites for eating and drinking well despite taking a vow of poverty. What I remember is the joy from that dining room. The place roared with laughter, good cheer, and lively, argumentative conversation.

Where is the joy at Saint Paul's dinner hour? Hard to find. I want to linger, but the last dish is cleared quickly, and the place empties out in a hurry. The entire meal, from hand washing to dessert, takes barely thirty minutes.

Outside the dining room, I thank the abbot for allowing me to join the Benedictines. I want to compliment him on the wine, but I'm not sure if that's appropriate. He dashes off, saying he may not see me in the morning. I'm left alone with the Frenchman in the hallway. Our conversational dam, backed up during the silent supper, bursts quickly. He knows a lot about the Saint Paul monastery, and every one of the brothers here. They don't mind being forgotten, hidden at the northern edge of France in a village of a couple of hundred people, or being thought of as archaic, he says. But they do feel like they are under relentless persecution.

"If you're a Catholic in France, you have to be very careful."

How so?

"Hundreds of anti-Catholic incidents. It's far worse than the anti-Semitism of the past."

This strikes me as an exaggeration, and an insult to history. When I ask him for examples, he cites the murder in 2016 of a parish priest in Normandy. Father Jacques Hamel, a much-loved eighty-five-year-old, was saying Mass one morning near Rouen. Two men burst into the church and grabbed a nun and a pair of worshippers as hostages. One of the men forced Father Hamel to kneel, and then slit his throat at the altar. The killers shouted *"Allahu Akbar"* and filmed the carnage. On their way out, they were shot dead by police.

God is certainly not great if he accepts praise from people who would butcher a kindly old man in a church. And those killers would not have taken the life of Father Hamel had they not believed they were serving God. The logic is as twisted as it is ancient. What did God ask of Abraham? To kill his only son, Isaac. It was a test of his faith, as it turned out—and the boy's life was saved at the last minute. But today, we would rightly lock up Abraham after he tied his son to a wood bundle and raised a knife over his throat.

We talk about my fellow pilgrim's experience at Saint Paul. He likes this refuge from modernity. He enjoys the silence, the Latin Mass, the Gregorian chants, the rituals, the fraternity.

I tell him a story about my mother, frayed and exhausted while trying to raise seven kinetic kids, each barely one year apart. At age nineteen, she was a fashion model for a department store, studying art, her life full of promise. I saw a picture of her in a bathing suit posing in front of a cedar tree; a gorgeous and confident young woman. She loved books. She loved music. She loved the outdoors. She loved history. When my grandmother took her to school for the first time, she handed her off to the nuns with these words: "She's all yours. She's too smart for me." But not long after her twenty-first birthday, she fell in love with a soldier from

Chicago, dropped out of college, married. A surfeit of kids soon followed. To us, she was a whir of diaper changing, clothes washing, and dinner preparing, all on her own. Often she broke down, lashing out at the kids, saying she couldn't take it anymore. I would find her crying, alone in her room, and when I asked her what was wrong she said, *Nothing, don't bother, honey.* Her only relief came at the end of the day, when she poured herself a glass of wine and opened her book.

But once a year she would disappear, away to a former seminary in Spokane, now used as a retreat house. For a couple of days, she would pray and read and walk and sleep—but mostly sleep. They didn't charge her anything. She had minutes, hours, entire mornings to herself. In her absence, my dad cooked meatballs and loaded a stack of Frank Sinatra records on the turntable until he fell asleep on the living room floor. . . . *Fly me to the moon.* When she came home, she was a new mom. She looked pretty and youthful, and she hugged us all and said how much she missed us and loved us. I always thought that was one of the better things the Catholic Church did for her.

I bid my companion good night and retire to my room. It's still light outside, too early for sleep. I start another book, a story of intrigue and backstabbing among cardinals selecting the next pope—*Conclave,* a fictional thriller.

In the middle of the night, I'm startled awake. A door slams. And now . . . footsteps. I'm sure of that; it's not my imagination. This gives me the chills. My door has no lock, so I tighten defensively. Logically, there's no reason to be afraid. But I'm alone in a big monastery, surrounded by strange men. As I'd dozed off, the book left me with the impression that anyone in a cassock has a creepy motive. The footsteps get closer, closer, louder, louder in approach. Now, the intruder is just outside my door. And then, just as quickly, the steps move on, the midnight walker passes by, the sound fades, another door opens and closes, and I'm left with my scramble of nighttime thoughts.

I RISE WITH THE BELLS of Saint Paul's, sometime around five a.m. Outside, there's enough light to watch the dawn unfold, birds fluttering from tree to tree, streaks of pink and salmon coloring the horizon. Another hot day is ahead. For breakfast, in an empty room one floor below me, I boil water in a kettle and make a cup of instant coffee. I nibble on some tough bread. Back in my room, I pack, fold my sheets, and leave money on the pillow. Walking through the monastery, fully saddled for the day, I pass a small side chapel, barely larger than a bathroom, with statuettes, candles, and pictures of saints. One of them is the Vagabond of God—Benoît Labre. If I go inside, what will I find? And why should I need a closed space for a spiritual lift? Better to keep moving, to get out into the world that presents itself along the Via Francigena. I'll take the advice of Labre, the patron saint of wandering souls, who grew up not far from here: "There is no way. The way is made by walking."

The morning is exhilarating. As much as I hated this trail coming in, I love it going out. The countryside is just coming to life, doves cooing, bees buzzing off to their labors, a light breeze carrying the fragrance of fresh-cut hay. Yesterday, I never noticed the row crops of the farms along the road. But now, everything stands out. Ahead, I can see Saint-Omer on a rise above the thinnest veil of dew, and beyond—I can see for miles and miles. Off in the immediate forever, the days have no past, no future, only present, only the moment.

SEVEN

WAR AND PEACE
ON THE WESTERN FRONT

The great powers of Europe had been talking about a way to end all wars well before the actual War to End All Wars. Killing for tribe and state was intuitive. Christianity changed nothing. No sooner had the kingdoms converted to a God known as the Prince of Peace than they took up nearly nonstop war for a thousand years. Most of the bloodletting was blessed. The biblical Jesus who never lifted a hand in violence was unrecognizable among the armies who murdered thousands while summoning his name. Romans killed Goths. Goths attacked Byzantines. Normans conquered English. Franks butchered other Franks. And the Holy Roman Empire—a loose confederation of mostly Germanic people, neither Holy nor Roman, as the old joke has it—killed fellow Christians east and west, north and south, all under the banner of heaven.

But after another drawn-out war was followed by even more intra-Christian killing, the nations of Europe finally tried to do something about it. All the kings' men put their swords down and assembled in peace to sign the Treaty of London in 1518. Under the terms, the countries that pledged fealty to Christ would no longer go to war with one another. Their archers, their cannons, their cauldrons of oil and chambers of torture, their fireballs, their lances and knives, their catapults, concussion hammers, and cat-o'-nine-tails would be put aside in a part of the world whose people worshipped Jesus. Spain, England, France, Burgundy, the Habsburg Netherlands, the Holy Roman Empire, the Papal States of Italy, and others signed. War between Christians was outlawed. Forever.

I came upon this grain of historical sand while researching the best route to take on the northern Via Francigena. Midway between Calais and Saint-Omer, on French road D231, is a small plaque commemorating a showy summit between the royal families of England and France in 1520. For several weeks, they outdid each other with gift giving and feast hosting, a Renaissance-era version of a Northwest Indian potlatch. The meeting was supposed to further along friendship between two nations that hated each other—an attempt to shore up the brotherly sentiment of the fledgling Treaty of London.

I hadn't given the Christian peace pact a second thought until my visit to Arras. I'm here on a warm evening, in a part of France known for its sodden, postindustrial gloom. Everyone is out, coatless and carefree, in this masterfully reconstructed city. Arras has a distinctly Flemish look, gabled houses and ornamentally carved buildings shoulder by shoulder around the Grand'Place. Despite the happy pantomime of people eating their *moules-frites* and children kicking a soccer ball, it's a springtime to be solemn. For the square is packed, also, with those who are here to commemorate the young men who never got a chance to be old men taking in the awful gravity of the fields around Arras. A hundred years have passed since a spring when nations that shared a Christian heritage annihilated one another over a few miles of mud.

This pilgrim path that I'm on goes directly through one of the heaviest concentrations of organized killing in the world. Arras sits on a rise above infinite rows of graveyards from the Great War—mass burial grounds of English boys, Scottish boys, Australian boys, Canadian boys,

German boys, American boys, and French boys. Between the craters and white crosses, signs warn of the occasional unexploded shell. The fields are a churn of rust from carnage that killed more than 17 million worldwide, led to the collapse of four empires, and set the stage for Hitler's rise and the unleashing of Nazi genocide—"the great seminal catastrophe" of the twentieth century, as George Kennan called World War I.

The numbers are too enormous. What hits me on this otherwise sublime evening is a series of photographs mounted outside the Arras cathedral. The exhibition shows how Germans leveled one of the premier houses of worship a century ago—space devoted to the same God the destroyers worshipped. Shelling reduced that prodigious space to rubble in 1917. It has since been reconstructed. An obvious question is why Germany, which produced many a brilliant Christian philosopher and legions of reasonable Lutherans and Catholics, would pulverize the cathedral to dust. This, mind you, was not Hitler's war. He was a corporal at the time in the trenches not far from Arras, his stew of pathologies at a low simmer.

A larger question, then: How can you join a faith whose nation-state followers have spent most of their years killing others of that same creed? How can you believe in a savior whose message was peace and passive humility, when the professional promoters of that message were complicit in so much systematic horror? As for that pact to end all Christian-on-Christian killing, it lasted barely two years. In 1521, the nations that signed the Treaty of London commenced a quarter century of new and more awful wars, unleashing terror against civilians and their sacred places.

My fellow pilgrim at the Wisques monastery was horrified by the killing of a priest, as we all should be. He would be horrified at what a devout Catholic, Charles V, did to the cathedral of Thérouanne, a few miles from here on the Via Francigena—just to name one random bit of religious fratricide. This Holy Roman Emperor—though crowned by a pope, he was a nominally secular ruler of a cluster of fiefdoms in central

Europe—burned the cathedral of his faith to the ground and ordered the town razed in 1553. In the same century, mutinous Catholics who'd been under Charles's command sacked Catholic Rome, drunkenly pillaging for eight days while the pope cowered inside the Castel Sant'Angelo. The entire Swiss Guard was wiped out defending St. Peter's Basilica.

European Christians would make war with one another for the next four centuries, expanding the savagery and brutality, the loss of innocent life, with each new conflict, culminating in the high crimes of the twentieth century, the bloodiest in the history of humanity. Nationalism, a scourge that has made a comeback of late, and cancerous ideology were at the root of the two world wars. But even then, and for most of European history, faith in Christ didn't stop Christians from trying to destroy one another. "The truth is that the greatest enemies of the doctrine of Jesus are those calling themselves the expositors of them," said Thomas Jefferson, who struggled with this incongruence all his life. Only now, with Europe at its most secular, is the Continent experiencing one of the longest epochs of peace.

I DECIDE TO USE Arras as a base for a few days of exploring. I like the city. The people are welcoming and easygoing, the food is hearty and lovingly prepared, the place full of UNESCO World Heritage sites ignored by most visitors to France. I'm currently occupying a corner room on an upper floor of the Hôtel de l'Univers, a former Jesuit home dating to the sixteenth century. It's a startling change from the abbey at Wisques. Breakfast of cheese, berries, and pastries is served outside, in a cobbled inner courtyard where priests once clustered for theological debate. I could spend a morning in the arcaded squares of Arras, afternoon in the airy reaches of the town belfry, evening sampling Belgian beers in the Grand'Place. But I'm not here for pleasure, tempting as it is. I'm here for war, and Arras is a place where no stone is without a military scar.

My original plan was to walk from Wisques to Arras, with an overnight in the rebuilt village of Thérouanne. But after a day hoofing it from the abbey, the heat got to me. A morning that had started out perfect morphed into an afternoon of pain. The temperature was in the upper 80s when I stumbled back to the Saint-Omer train station. Water stops are scarce on the northern Via. Scarcer still, at least on the next leg, were places to sleep and eat. The train to Arras, with a transfer, took an hour and a half. Ten minutes from the station, I found the Hôtel de l'Univers. They had me at *bonsoir.*

There's news on my outreach to the pope. After Father Sundborg had a chance to look over my request, he suggested translating the letter into Spanish, the pope's native language. He had someone at his university do it for me, and then made sure it got into the Vatican pouch, as he called it, via the Jesuit back door. *The Vatican pouch!* A glimmer of hope.

THE NEXT DAY, I follow the sound of bagpipes to a ceremony. The Scots lost 46,000, killed or wounded, in the Battle of Arras—a terrible toll for a tiny nation in a single clash in a spring offensive on the western front. Descendants of the dead, their rosy cheeks puffed in making mournful music on a cloudless morning, are here to remember what most of us have forgotten. World War I was a senseless grind of human flesh. Its origins are still baffling, its ending cataclysmic and still felt. Civilized Europe, enlightened Europe, Christian Europe showed that it could be at its most creative when fashioning new ways to kill. These nations gave the world poison gas and bomb-dropping biplanes, flamethrowers and rapid-firing tanks. After a month, the Allies suffered 159,000 casualties in the Battle of Arras—heads crushed, limbs severed, lungs collapsed in trenches fetid with misery.

As the twentieth century dawned, the intermarried monarchs of Europe would seem to have had no reason to destroy one another's nations. The Kaiser of Germany, the Tsarina of Russia, and the King of England were all grandchildren of Queen Victoria. With the 1910 funeral of

Edward VII in London, a prescient time-traveler saw a pivot. The British Empire covered a population of 400 million. "On history's clock it was sunset, and the sun of the old world was setting on a dying blaze of splendor never to be seen again," wrote the historian Barbara Tuchman. The assassination of an obscure and vainglorious archduke in the Balkans set off a domino of chest puffing, saber rattling, and troop moving. It would all be over by summer's end, the generals said. But by the close of 1914, that first year of the war, almost a million Frenchmen had been killed or wounded. By war's end, there were 630,000 young widows in France.

I GET A LIFT from a man at the hotel, taking me farther inland, through more Flemish-flavored lowlands. My destination is Péronne, on the Somme. The river is wide and slow-moving today, lazy in its retirement from industry. Too bad the Somme is saddled with infamy. In the third year of the War to End All Wars, the Allies lost 600,000 men and the Germans almost 500,000 in the four-month Battle of the Somme. In the first day alone, Britain suffered 56,000 casualties. It resulted in no breakthroughs, only a vast harvesting of young men in the scythe of advanced human destruction.

Having survived pillaging from many a medieval marauder, Péronne could not live through the Great War. The town was completely destroyed by the Germans in 1917. When it tried to come back one more time, the Luftwaffe finished it off in 1940. What is left today is a huddle of seven thousand people, and two of the best tributes to the worst impulses of man. One is a carving of a woman leaning over the dead body of a loved one, shaking her fist in defiance: *The Monument to the Dead.* One life taken. One life bereft. In a single casualty, this sculpture says as much about war as a graveyard stretching to the horizon's edge.

The other site is the Museum of the Great War, inside the walls of a crumbling château. War evolved quickly in the twentieth century. Poisonous gas could leave a boy blind, lame, psychotic, or quivering for the rest of his life—that is, when it didn't kill by toxic asphyxiation. Wooden prosthetics were mass-produced for the legless legions of the Lost Generation. Men without faces returned home and found that their loved ones didn't recognize them, in body or soul. Among the displays here are fake noses and fake eyes for the faces scraped of their features. It's dizzying, this mass destruction.

On my way out of town, I come upon a final reminder of the crude evil that civilized people can do to each other: Péronne's main church, Saint John the Baptist. It was destroyed, just like the cathedral of Arras, by hellfire rained down on one Christian nation from another. So where was God? It's the same question asked by the earnest woman in the oldest church in the English-speaking world, regarding the Holocaust—the same question any sentient human should insist be answered, no matter how many times it's posed, no matter how basic the query, no matter how much ridicule it prompts from eminent theologians who've moved on to more arcane subjects. God is nowhere in this former no-man's-land. And if God was here—why allow it? A test of free will? At the price of unfathomable cruelty, that explanation cannot hold up. Why not "interfere" with this fatal folly, and answer a million prayers? Why not?

Solace comes in a thimble, from a well-known poem the Jesuits made us memorize in ninth grade. It's from John McCrae, a Canadian soldier and medical doctor who had just buried a dear friend in this ground, and would soon follow him to an early grave. One stanza stays with me at the end of the day:

> We are the Dead. Short days ago
> We lived, felt dawn, saw sunset glow,
> Loved and were loved, and now we lie,
> In Flanders fields.

EIGHT

THE MIRACLES OF LAON

I arrive late in Laon, deposited at the pedestal of a city of shimmering stone three hundred feet above the plains of Picardy. It's an illusion in the sky, a fortress of wedding cake white. The eighty miles between Arras and Laon held little in the way of scenery or inspiration. And what had been a spell of unusual weather is now a certified heat wave and cause of concern among the *vignerons* as I inch toward Champagne country. I did the sensible thing and took two local trains to get here. Laon—settled since the time of Julius Caesar, a principal town in the kingdom of the Germanic Franks who gave their name to this nation, occupied by the English during the Hundred Years War—was clearly not going anywhere. Nor was I. My hope was that the Laon lift, said to be the world's oldest automated cable car, would carry me to the top. But upon arrival I find that the transport has been retired, leaving no option but to hike more than a mile uphill.

Beyond the ramparts is a plateau crowned by the Seven Wonders of Laon—part of an intact medieval city that instantly enchants. Within the four-mile enclosure of the town walls is the story of a country tied to the heavens and the densest clot of historic monuments in France. In my sweaty stupor, I come across the first of many explanations for Laon's miracles. In the twelfth century, another exhausted man was trying to coax oxen carrying a load of cathedral stone to crest the hill. The beasts would not budge. Then, out of nowhere appeared a large bull, strong enough to deliver the blocks on the cart to the holy construction site. The astonishment is commemorated in giant carved oxen perched along the corners of each of the cloud-busting towers of Laon's Cathedral of Notre-Dame, which dominate the skyline. As animal legends go, Paul Bunyan and his blue ox Babe is a better tale. Still, the supernatural runs deep here, making Laon the perfect place to delve into two millennia of miracles. Why did the finger of God so often touch this promontory, and not the ghastly fields I had just left behind?

Off the Rue Franklin Roosevelt is a small hotel owned by a family of immigrants. The street is a rare New World name in this part of the Old World, a tribute to a liberator. My room is up two flights of creaky steps, with a view out toward the plains. There is no air-conditioning. But I'm assured that I can catch a night breeze with the windows open. I catch the noise instead, the sound of Europe's ubiquitous scooters. For a ration of time—maybe three a.m. to six—all is quiet on this part of the western front.

After coffee and croissant at the hotel, I'm off for the day. It's a thrill to watch Laon rouse itself. While walking along the storefronts, I feel drips. I look up: as if on cue in a musical, shutters open and people lean out to water happy-looking flowers in hanging baskets. At the top of the hour comes a chorus of unclamping of metal grates and opening of shop doors. Merchants take to the sidewalk with whisk brooms. Huge, battery-powered municipal vacuums inhale crumbs on the street, like boars on a truffle hunt. Now, every window at sidewalk level has something enticing for the eye—fresh-cut rabbit loins in the *charcuterie*, adorable matching shirt and pants in the shop for the well-dressed toddler, an artful spread of strawberry tarts and chocolate éclairs at the *pâtisserie*. You can imagine chucking it all in the U.S.A. and taking up a new life here.

The artistry of the everyday is enough to delight. But what sets Laon apart is an urban plan that dates to Charlemagne, more than twelve hundred years ago. The center of the old city is medieval without the dark corners and damp interiors where so much superstition was allowed to fester. All is luminescent. If you wrapped the whole of Laon in Costco plastic and dropped it anywhere in North America, people would be lining up at its doors, year-round. They would have much to marvel at: a sundial held aloft by Saint Michael the Archangel. A commandery built by those ass-kicking, treasury-hoarding, secrecy-loving monks the Knights Templar, in 1134. A hospital for recuperative mental care, constructed about the same time—the oldest such building in France, twice the age of anything built by human hands in the United States.

These little oddities of place are not even among the Seven Wonders. The city was long a stop on the Via Francigena—both fortified and heavily consecrated, the ideal combination for a pilgrim restorative. A book about Laon's miracles published in the 1700s brought even more seekers to town, and Laon today still welcomes the spiritual straggler. The half-dozen-plus-one major miracles are a bit of a disappointment, though a few of them stand out. One is the pond belonging to the monks of Saint Vincent; the waters in the abbey never go down. The second is the Leaning Tower of Lady Eve, which slipped off its foundation eight hundred years ago but is still standing, precariously. The other is a rock from the year 1338, studded with nails driven into it by a mother who was protesting the hanging of her three innocent sons.

There are explanations for each of them. Perhaps the water is spring-fed, an eternal flow having more to do with geology than Jesus. The tower has yet to tumble over, thanks to superior construction; gravity will ultimately win. The rock—well, a good nail can penetrate sandstone. So why not let it go at that? Are lifelong Christians going to lose faith when the tower finally falls, when Saint Vincent's pond shrinks, when the nail crumbles to rust, as it must? Miracles are for doubters. They're faith converters and skeptic convincers. Saint Augustine, a hedonist for much of his life in fourth-century North Africa, said he might not have become a Christian without the wizardry of the faith. After converting, he explained the supernatural as short-term inducements: "Miracles were necessary before the world believed, in order that it might believe." I can also believe most miracles are fraudulent, as Hitchens says in his argument for atheism. As a journalist, fact-based reason is my crutch. But as a pilgrim, I have to dampen down my skepticism, to try to see things in another dimension. I cannot easily dismiss the children who leave their shoes atop the tomb of Saint Erkembode.

Why do more than 5 million people a year make the pilgrimage to Lourdes, in the French Pyrenees, where the apparition of the Virgin appeared to a fourteen-year-old girl in 1858? Because something, somehow, some way, does happen to a handful of lucky supplicants. Since 1883, the Lourdes Medical Bureau has documented sixty-eight cures at the site, the same number recognized by the church as certifiably divine interventions. The doctors will not pronounce them miraculous—they use the term "medically inexplicable," as well as the placebo effect. More recently, after taking a deep dive into these cases, a prestigious Oxford medical journal came up flummoxed. "The Lourdes phenomenon," the authors wrote, "still awaits scientific explanation." The best they could conclude is the cures "concern science as well as religion."

Christianity was born in the realm of the supernatural: the virgin birth and incarnation. And it took flight on the resurrection of a man killed by the Roman Empire for political sedition. If you doubt that Mary conceived without a human sperm donor, that God became man, or that Jesus rose from the dead, you doubt the foundation of the faith. The four major Gospels record a total of thirty-seven miracles by Jesus, beginning with that water-to-wine conversion at the wedding party in Cana, just north of Nazareth. He was hesitant, at first, saying that his time had not yet come. "But they have no wine," pleaded Mary, ever the Jewish mother. Water in six large stone jars was then converted to 150 gallons of wine that the steward pronounced the best he'd ever had. Oh, for a taste of *vin de Jésus!* After that, his powers moved doubters all over Judea. And unlike the many charlatans working the supernatural circuit, he didn't charge money for cures. He gave sight to the blind, hearing to the deaf, health to lepers. He raised the dead. He cast out demons, walked on water, calmed a storm when waves turned the lowest freshwater lake in the world, the inland Sea of Galilee, to white-capped fury. Only a single miracle, the transformation of five loaves of bread and two fish into enough food to feed five thousand people, is recorded in each of the four major Gospels. The others are specific to the narrator. And therein lies the conflict: the accounts of these celebrated deeds, written decades after the death of Christ, are unreliable and full of contradictions. Would the lone miracle that the books of Matthew, Mark, John, and Luke agree on have been enough? How about none? Can we take the philosophy of Jesus without the miraculous?

Certainly, the early church did not believe so. Saul of Tarsus became the most influential of first-century promoters of an underground faith only after he was temporarily struck blind, while on his way to harass the Jesus cult in Damascus. A small, Greek-speaking Pharisee, Saul had been complicit in the stoning of the first Christian martyr, Saint Stephen—"and Saul approved of his murder," the Bible says. The killing had its intended effect, scattering the followers of Christ away from Judea and neighboring Samaria. Saul was a violent, hate-filled zealot. He claimed that the voice of Jesus asked him why he was attacking Christians. Skeptics have a different take on the conversion. The blinding light could have been an epileptic seizure or acute dehydration. Maybe it was sunstroke.

What we know for sure is that Saul became Paul, persecutor to proselytizer—abandoning an ancient, monotheistic religion for a struggling spiritual start-up—because of a life-altering event. No conversion was more significant, no miracle more influential. Almost half of the New Testament was written by Paul or his followers. His letters are among the earliest surviving documents of Christianity, predating the Gospels—though still written two decades after the crucifixion. And we know that a religion that sprouted from a small provincial sect, a religion that should have died with the killing of its leader, took hold throughout the Mediterranean—an area already rich in its own gods and backed by the mightiest army on earth. The odds were not good for the survival of this faith. Thirty years after the death of Jesus, Christians numbered fewer than two thousand, by several estimates—total, in a Roman Empire of more than 50 million. Few would have predicted that this obscure, marginalized movement would become the world's most popular religion.

Thereafter, miracles converted monarchs and military leaders. Constantine, the first Roman emperor to embrace Christianity, did so only after giving the new deity a try as he went into battle in the year 312. He saw the image of a cross in the sky, the IHS Christogram, with a message, "By this conquer," according to church tradition. One year later, he issued the Edict of Milan, decriminalizing Christianity. In time, Constantine established a new seven-day calendar, with Sunday as the Day of the Lord, and built a new form of temple for the new god—the Christian basilica. But let's not forget that the emperor also had his wife boiled to death in a bath, and a son assassinated—an un-Christian reaction to a twisted round of family treachery. Another military-miracle convert was Clovis, the fifth-century king of the Franks, who reigned over what is now northern France, Belgium, and western Germany. While slaying members of a rival Germanic tribe, Clovis fell behind, and looked to the heavens for help. "If thou shalt grant me victory over these enemies," he said, "I will believe in thee and be baptized in thy name."

Over the centuries, miracles have been institutionalized, requiring scrutiny from a slow-moving Vatican bureaucracy. In 2016, Pope Francis introduced tough new guidelines, banning cash payments to doctors who examine cures attributed to Christ. The new process is designed to be more transparent, with a group of medical detectives applying the ecclesiastical equivalent of peer review. Most of the saints—those who were not martyred directly into heaven—had to have at least two miracles attributed to them. This is still the case, though there are exceptions. It can take several lifetimes for the Congregation for the Causes of Saints to verify the miraculous. But those who passed the sanctification test had some amazing superpowers. One saint could fly! Another walked around Paris while holding his severed head!

And many a saint, in death, became an ongoing miracle: a body that does not decompose, a condition defined as incorruptible. These corpses are not "natural mummies," wrote Joan Carroll Cruz in a study of the phenomenon. "The bodies are quite moist and flexible, even after the passage of centuries." Other corpses smell of roses, known as the odor of sanctity. In the modern era, a Stanford University graduate in engineering, Michael O'Neill, keeps a running tab of apparitions, cures, and other mystifying things through his website, miraclehunter.com. He is in high demand, for 80 percent of Americans believe in miracles. O'Neill does not pass judgment on the veracity of extraordinary events. But he doesn't strike me as a skeptic either. He notes the words of Saint Augustine parsing the supernatural, which seems about right: "Miracles are not contrary to nature, but only contrary to what we know about nature."

I DOUBT THAT THE OX immortalized atop the towers of Laon's cathedral would have survived a contemporary vetting process. The cathedral is a colossus of creative persistence, an early Gothic masterpiece dating to 1150. Like the city, it's full of light, exuding a cheery glow throughout its impressively long and superbly symmetrical nave. There are no saintly body parts or scraps from the heaven-sent that I can see. It's not pickled in the past, or haunted like so many of Europe's largest holy palaces.

Today, a priest is hearing confession. His flag is up—the light is on in the confessional. It's been, mmmmm . . . many decades since I last tallied up my misdeeds for a stranger in a clerical collar behind a screen. On impulse, I decide to unload a truck bed of sins and ask *le prêtre* for forgiveness. If I wait any longer, I'll lose my nerve. I go inside the tiny enclosure and close the curtain.

"Bless me, Father, for I have sinned. My last confession—"

"*Qu'est-ce que c'est?*"

"*Mon* . . . confession, Father."

"*Mais je ne parle pas anglais.*"

"*Et moi* . . . *je ne parle pas bien français.*"

"*Au revoir.*"

"*Merci!*"

I settle for a pilgrim stamp on my V.F. passport. Near the exit is a small side shrine to a thirteenth-century juggler named Jo, who scandalized clerics of the cathedral with his bawdy sayings while performing before a statue of the Virgin. They banished him from Laon. But then the mother of Christ appeared, shaming the men of the church for ousting Mary's entertainment. Jo now has his own place in the church. The juggler's tale is the quirkiest miracle of Laon, and you have to wonder how it made the cut. But again, I'm glad it did. A little whimsy is not a bad thing among the miraculous.

At dusk, the ramparts of Laon are still warm to the touch, holding the Picardy sun well after the walls have been overtaken by shadows. The plaza is full of life. Dinner outside at a small bistro is duck with cherry tomatoes on top. It is perfectly presented, burnished in buttery twilight. It's well past nine p.m., and yet the west façade of the cathedral is aglow with the loveliest part of the longest days of the year. The church is like a totem pole, in that each layer tells a story. The first floor is a crowd of Gothic characters, feudal lords lost to the years, their heads intact. The second is dominated by an expansive rose of glass, circles within a circle, which allows ample sun into the cathedral. Next are arches, each a perfect match of the other, beneath a Virgin Mary holding the Christ child. The towers rise above it all, with the miracle ox. At the very top are nasty-faced gargoyles. They represent the seven deadly sins—pride, envy, sloth, anger, gluttony, greed, and lust—and stare accusingly down at the former bishop's palace, where many an overfed cleric indulged in all of the above.

I want to hold this moment, this hour, this day, like the dawn walk out of Wisques. Back when the serfs of Laon were laboring over this cathedral, the everyday was mostly miserable. Today, it can seem miraculous, something my father tried to teach me. Though my dad suffered through plenty of disappointments, though he was raised without a father of his own, living above a bar on the South Side of Chicago, he was barely bruised by life's poundings. The smallest things could make him happy—a trait that eludes many of the wealthiest and smartest among us. He once found a pair of used shoes at a thrift store—"Rockports! Do you realize how much these would normally cost?" Already broken in, and didn't smell. He'd lose his ass in bingo at the church gym but come home happy because he laughed all night with nuns who drank him under the table. Neil Diamond's songs could make him weep. Watching him die, as with watching him live, I learned a lot.

But as it turns out, I need something more on this stop along the road to Rome. I have an ulterior motive for investigating miracles. My sister-in-law is struggling through late-stage cancer. She's far too young, too vibrant, too full of fresh ideas, with too many songs still to teach her piano students. She is known in Los Angeles as the Piano Teacher to the Stars. When Holly Hunter won her Best Actress Oscar for *The Piano*, it was Margie Balter who taught her how to play. She doesn't smoke. She swims every day. She rarely drinks. Her diet is fruit, vegetables, bagels, and the occasional burger. Why her? Her mother is 102, born when World War I still raged and Woodrow Wilson was president; she's in good health. For months, Margie felt terrible and weak, with no appetite and powerful headaches. A scan showed cause for concern. A biopsy confirmed the worst. When they cut her open, they found tumorous growths in eleven different organs. The cancer is eating her up. She's in constant pain. She can't sleep or even find a position in bed that's comfortable. She's been bombarded with radiation and poisoned with chemo until she cannot sit up or hold down a few sips of a milk shake. The oncologists have almost killed her, in the perverse way of modern cancer treatment, while trying to save her. She's open to any alternative therapies that she can qualify for, but her medical team has told her to close out her affairs. Her cancer is stage IV.

Though the doctors may soon give up on her, my wife, Joni, will not. The sisters are inseparable, as they have been for life. What happens to one is felt by the other. In a hurry, Joni has dropped everything and become cancer literate, an instant expert in the awful details of her sister's sarcoma. She has used her journalistic Rolodex, and all of her powers of persuasion, to get phone calls and emails returned from some of the best cancer docs in the United States. But nothing is working. We find ourselves desperate, wondering what else is out there. And I find myself, as with so many pilgrims on this road over the last thousand years, in need of a miracle. If that sounds expedient, last minute, an opportunistic misuse of prayer, so be it. If it means suspending rational thought, consider it done. If there is a force that can produce the scientifically inexplicable, I will beg for it on bended knee. If there's a power that can help a juggler, an ox tender, the seekers at Canterbury, the pleaders at Lourdes, the children of Saint-Omer, bring it. We need one more miracle out of Laon.

NINE

SLUTS AND SAINTS ALONG
THE CHEMIN DES DAMES

For a village of fewer than a thousand people, tiny Corbény has been trampled on by more history than some of the best-known cities of the world. The archers of England and the army of Napoleon grazed their horses nearby in pastures of poppy and tall grass, the same fields that were dug into trenches for the Great War. Many a newly crowned king and his mistress bedded down in this stop along the Chemin des Dames—the Way of the Ladies, a section of the V.F. named for the well-born women who came this way from Paris to Reims. But today, I'm only interested in the overnight stay of a single teenage girl who changed the world, an illiterate peasant from a small town: Joan of Arc. After walking thirteen miles on mostly flat roads with plenty of leafy canopies for shade, it gave me a chill to plop my tired ass down on a piece of ground next to a plaque honoring the national saint of France. Joan and Charles VII, the king who owed his crown to her, slept in Corbény on July 22, 1429, five days after his coronation in Reims. They were in separate quarters, for Joan the Maid wore her virginity as no other woman save the mother of Christ.

I am here on the same day, May 30, that Joan was roasted at the stake—burned twice over after she was already dead, to ensure that nothing of her mortal remains would find its way into a cathedral reliquary. Her ashes were dumped in the Seine. The church authorities who pronounced her a harlot and a heretic, a sinner and fraud, a bloody tart and cross-dresser, did her one favor before they tied her to a pyre in the town of Rouen. They examined her carefully at the fortress where she was held and determined that she would take her virginity to the stake.

But what if Joan *had* made love to one of the men who worshipped her? What if she *had* spent a night with a soldier impressed by the greatest woman warrior of Europe? "We were all in the straw together and sometimes I saw Joan prepare for the night," wrote the Duke of Alençon. "Sometimes I looked at her breasts, which were beautiful. And yet I never had any carnal desire for her." Would she still be a saint—with the sanctity given her in 1920 by the same church that condemned her to hell nearly five hundred years earlier? Not likely. For the story of Joan the Virgin is also the story of a faith trapped in logical and biological incongruities.

One of the joys of sauntering along the Via Francigena is letting your mind loose for the same purpose. When you can stop thinking about shoulder straps rubbing deeper into your skin, crotch chafing, or how far it is to the next *boulangerie*, the open road is liberating. Something random and obscure pops up, leading to random and obscure thoughts. Wonderful. And so here we are on the Way of the Ladies, and those stray thoughts turn to sex—the obsession with it, the repression of it, the lack of free expression regarding it. As saturated as this walkway is with the artistic and spiritual glories of Christianity, it is also thick with evidence of a confused and conflicted view of sexuality.

I don't blame Jesus, not in the least. He refused to stone a woman accused of sexual immorality, saying only those without sins should cast a killing rock. In that bold act, he was implicitly rebuking an Old Testament command in Deuteronomy, which called on men to execute women who had sex before marriage. The first half of the Bible, for what it's worth, is stuffed with stories of predatory patriarchs, wily prostitutes, and any number of revered men cavorting with women not their wives. It's a mass of contradictions. Indulgent towns of Sodom and Gomorrah, bad. King Solomon and his 700 wives and 300 concubines, good. In his preaching, Christ condemned adulterous behavior, but otherwise said nothing in any of the four Gospels about whom you could love, or how you could love. He said nothing about sex between people of the same gender. He said nothing about the superiority of abstinence over experience, nothing about the who and how of coupling, the timing of when to have children and when to practice birth control, all the forbidden sex later codified in exhaustive detail by celibate men. For that, you can blame his more censorious followers, those eunuchs on high moral ground looking down, turning natural pleasure into unnatural guilt, stoking ignorance into perversion, and on and on, up to the present day, in which the authorities of the Catholic Church are still trying to legislate rules of the bedroom while their biggest problem is priests who molest children.

In this part of France, the only woman more honored than Joan in statue or portraiture is Mary, whose name is given to nearly every cathedral. And Mary was likely not a perpetual virgin, as Catholics believe. I say that as a grade school graduate of Assumption of the Blessed Virgin Mary. And I say that with some trepidation, having just asked the good woman's son for help. But consider the evidence. Jesus never mentioned it. You would think the incarnated God, deploying the miraculous to convince skeptics of his earthy mission, might at least drop a hint that he came from supernatural stock. Born to a virgin! Try doing that on your own! Never said a word. It's mentioned by others in Matthew and Luke, but does not come from the mouth of Christ. In the earliest accounts of his life, the Gospel of Mark or Paul's letter to the Galatians, the mother of God is not specifically asexual. In two of the four Gospels, the origin story of Jesus is a complete mystery. He just appears, a fully grown thirty-year-old man, having spent too much time living at home with his parents. Even when he had a prompt to tell the story—after a woman shouted to him, "Blessed is the womb that bore you and the breasts at which you were nursed"—Jesus passed up the chance for a supernatural shout-out on behalf of his mother.

Also, Jesus had an older brother, and possibly other siblings, in the view of a sizable number of scholars. The earliest nonbiblical account mentions "James, the brother of Jesus, the one they call the Messiah." That was written by a Roman historian of the Jews, in the first century. "James, the Lord's brother" is cited in Mark's Gospel, very specifically within a family context, not a bro in Christ. Matthew quotes the reaction of those who heard Jesus preach early on: "Isn't he the carpenter's son? Isn't Mary his mother, and aren't James, Joseph, Simon and Judas his brothers?" James could have been Mary's son out of wedlock or born to an earlier wife of Joseph who later died. Speaking of which—what does the Catholic Church make of Joseph, Mary's husband? A long-suffering celibate? A good handyman there to fix the stone wall and haul out the fish bones, with nothing more than a peck on the cheek at night? Apparently so. Joseph never consummated his marriage to Mary; according to canon law, she was a virgin till death.

Completing the sex-free family is Jesus. He's a man, let's not forget. A man in his prime. Attractive. Vigorous. Charismatic. He eats. He sleeps. He weeps. He sweats. He aspires. He gets angry. He gets thirsty. He gets tired. His feelings get hurt. But lust? Not part of the human package. Well, there was Mary Magdalene, the most interesting woman in the New Testament.

The last century has been good for Ms. Magdalene, and bad for the attempt to scrub sex from the founding story of Christianity. In December 1945, a farmer made a globe-shaking discovery near Nag Hammadi, in Upper Egypt. While digging away at soft soil, the man hit a red earthenware jar, almost three feet in height. Inside were thirteen books, remarkably well preserved, the pages made of papyrus, the covers of leather. They were Coptic translations, about 1,500 years old, of original stories written in Greek, up to 1,900 years ago—the Gnostic Gospels, as they would be called. Of late, some scholars have suggested that the books predate the four canonical biographies of Christ in the New Testament. Taken as a whole, much of the newfound gospels read like Buddhism, with an emphasis on finding God within yourself. Some of it is wild stuff—sex orgies, talking snakes, and bizarre rituals. But then again, the Old Testament is about as lurid and violent a book as can be found anywhere in proper literary company. The main characters of some of the gnostic stories are basically those we've long known about—Christ and his apostles, his mother, and the other Mary—but with very different dialogue. There's far less emphasis on sin and sex, and more on tolerance and finding a way to enlightenment.

"These are the secret words which the living Jesus spoke," begins the Gospel of Thomas. The most convention-defying revelation pertains to Mary Magdalene. The Gospel of Philip states, "The companion of the Savior is Mary Magdalene." Jesus loved Mary "more than all the disciples and used to kiss her often on the mouth." This last statement is hearsay, and also heresy to the gatekeepers of Christian orthodoxy. But who's to say it has any less veracity than the spoken words transcribed from Matthew, Mark, John, and Luke? About two hundred years after the birth of Christ, a group of well-placed bishops and priests were to say. That is, they settled on a patriarchal view of the faith and dismissed the other interpretations as false. To be fair, they were up against many frauds and characters claiming a direct connection to the words of Christ. The early messiah racket had no small number of hucksters playing on the Jewish prophecy of a savior and the "secret" texts about his ministry. But if the Gnostic Gospels were just another fairy tale, posing no real threat to the conventional narrative, why the exhaustive attempt to bury them? As Christianity emerged from persecution and took hold in the Roman state, copies of these gospels were destroyed under civil authority, and people were imprisoned for being in possession of them. They were hidden underground in that earthenware jar to keep the alternative words of Christ from disappearing altogether.

In the stories that most Christians were raised on, Mary Magdalene has a prominent role, the second most-mentioned woman in the New Testament—though it's never implied that she might have been Christ's lover. She was a person of independent means who helped out the working-class, largely illiterate apostles, a benefactor of sorts. She was always there in a pinch. In the Gospel of Mary, an earlier Gnostic discovery, Christ entrusts her with keeping his words alive among the disciples. She followed the Hebrew rebel from rural Galilee to Jerusalem, witnessed the lurid homicide of his crucifixion, and arrived at the tomb of Jesus just days after his death. The apostles were hiding. Not Mary Magdalene. Her intention was to assure a proper Jewish burial for a man she loved. Instead, she found a big boulder rolled away. The risen Christ then appeared to Mary and told her to spread the news: He was back! She thought he was the gardener.

"Woman, why are you crying?" said Jesus, according to John. "Who is it that you are looking for?"

At the time, women had such low social status that their testimony was not admissible in courts. And yet, Jesus chose a woman to be the first witness to the greatest miracle and central event of Christianity. And it was another woman—unnamed in the Gospel—who was the only person ever to win an argument with Jesus, cajoling him into healing her daughter, as both Mark and Matthew tell it. How Mary Magdalene, one of the most trusted and loyal of all the early followers, came to be cast as a slut is central to the Catholic Church's impoverishment of thought on half of humanity. Writing women and sex out of the story started with Saint Paul, an early celibate, whose letters became Scripture, if not statutes of the faith. "It is well for a man not to touch a woman," he wrote to the Corinthians. "To the unmarried and the widows, I say that it is well for them to remain single as I do. But if they cannot exercise self-control, they should marry. For it is better to marry than be aflame with passion." Married people can't be aflame with passion? No, apparently not. And certainly not unmarried people. Passion is a forbidden fruit, though Paul had no directive from God on this, which he admits. "I do not have a command from the Lord, but I give my opinion as one who by the Lord's mercy is worthy of trust."

For centuries, some clerics followed Paul's example, while others married or had lovers. When mandatory celibacy came up for discussion before the Council of Nicaea—convened by Emperor Constantine in 325 as conclave to settle doctrinal questions—it was rejected. But the abstemious would not let it rest. And there was always a heavy overlay of hypocrisy among the leaders. Thus Charlemagne, crowned by the pope as the highest ruler of Western Europe in the year 800, married four times—but forbade his daughters from marrying at all.

The two most influential early philosophers in the history of Christianity, Saints Jerome and Augustine, contemporaries and correspondents, busied themselves with a body of work that demonized sex. Their words became doctrine, and heavily influenced the accepted version of Scripture. But both had experience, much more than the average man, by their own accounts. Jerome, born around 347, chased women with abandon while studying in Rome. He was fussy, ranting against men with trimmed beards and women who wore perfume. He himself was long-bearded, elegantly robed, and fragrance-free. After entering the monastery, he could not contain his carnal urges. "I often imagined myself among bevies of girls . . . my mind burned with desire, the fires of lust leapt up before me." His was a typical monastic musing for a young man, but Jerome considered such desire to be a moral crime of the highest order. And then he went even further. "Marriage is only one degree less sinful than fornication," he wrote.

And why should the tortured nocturnal fantasies of an ancient theologian matter? For one, Jerome was the biggest early promoter and defender of the idea of Mary's perpetual virginity—and sexual purity in general. He did this while possibly pursuing an affair with a well-off widow, Paula. More important to generations of Christians, he also *wrote* the Bible. His translations from Greek text, based in part on Aramaic and Hebrew oral traditions, to Latin eventually became the accepted Word of God for almost a thousand years. "There is no other person who has had a greater influence on the way Catholics read the Bible than St. Jerome," wrote Leslie J. Hoppe, a professor at Chicago's Catholic Theological Union. Translations never produce precise copies; they are filters. If someone like Lucretius, the Roman poet who celebrated the good life, had been tasked with turning Scripture into the language of the time, the Bible might be lighter on the condemnation and heavier on the delights of this earth.

Like Jerome, Augustine loved sex before he hated it. As a boy growing up in North Africa, he said, "our real pleasures consisted of doing something that was forbidden." For him, that was sex. "I was inflamed with desire for a surfeit of hell's pleasures," he wrote. "Love and lust together seethed within me." He "fell in with a set of sensualists." This pattern held after he moved to Rome, and his renown as a first-rate philosopher grew. He took many lovers. Through one mistress, a longtime girlfriend, he had a child out of wedlock. And then he turned against himself, lamenting "the abominable things I did in those days, the sins of the flesh which defiled my soul." Although he said, "I could not possibly endure the life of a celibate," he tried to do just that—but not before pining for one last fling. "Give me chastity and continence but not just yet," he prayed. This was a very confused man.

In his struggles with the most human of urges, nature usually won. Observing that his penis had a mind of its own—"sometimes it refuses to act when the mind wills, while often it acts against his will!"—led Augustine to theorize that we were born flawed. Looking for pleasure, for beauty, for sensuality, could be selfish and sinful, and may doom a person to everlasting lockup. It's worth repeating that this philosophy came not from Christ, but from one mortal man—and became a foundation of the faith. Augustine, brilliant in so many ways, the thinking person's Catholic, the accessible writer, is a dreary scold on lovemaking. Guided by Augustine, what could have been a religion of healthy physical joy became a bulwark against human nature. The monks who took up the Rule of Saint Augustine were forbidden from "fixing your gaze upon any woman" or wearing an article of clothing that might attract attention. Lust, love, the outer dimensions of passion—they were banished.

But "if god really wanted people to be free of such thoughts," as Christopher Hitchens notes in his polemic against religion, "he should have taken more care to invent a different species." Precisely.

What if Augustine had been happily married to the mistress who bore him a child? What if he was delighted by sex with this life partner, rather than tormented by it? What if he learned to love sexual intimacy, rather than bemoaning it as a guilt-soaked side duty—the drab job of procreation for grim-faced Christians? The what-ifs matter, because Augustine, like Jerome, mattered. "There has probably been no more important Western thinker in the past 1,500 years," wrote Stephen Greenblatt in a profile in *The New Yorker* on the invention of sex as a modern construct of Western civilization.

Benedict, the founder of the monastic order that colonized much of the Western world, was of the same mind, and hugely influential, at about the same time. The Italian monk feared sex so much that whenever he was aroused he threw himself into a patch of nettles or a bed of thorns. Better to be bloodied and skin-torn than visited by an erection. Legions of good men followed him into abbeys for lives of prayer, contemplation, and benevolent deeds. Their celibacy was a mark of discipline and principle. But so, too, did men who developed a sick obsession with young boys. For these monsters of the cloth, monasteries and parishes were a place to prey.

As for Mary Magdalene, her loss of stature is largely the fault of one pontiff who was influenced by Augustine, Jerome, and Benedict. Magdalene was a relatively benign figure until Pope Gregory took it upon himself to ruin her reputation in 591, with a single homily. The Gospels tell of an unnamed woman washing the feet of Christ with ointment. "It is clear, brothers, that the woman previously used the unguent to perfume her flesh in forbidden acts," Gregory wrote. With this proclamation, the mystery foot-cleaner was no better than a whore. But Gregory went further, calling her out by name. In identifying the woman at Christ's feet as Mary Magdalene, and implying that she had taken many lovers, this pope single-handedly, and without new evidence, redefined one of the most prominent early Christians. But why, for argument's sake, could this helpful, loving, radiant woman not be reinvented as Our Lady of Perpetual Promiscuity? Because sex was bad. The only good Mary was the sainted virgin. And so it followed that the women in Christianity's hall of fame were, invariably, women who never made love to another person.

The early church was a strong draw for women. If not quite exalted, they held a higher place in the faith's structure than they did throughout the secular part of the Roman Empire. But that soon changed. And within two hundred years of the founding of the faith, women were banned from the ministry. Outside the walls of orthodoxy, it was a different story. In Ireland, the legend of the sixth-century Brigid of Kildare reveals an independent woman of faith, and a beautiful one at that. She founded a monastery for women, but also for men. She took the words of Christ regarding the hungry and desolate to heart, and stood up to a king who did not. Later mythic tales of Brigid had her praying for ugliness to ward off suitors. As the Roman church co-opted her, she was made to be a virgin for life. Orders of nuns, committed to prayer and reflection, and sisters, who established schools and hospitals and worked like Brigid to comfort the afflicted, spread far and wide. Though given little say in shaping Christianity, women own a big part of the story of why this faith has prevailed—from the dual Marys at the time of Jesus up to present-day nuns willing to put their health at risk to aid the sick in the poorest parts of the world.

———

JOAN OF ARC FITS the mold, but also complicates it. It's easy to be enthralled by her story. Mark Twain spent more than a decade obsessing about her for a fictional retelling of Joan's life. He fell hard for the holy avatar. "She is easily and by far the most extraordinary person the human race has ever produced," he wrote. While the child Joan was pulling weeds in a hamlet in modern-day Lorraine, France was without a true king, and under occupation. The English, more than halfway through the Hundred Years War, held much of the country, aided by an alliance with Burgundy. At thirteen, Joan started hearing voices telling her to liberate her country. At seventeen, she began pestering the captain of a nearby castle, insisting that she be allowed to see the young man who would be king, Charles the Dauphin. The audacity. Not only was she a peasant girl, unschooled and clueless in the ways of power, class, and theology, but she claimed God as the source of her mission. She was ignorant of military strategy, weaponry, the mechanics of a siege, but was determined to go into battle.

What she had was courage. Meeting with Charles, she convinced him of her calling. On horseback, with a banner lifted high, dressed as a man armored for war, she inspired numerous charges against the English who had held the city of Orléans in a death grip for six months. Though wounded by an arrow in the neck, she attacked the enemy—known as *les goddams*, for their foul mouths—until the city was freed. The legend, tied to historical fact, was born: an ignorant country girl had whipped the occupiers—the Miracle of Orléans. Another major victory followed at Patay. After that, it was on to occupied Reims, the traditional site for coronation of French kings. As Joan approached, Reims and nearby Laon gave up rather than try to blunt the momentum of men inspired by the Maid. On July 17, 1429, Charles the Dauphin became King Charles VII at the cathedral of Reims. Five days later, he and Joan spent the night in Corbény.

Charles ruled for thirty-two years. Joan lasted less than two more. Captured by the Burgundians, she tried to escape by jumping from a tower; the impact left her nearly crippled. She was sold to the English, and prosecuted by their state-assisted Catholic Church. Under one flag, the protectors of the faith had embraced Joan; under another, they sought to destroy her. She was poked, slapped, spit on, insulted, interrogated ceaselessly. Confined to a dungeon in Rouen, with a diet that weakened her into sickness, she was tried as a witch. The main charge against her was that she claimed to have heard voices from God's representatives, the angels and saints. Many a child who had heard a voice or seen an apparition has been elevated to sainthood by that same church. Schizophrenic delusions were venerated. They still are. But Joan's problem was that she did not dress as a woman, an appalling offense. She wore pants and a man's breastplate, cut her hair short, and refused to put on a proper dress. She was a young woman with true power, an even bigger threat to the forty-two male clerics who judged her. Just before they killed her, Joan's executioners made her wear a cap inscribed with the words: "Heretic, relapsed. Apostate. Idolater."

Joan's love life, or lack thereof, continues to fascinate. Voltaire was convinced Joan was not a virgin, citing her zest for wine and celebration in the heady days of the coronation in Reims. One cover of his outlawed poem, *The Maid of Orléans*, showed a naked Joan in full frolic. Modern authors suggest that she had taken several female lovers. But the one fact that the revisionist takes have in common is Joan's faith—she never wavered. And so, as her legend grew, the church was forced to come around. Still, when a second, posthumous trial, and later Vatican examinations of her life, reversed the earlier condemnation, church authorities played down her guts in battle and played up her virginity—as if abstinence made the warrior. It should not have mattered. Joan was a visionary. She smashed class barriers and sexual barriers and English-fortified town barriers on the way to a remarkable series of triumphs. For good reason, she was a heroine to French Resistance fighters trying to break the hold of Nazi tyranny in their homeland five hundred years after her death. As well, she is the only person ever condemned to death for heresy by the same faith that made her a saint—evidence of the deep bewilderment about women in a church run by men.

I don't know why so many of the church elite were afraid of women with power, and why so many still are. The elevation of one sex does not have to be the diminishment of another. This attitude is certainly not unique to Roman Catholicism. And when the Reformation led, eventually, to the founding of Christian churches with female ministers, female deacons, female bishops, the world did not fall apart. Nor has Reform Judaism crumbled with female rabbis. The desire among women to be a guiding part of this faith is great. Today, as it has been for some time, there are 50 percent more nuns and sisters in the world than priests.

Sex got stuck, just like those clerics who were never able to move beyond the boyhood trauma of arousal. The best women—Mary the mother of God, Joan the Maid, and Brigid of Ireland—were virgins. The best men—Augustine, Jerome, and Benedict—renounced sex. Pope Gregory VII issued a decree against clerical marriage in the eleventh century, a rule that was formally established in 1563 at the Council of Trent. At the time of that earlier edict, up to half of all clerics had "wives" or mistresses. The Reformation hero Martin Luther thought celibacy led to masturbation. "Nature never lets up," he said. "If it doesn't go into a woman, it goes into your shirt." He should know, as a formerly celibate monk with some strange ideas about marriage, insisting that a witness watch him have sex on his wedding night, per the local custom.

Pope Francis could turn the clock forward. The Vatican encyclical against birth control, written in 1968, is almost universally ignored by Western Catholics—and has little basis in the philosophy of Christ. Priestly celibacy is not one of the "infallible" truths, and also has no links to the words of Jesus. As a seminarian, the young man who would become Pope Francis struggled for days after running into a woman he knew and liked at a wedding. Had he married, he would never have been

pope, yes, but he might have been a Christian with a different understanding of the human condition. He said in 2016 that women could not
be priests because Jesus chose only men as his apostles. This logic is
flawed, and a good Jesuit mind should know better. For Jesus also chose
fellow Jews as his original twelve disciples, and you don't see a lot of Jews
entering the Roman Catholic priesthood.

I FIND A SIMPLE ROOM in a simple hotel in the quiet embrace of the
Chemin des Dames. The heat has not lifted. At dusk, waiting for the
stars to appear overhead, I imagine Joan and the king sharing this view
on a similar evening. How far she had come in so little time, and how
little time she had left. She was dead at nineteen. The years have not di-
minished her. Joan is with us still, her gilded bronze statue prominent in
Paris, her life immortalized on the screen by Ingrid Bergman, among
others, and renewed on a New York stage in 2018, but not because of her
virginity. Joan is a hero to any teenage girl whose ambition is ridiculed, a
hero to someone who is told she is no one, a hero to a woman who is
called a witch, a hero to a loner who follows a mystical path. Her faith
was real. "She was not flesh," Twain wrote. "She was spirit." Perhaps
God used her to liberate France from the English, as legend has it. More
likely, the French used her, and needed her, and still do.

TEN

WHEN GOD ANOINTED KINGS

On the road to Reims, I wish I had a companion. It's lonely on the Via Francigena at this hour, at this mark on the map, more than two hundred miles from Canterbury, a few weeks into my camino but many days until the Alps appear in the distance. Young Joan had a king and an army to accompany her, plus the voices from God. All I've got is a horrible song lodged in my head. My son is supposed to join me in Switzerland, a break from graduate school. I could use some banter with him now. The sun rose at 5:44 this morning, and I was out the door an hour later. On another day when the heat is my worst enemy, an early start is the only way to get through the nineteen miles from Corbény. The forecast is for a high of nearly 90. Most of the weight on my back is water: a plastic bladder of two liters with a long suction tube, and two large neoprene bottles. Medieval *pèlerins* traveled with little more than gourds filled with fluids, and those fluids were often wine. Bread was their main source of carbohydrates. And the lack of fresh fruit and vegetables, particularly in the cold months, could lead to scurvy and crippling muscle cramps. I can't count on finding water along the trail; I've yet to see a *point d'eau*. Carlo, the Brit traveling ahead of me, was so desperate he banged on the doors of farmhouses until someone took his empty bottle. The drink he was given was rancid, he reported later—filled with horse piss, in Carlo's guess. "The problem with the French," he said, "is that they hate everybody." Well, he's English.

I considered following a quicker route, a straight shot on D1044— under six hours of walking time and five kilometers shorter. But the road has no shoulder. I'd be hiking against faceless cars, constantly ducking into the ditch to avoid the texting and gabbing motorists of the Marne. And I have a history of taking shortcuts that become disasters. The guidebook route is varied by surface—part road, part gravel path, part field—and scenery. Clean rectangular farms give way to compacted forests enclosed in squares. Here's a canal. There's a castle. And, best of all—vineyards. I'm at the edge of Champagne, the terroir of the most celebrated vines in the world. These rumpled rows of grapes are such a lift. In the first light of day, it's like walking through a painting by early Impressionists.

At Saint-Thierry, a village of 572 people, I'm ready to call it quits at four in the afternoon. The town has an intriguing history: William of Saint-Thierry wrote *On the Nature and Dignity of Love* here in the twelfth century. How does it hold up? A bit dense, but provocative still. The highest form of love is charity. Wisdom is being close to God; the more intimate you are with the divine, the smarter. And humans "have a natural bent by which the spirit tends toward higher things." He was a much sunnier monk than his contemporary, the jihad-provoking Bernard of Clairvaux. The monastery where William of Saint-Thierry did his heavy thinking is gone, seized by French revolutionaries in the 1790s after twelve centuries of existence, and then razed. A new house of contemplation, run by Benedictine nuns, has beds for pilgrims. I looked them up earlier. To judge from their website pictures, they seem cheerful—happily shelling peas and singing with a guitar-playing sister who doesn't look anything like Julie Andrews. I walk up to the edge of the gate outside their quarters, stare blankly at the impressive Georgian entrance, but

can't take another step. The guitars. The peas. Those memories of pugi-
listic penguins slapping me around in third grade at Assumption of the
Blessed Virgin. Reims, the city of kings, with nearly a quarter million
people in the metro area, is ten kilometers in the distance—six miles. It's
too tempting not to suck it up and finish.

THOUGH THERE ARE countless things to do in Reims, I'm here for the
Holy Ampulla. The widest triumphal arch of the Roman Empire stands
strong, not far from the train station. That would be the Porte de Mars,
named for the god of war, carved with near-naked and mythic characters
across its 105-foot length. The champagne houses—Veuve Clicquot, Ru-
inart, Taittinger, among the better known—beckon with come-ons to
their gilded *maisons* here in the Vatican of sparkling wine. An evening
stroller can wander along wide boulevards and pedestrian-only side
streets, eat pink cookies made daily since the seventeenth century, or try
a blood sausage without the blood. This is a real city, sparking at all
hours. But I want to see the Holy Ampulla, the tiny glass vial that holds
the sacred oil used to anoint nearly every king of France. Reims is where
church became state, the birthplace of this nation's creation myth.

The tourist office is bustling; for the first time my trail is full of pilgrims. Since Calais, I've seen no more than six people walking to Rome.
But here at the crossroads of the V.F. and a route leading to the Camino
de Santiago, the place is crawling with holy hikers—Brits, Germans,
Russians, Dutch, Italians. Most people are going south to Spain, through
a network of trails that ultimately lead to the tomb of Saint James. The
pilgrimage, they say, begins wherever the pilgrim does, which makes it
fairly easy. They have traditional scallop shells draped around their necks,
which also served as a medieval eating tool in the pre-cutlery age. And
they exude a sense of superiority. When I explain to a sunbaked Scandi-
navian that I'm taking the camino less traveled, he gives me a dismissive
eye roll, as if I'm on an inferior road to revelation.

The office finds me a hotel named for the conspiratorial Knights Templar, the monastic order founded in violence. They had wealthy donors, and worked in the shadows, assassinating rivals, hoarding sacred relics. The Templars came to their inevitable end when fifty-four of their leaders were tortured and executed in 1310 by a church that had once relied on them, but then turned against them. That said, the Grand Hôtel des Templiers is a fine tribute, a nineteenth-century home built around a peaceful courtyard, with a tub in my room for soaking sore muscles. My legs have started to cramp at day's end, from a combination of heat and strain. I'm a long way from Rome. I'll need heavy maintenance to make it. I decide to stay for a few days to wait out the hot weather. The front desk clerk even helps me with my French. Reims is pronounced *Rahns*.

Catching up on correspondence, I light up at an email from the pope. Francis—it's about time! Actually, it's the pope's spokesman, Greg Burke, director of the Holy See Press Office, who was forwarded my request through the Vatican pouch of the Jesuits. He's encouraging on the pilgrimage, calling it "brilliant" for an American to get away from our screens and see the ancient Christian world on foot. This alone makes me pause and cherish the word "brilliant" and, before reading further, allow my hopes to rise. But then, just as quickly—deflation. Regarding my interview with the Vicar of Christ, he can't promise anything. "Longshot," he writes, "but will pass it on." I'm also still working the Jesuit back channel, and send another note to Father Steve.

The papal representative suggests picking up Hilaire Belloc's *The Path to Rome*, which I've already read. Belloc was a French-born Anglophile, educated at Oxford, who stirred a million philosophical pots during a long career through the first half of the twentieth century. In 1901, he followed the same route that I'm on, walking through France, Switzerland, and Italy. It was overgrown and not marked, but he found his way. "I vowed a vow to go to Rome on a pilgrimage to see all of Europe which the Christian faith has saved," he wrote. Belloc was an uncompromising Catholic, an apologist for the Crusades, someone who would have been welcomed by the Templars at one of their heretic roasts. "The faith is Europe, and Europe is the faith," he wrote. Certainly that was true of his age, when the crucifix could be seen in nearly every corner of the Continent. It's not hard to guess what he'd think of the Europe of today—"a heathen continent with a Christian residue," in the estimation of the German American evangelist Dietrich Schindler. Less imperiously, Belloc noted: "Wherever the Catholic sun does shine, there's always laughter and good red wine." His faith seemed genuine and deeply rooted, but the modern mind chafes at his casual anti-Semitism. Nor did he anticipate the beast that would rise from the nation to my east. "A great sea of confused and dreaming people, lost in philosophies and creating music," he said of Germans at the dawn of the century in which they would nearly destroy the world. I give him credit for his physical stamina. Belloc says he walked thirty miles a day.

WELL SLEPT, I'm up and outside just as the first steaming cup of *café au lait* is produced in the courtyard. Then I hit the ampulla trail, strolling to the place where the oil that baptized Clovis has long been stored, the Saint Rémi basilica and abbey, a UNESCO World Heritage site. The large sculpture out front depicts a very ripped-looking Clovis, naked but for a loincloth, getting anointed by Bishop Remigius on Christmas Day in 496. With this sacred sealing, the King of the Franks was linked to the kings of Israel, back to David. The story is that a dove of the Holy Spirit descended from the heavens bearing a vial of oil. It's been called the Baptism of France. At the time, there were plenty of Christians living among the ruins of the northern Roman Empire. The faith had spread through peaceful means. And the church, with its new network of bishops, deacons, priests, and monks, with its monastic centers and increasingly large property holdings, held many communities together after the fall of Rome. What Clovis did was unite the tribal Franks under the banner of one rule—a kingdom blessed by the highest Christian authority. The anointment sealed God to crown. The Divine Right of Kings, the idea that monarchs get their authority from the creator, can be traced in part to the union of the militant Clovis to the mostly pacifistic Christians scattered on this side of the Alps. Clovis is considered by many to be the founder of France.

But the conversion of Clovis, we shouldn't forget, was purely mercenary—conditioned on victory over one of his enemies. While waging pagan-on-pagan war, Clovis was persuaded by his Christian wife, Clotilde, to give her god a try—just as Bertha had talked Ethelbert into her faith in Canterbury. When it worked, Clovis switched. Though, as a fresh-minted Catholic, the King of the Franks ignored a central tenet of his new religion and killed off most members of his family. To be related to him by blood was to know your days were numbered. "After each murder, Clovis built a church," wrote the novelist Maurice Druon.

This wasn't the first time a ruler had tied his realm to religion in Europe. That occurred nearly two hundred years earlier. The Roman Empire had been mostly tolerant of other faiths through the years, with the exception of some binges of gaudy violence against Christians by sociopaths like Nero. By one scholarly estimate, the total number of Christians martyred by Romans was fewer than a thousand. As a convert to the words of Jesus, Emperor Constantine continued the open-worship tradition. His Edict of Milan promised that "every man may have complete toleration in the practice of whatever worship he has chosen." But it would not last. After the Romans made Christianity the state religion, the persecuted became the persecutors. By the end of the fourth century, under Theodosius, Christianity was cemented as the Empire's official faith. And within a generation's time, more Christians were killed by other Christians—orthodox believers versus "heretics"—than all those slain during three hundred years of Roman mistreatment. In addition, classical statues, temples, and libraries holding the collected wisdom of Greek thinkers were destroyed as pagan artifacts. Communal Christian gathering places gave way to great concentrations of wealth and power. A papal saying was coined: *Roma locuta est, causa finita est*. Rome has spoken, the case is closed.

It was a breathtaking transition, almost unfathomable: the Roman Empire adopting the religion of a small creed that had no armed legions, no great royal families, its followers making up barely 5 percent of the population. Christianity had spread by word of mouth, not organizational muscle. The Word was powerful, a gospel of humility and love of fellow humans. A slave could be a Christian. But while this union of Empire and God aided the rapid expansion of Christianity, it might have been the Original Sin of the church. With power came intolerance, secular control, and organized killing. After Constantine, every Roman emperor but one was Christian. The exception, Julian, converted back to paganism in 361. "You keep adding corpses newly dead to the corpses of long ago," he complained about Catholic proclivity to sanctify the deceased. "You have filled the whole world with tombs and sepulchers." The old religions were doomed.

And so, too, was Christian Rome. The Empire grew sickly, feeble, unable to defend itself. After being split in two by Constantine, the eastern half, Byzantium, became the stronger sphere. The city of Rome gradually emptied out. No emperor after Constantine would live there. The capital was moved to Ravenna, on the Adriatic coast, leaving behind a graveyard of saints and a haunt of imperial slogans on chipped marble. Soon, sheep would graze on the Seven Hills, or such was the prediction. The wonder is that it lasted so many centuries. "It's easier to explain Rome's fall," wrote Will Durant, "than to account for her long survival." He was seconding the point made by Edward Gibbon, whose six-volume *Decline and Fall of the Roman Empire* appeared about the same time that Thomas Jefferson penned a declaration that would give rise to another great power.

The last emperor of the West was a fifteen-year-old boy, a puppet and usurper. He took the name Romulus Augustulus. The imperial power that had stretched from Hadrian's Wall in the far reaches of England to the River Euphrates in Iran, from the North Sea to North Africa, ruled by giants—by *gods*—ended on the soft shoulders of this child with a high-pitched voice. Within a year he was forced to abdicate, in 476. The West was gradually dissolved, its parts subsumed by the Eastern Empire, by fresh waves of soldiers for hire, by Germanic Lombards and Goths, Vandals and Huns. The Eastern Empire lasted another thousand years, though it lost territory to Persians, as well as to Arabs waging holy war in the name of Allah.

Gibbon famously blamed Christians for the fall—terrible at war, worse at diplomacy, too chaste by half. "The active virtues of society were discouraged, and the last remains of military spirit were buried in the cloister," he wrote. The emperor lost much of his authority when he was no longer a god; he had no clothes. What came after Rome's fall, in Gibbon's view, were loathsome clerics and ignoble lords overseeing primitive peasants. The sun stopped shining. In the Dark Ages, living well for the present gave way to living piously for heaven, or trying to game your way in. Riches and estates were given to those who could grant eternal life, the entity that filled the power vacuum—Pontifex Maximus, soon the largest landowner in Europe.

The church issued waves of edicts against other faiths and subversive theologies. Charlemagne, not long after being crowned by the pope as the first Holy Roman Emperor in the year 800, gave Saxon rebels north of Italy a choice between conversion to Christianity or death; almost 5,000 were beheaded on his orders. Jews were marginalized, attacked—in places prohibited from sharing a meal with Christians or holding minor offices. It would get worse. In 1180, King Philip Augustus of France expelled the Jews from Paris and took their property. A decade later, he had sixty Jews burned at the stake. In 1215, Pope Innocent III decreed that Jews must be "publicly distinguished from other people by their dress"— an order with lineage all the way to the Nazi mandate to wear Star of David armbands. In Spain, at the same time that Columbus was getting his patronage to sail the open Atlantic, the Crown ordered all Jews to give up their faith. Those who refused were tortured, executed, or banished. Up to 60,000 Jews were run out of the country. In Portugal, 4,000 were slain on a single night.

THE BASILICA OF SAINT RÉMI is cavernously dark, and at the moment I'm the only visitor. I actually get lost for a time, and have trouble finding an open door that would lead back to light and fresh air. For such a big place, it feels claustrophobic. I wander around in the pre-Gothic gloom looking for a singular treasure. After Clovis was baptized, the holy oil disappeared for centuries. Then it reappeared, in its original one-and-a-half-inch glass vial, the all-powerful Holy Ampulla, and was kept in a vault somewhere in this high Christian compound. Whenever a new king of France was crowned, the oil was carried in a procession to the majestic Reims Cathedral of Notre-Dame, and rubbed on the skin of the sovereign. He took an oath to defend the faith and "extirpate heretics." From 1027 onward, all but two of the kings of France were crowned in Reims and dabbed with oil brought to earth by God's winged carrier. Some very odd men were sealed in this way. Charles VI was anointed in Reims at the age of eleven. He was insane, or more precisely, schizophrenic. He went weeks without changing his clothes. He sat for days at a time, frozen in place, saying he was made of glass and that any movement would shatter him. The Divine Right of Kings certainly had its privileges.

The Clovis tale is mostly mythic—that is, the dove and the oil, the *moment* that gave birth to France. Nobody in this city can say for sure exactly where Clovis was baptized, when, or how. The oil was likely conjured up in the early eleventh century, scholars now believe. But it's not crucial whether the story is true or not. What's important is that people *believed* it to be true, and still do. For centuries, wars were waged, dissidents killed, land seized, edicts issued, entitlements justified (need I mention droit du seigneur, the right of a Christian lord to rape a peasant bride on her wedding night), all in the name of monarchs with the imprimatur of God. While the state-backed Inquisition was terrorizing Spain, Catholics with a conscience looked the other way. "The most ardent defenders of justice here consider that it is better for an innocent man to be condemned than for the Inquisition to suffer disgrace," wrote a group of official observers that included three future popes.

In 1793, newly secular rulers in Paris sent Philippe Rühl to Reims with a mission to eliminate the symbol at the center of Christian France. He seized the Holy Ampulla, placed it on a pedestal in a public square, and smashed it with a hammer. But he couldn't kill the legend. Some of the oil had been put aside beforehand, and that, along with shards of the broken glass covered with balm, was rescued. It was to Reims that Pope John Paul II came in 1996—exactly fifteen hundred years after Clovis was oil-rubbed—to recall the story of the bird and the vial and the first conversion of a monarch in Western Europe. More than 200,000 people turned out to hear the creation myth retold.

I'm told by an old man at Saint Rémi that I can find the restored vial at Reims Cathedral of Notre-Dame. Off to the big house of worship it is, then. This is another architectural wonder, originating in the thirteenth century, the model of Gothic symmetry and beauty. In the place where kings got their crowns, everything is designed to project power. You can imagine feathered and silk-robed nobles gathered up front, peasants and pilgrims in the cheap seats. General Eisenhower chose this cathedral to receive Germany's surrender on May 7, 1945. And it was here, a few years later, that a reconciliation ceremony was held between France and Germany—heralding the European Union.

WHEN I WAS GROWING UP, my first church was a modest, ranch-style building plopped down amid the tumbleweeds and ponderosa pines off

Indian Trail Road in Spokane, but with a cathedral-like distance between pastor and flock. Father Ralph Schwemin was Gothic, his cassock stretching nearly the full length of his six-foot-four-inch frame, the high altar of his immense forehead gleaming under fluorescent lights, his gloomy scowl. At Mass, in the days after I'd just lost my two front teeth and before Vatican II changes had arrived in our distant province of Catholicism, this priest would mumble in Latin for fifteen minutes, his back turned to us. Then silence but for the squeak of his size 13 shoes on linoleum tile. He slowly ascended to a podium with a sermon designed to make us feel small. He looked like a man on stilts. The theme was always the same. "God is up there," said Schwemin, unfolding one-half of his condor-length wingspan over his head, "man is down here." Way, way, way down here, as my mother would soon learn.

We trembled with fear whenever Father Schwemin came near. I tried to avoid all eye contact. Or I hid. But he knew me, because our house was across the street from the parish compound. He was building a physical church at the dusty fringe of north Spokane, not a human parish. Nothing else mattered to him. When someone stepped on a newly installed flower bed, Schwemin went into a squall of rage. He got on the school intercom, in his deepest, most child-withering tone. "I want to know which one of you miserable little kids did this!" he thundered. It was a red-alert emergency, broadcast to all eight grades. "I'll find out. And I will punish you." We expected the school to go into lockdown until somebody snitched on the culprit.

A month or so later, I was in the confessional, which was supposed to be a witness protection booth, the sinner shielded by anonymity and a screen. At the end of reciting my list of offenses, I mentioned to Father Schwemin that I might have been the one who trampled the tulips while playing kickball.

"Egan—you worthless piece of shit!"

You wonder why I haven't been to confession since. Now you know.

———

MY RETURN TO THE REIMS CATHEDRAL, on a Sunday morning, is much better. How did I not notice the stained-glass windows of Marc Chagall, the great Jewish artist of dreamy spirituality? Is there a more sublime fusion of sunlight and panes, of twentieth century and twelfth? Mass with Gregorian chants and music is under way. I join about seventy people in the pews behind a side altar. I can't explain much of what is going on in these ritual flourishes, dating to Clovis's day. But it's very hypnotic. The priest, who is black, as are most of the worshippers, faces us and holds his hands at a calming distance. It is—dare I say—most welcoming. I take it as an invitation to pray, and I offer up another plea to stall the cancer that is killing my sister-in-law.

Still, no Holy Ampulla. I was misinformed yet again. The sacred vial is actually next door in the former bishop's residence, the Palace of Tau, according to a church employee who stamps my pilgrim passport. After threading through a banquet hall once used for postcoronation feasts, into rooms where royalty slept and plotted, then bigger rooms where bishops slept and plotted, anterooms stuffed with tapestries of nobles and sculptures of same, I arrive at a red-walled gallery in the rear of the palace. At the center, under very thick glass, overseen by a guard, is the reliquary holding the Holy Ampulla. At last! You can't see the oil, or what is left of the shattered vial. What you see is a small, gold-lined treasure chest, with a dove on top, and carvings of kings, popes, and cherubs all around, also in gold. It's a piece of art, very Baroque. What is left inside has no power, for the last king of France from the unbroken line was beheaded by his own people in 1793. The oil did him no good. The ampulla is memory in a golden box, the years layered with meaning until myth became mist.

While the ampulla is a letdown, Reims is not. Outside, on the cathedral steps of the west façade, I lock eyes with the Smiling Angel. She is life-sized plus and pretty, carved of soft stone, wings at rest, slender arms under a tunic, a pageboy haircut. Almost eight hundred years ago, someone was allowed to chisel a figure that would stand out among the 2,307 statues of this cathedral—singular, because of the expression. A smile. When the Germans bombed Reims during the Great War, the head was knocked off the angel. It fell to the ground and broke into pieces. A monk scooped it up and put it in safekeeping. The restored head looks unblemished today, aglow in the sun, a more lasting image of the city of kings than the flourishes of royalty anointed with oil from God. But you wonder, looking at the big angelic grin surrounded by all the columns of facial solemnity and the trappings of the place where kings were crowned—why is she smiling? Clearly, she knows or represents something that we don't, something that the anointed monarchs never did. *That's* the best-kept secret of Reims.

ELEVEN

THE HIGHEST USE OF MONKS

It would be a stretch to say that Sigeric's millennia-old route to Rome leads a pilgrim straight to the Avenue de Champagne in Épernay, eighteen miles from Reims. But not by much. The mortal remnants of Helena, mother of Constantine and finder of the cross on which Christ was crucified, were once stored in the same church where Dom Pérignon is buried. Faithful masses hiked through undulating vineyards just off the Via Francigena in search of something miraculous from the sainted mom of Rome's first Christian emperor. Now, very few people kneel at the longtime rest home of her relics, most of which were scattered after the French Revolution. Fewer still could say who Helena is. But I have never seen so many pilgrims of a different sort in one place in France, all radiantly happy to be meditating on the fine points of the life ambition of a seventeenth-century Benedictine. Like them, I've come to find out what I can of the founding father of sparkling wine, a man who put all his monastic energy into a masterpiece.

"Come quickly! I am drinking the stars."

Dom Pérignon's statue is outside the gates of Moët & Chandon. And so I assume that this burnished house of bubbly is the keeper of his story.

Those words of discovery are part of that story. I wait, along with two dozen other people from all parts of the world, to go underground into the tunnels beneath us. This room feels like a waiting area of a Rodeo Drive plastic surgeon's office: the cream-colored walls, the white marble floors, the perfect-looking hostesses offering rose-scented mineral water and speaking in hushed Jackie Kennedy tones. We stare at portraits on the walls of men in wigs and high collars, until an immaculately styled woman with an iPad emerges to call out names. This must have been what it was like to board the Concorde back in the era of supersonic luxury travel.

"Follow me. I will take you to the cellar."

Some cellar: seventeen miles of caves and tunnels carved into beige-colored chalk. The temperature today is 35 degrees cooler underground than above. The walls are moist to the touch, the sweat of Bacchus, producing humidity that is perfect for the slow development of the most famous wine in the world. Deeper into the darkened labyrinth we go, past horizontally stacked bottles laden with dust, bottles behind cages, bottles that haven't seen daylight for a century. If something has to get better with age, it might as well be champagne. Churchill drank it every day, a half liter for lunch, and went deep into debt to his wine merchant over a lifetime in which he consumed about 42,000 bottles. But then Churchill started his day with whiskey and soda—"mouthwash," he called it—and always had some alcohol in his bloodstream. Napoleon rarely marched off to battle without hundreds of cases of Moët & Chandon in tow. "I drink champagne when I win," he said, "and I drink champagne when I lose." The emperor's private vault here is intact. The wine bottled as the Dom Pérignon label was the first *cuvée de prestige* from this house, a 1921 vintage. It can sit ten years or more in the cellar before being released. In mediocre harvests, when the pinot noir and chardonnay grapes have been challenged by weather, no vintage is produced. The Dom himself hand-selected his fruit, and could taste which vineyards they came from with his eyes closed.

Monks made wine for Mass, for subsistence, and yes, for truth—*in vino veritas* were words to live by. A vow of poverty did not prevent over-indulgence. "It was, and is, the luxury and greed of our Christian world, displayed in our feasting and drunkenness, that has made the Muslims hate us," wrote William of Newburgh, the twelfth-century Augustinian cleric. The abbeys founded by the colonizing Brother Bernard were known for their deep-stocked wine cellars. Wherever his followers went, they pushed the frontier of fermentation.

But it was the humble Dom who would break barriers. Jesuit-educated, Pierre Pérignon took his vows at the age of eighteen. Making wine would consume him until his death at seventy-six. Whether he "invented" champagne is questionable. Benedictine monks in the Languedoc were making juice with bubbles by the mid-sixteenth century, and he was known to visit them. What the Dom did was refine a process, *méthode champenoise*. The cellar master's wines went through a second fermentation in bottles sealed in cork and wax, slow-releasing carbon dioxide without shattering the glass. He was also very particular about his grapes from the monastery's thirty acres, blending unusual combinations, aggressively pruning the vines to get the best fruit, and trellising for maximum sunshine in the oft-soggy Champagne country. While waiting for the perfect moment to harvest, nobody was allowed to taste the grapes but him. In the cellar, bottles were turned by hand, one-eighth of a circle at a time, to move the sediment around and ensure crystalline clarity.

At the end of this narrative of hard earth and time, when we emerge from the dark warren of wine to the bright Moët tasting room, you feel a reverence for the man who devoted his life to the grape. You feel grateful, also, that monks' pastimes evolved over the years, from self-flagellation to warmongering to manuscript illuminating to winemaking. I'm surprised, though, at the answer from our guide to a final question: Dom Pérignon never worked at Moët. For that matter, he had no connection to this house of sparkling wine. It was started in 1743—almost thirty years after his death. The prominent statue out front, the premier bottles bearing his name, select vintages selling for two thousand dollars or more—he's been co-opted. The monk who took a vow of poverty would be appalled at this tasting room. It's gold and brass and glitter, a bling-blast of Moët branding. It feels a little tawdry.

To pay my proper respects to Pérignon, I get a lift from a fellow champagne pilgrim up the hill from the valley in which Épernay sits, to Hautvillers. This is the site of the abbey where the Dom spent most of his life, founded in 650 by Irish monks. During the Revolution, the compound fell apart after the monastery was nationalized. It's been restored, at least the church has, in large part because of Moët's corporate benevolence. You wonder if at some point they may dechristianize the Dom himself. The holy man of champagne is buried at the foot of the altar, under a black marble gravestone embedded in the floor, next to a placard: *"Ici repose Dom Pierre Pérignon, cellerier de l'abbaye."* Like the monks at Saint-Omer, toiling in silence for years to produce a book that might lift a mind to higher things, his labors were a form of prayer—doing something good and well and dutifully until it was close to perfect, a tribute to the creator. He found meaning by having a great purpose in life. On this cloudless and searing day, there's quite a crowd seeking a few minutes with the grave of a Catholic cleric in little Hautvillers. Three centuries after the monk's death, he's been able to do what other members of his faith have not—get people lined up to go to church.

* TWELVE *

NAPOLEON WAS BULLIED HERE

June brings no relief from the heat. And now there's a chance of late-afternoon thunderstorms. That is, bolt-heaving, sky-cracking, fat-raindrop-pissing late-afternoon thunderstorms. It's about twenty miles from Épernay to Châlons-en-Champagne. I can't carry enough water, and after Carlo's story of the horse piss in his bottle, I can't count on the kindness of strangers either. My big toes are wrapped in thin gauze to prevent blisters. I've got duct tape on my heels, a trick I learned from an ex-Marine while climbing Mount Rainier. He used it on his severed limb, where the skin met the prosthetic above the knee. I could stay among these vineyards forever. By comparison, heaven sounds tedious, a space for souls without edge, albeit with the bonus of no crotch chafing. This is something even the pope has acknowledged, as he mused at a recent appearance: "Some may say, 'Isn't it a little boring being there for all eternity?'" Well, yes. On the whole, I'd rather be in Champagne. But I have to move. A pilgrim has no choice.

I'm making decent progress, traveling south and east, through a small part of the world that holds so many little unknowns, despite being one of the most known places on earth. But spiritually, I haven't gotten very far. If anything, I'm going in the other direction—doubts and disgust at so much of the history. I don't expect an *aha* moment, to be struck like Saul on the road to Damascus. Still, that stiff shot of no-bullshit spirituality would go a long way at this point.

Here's my problem: the deeper you unravel the layers of this faith, the more trouble you find. I respect the best thinkers of Christianity. Augustine is a maddening old fool with a beautiful mind. Once you get past his calluses of sexual guilt, he's brilliant. I'm using one of his best-known lines as a mantra: "The world is a book, and those who do not travel read only a page." My objections have been noted, most having to do with theological rejection of the sublime aspects of human nature. And women. They haven't figured out women at all. As for harnessing the gospel of Jesus into a vehicle for war—you can't just continue to explain that away. If it happened a couple of times, fine. Free will, bad judgment, cynical manipulation, the motivation of martyrdom, and all that. But this pattern repeats itself over and over, the Christian God in service of countless cruelties.

I'm impressed by what the early Christians did, against all odds. Their devotion to spreading a philosophy that gave meaning to their time on earth, while looking beyond themselves, is inspiring. There was no advantage, early on, to average people in abandoning an established set of deities in favor of a God of love and sacrifice. Conversion was a positive, emotional thing in its purest, noncoercive form. It's what William of Saint-Thierry wrote in the twelfth century, that the spirit, if allowed to breathe, will tend toward higher things. And I've been moved by small things seen along the way: defiant acts of charity from Catholics in Calais, the tomb for disabled children in Saint-Omer, the search for perfection by monks in Hautvillers, and the former scriptorium in the flatlands of Flanders. I haven't given up on this pope, and won't, especially now that he's facing some trouble from the doctrine monitors. What did Steve Jobs say? Don't be trapped by dogma, which he defined as "living with the results of other people's thinking." The Roman Catholic curia is geologic compression of other people's thinking, settled over the centuries.

I take to heart the pope's recent advice. "Allow yourself to be amazed," he said. "Do we let ourselves be surprised? Because the encounter with the Lord is always a living encounter, not an encounter at a museum." That, in essence, is the great challenge of Christianity in the Western world: to prove that it has a beating heart and not just a dead past. To that end, I will try to be more understanding of faith as a living thing, evident in the everyday along the Via Francigena. But for now, I'm making very little forward progress.

THE MORNING IS A DISASTER. While trying to find the way back to the signed V.F. route out of Reims, I make several terrible decisions, all in the interest of cutting time. I take one wrong turn out of a roundabout and lose two hours. I rely on the robo-woman of Google Maps and she mispronounces a key street, leading me to a life-threatening detour. There's another option: the train to Châlons-en-Champagne takes forty minutes. And it's on time.

So now I'm in a completely different part of France, and very well hydrated, thank you. Vines still tangle toward the sun on south-facing slopes. But there are more wooded areas, forests of poplar, oak, and beech. Other crops, mostly grains, are straining to stand in the withering heat. And more hills. And more water, the aged sloth of the Marne and its canals wrapped around Châlons, a city of 50,000. What stands out in the main square of this town is a huddle of handsome, half-timbered houses—exteriors of exposed structural beams, wearing the bra on the outside, as it were. A sleepy farmers' market is finishing up nearby. The strawberries! Small, red on the *inside*, a juice-burst when you bite into one. With a fistful of Gruyère in one hand and a packet of berries in the other, I follow signage to one of the oldest paths in Europe: the Via Agrippa, at least twice the age of the V.F.

It's a pleasure, though certainly no achievement, to add my footprints to those that have touched these smooth stones over the last 2,100 years—all the sandaled centurions, hooded pilgrims, and traveling merchants. The Agrippa, the Roman road from Milan to the north coast of France, was one of the main arteries of a network connecting the cities of Gaul. And it says quite a bit about the Empire's engineering skills that by the year 1500, as the historian William Manchester noted, "the roads built by the Romans were still the best in Europe." I once stood history-struck in the ruts made by wagon wheels over the Oregon Trail, in the Snake River plateau of Idaho. Touching the Via Agrippa for the first time is similar, with another 1,900 years of time-layered sensation to contemplate.

The high, singing voices of children draw me to another square. In the same place where Bernard of Clairvaux urged Christians to wage war against infidels in the Holy Land, about a hundred kids are lined up in the shade of a church, rehearsing a concert. Half the children, at least, are brown- or black-skinned, something I didn't expect to find in this old settlement, far from the bigger cities. At the prompt of a guitar-playing music teacher, one girl steps up to a microphone and sings "Black or White," in English.

THOSE KIDS IN THE SQUARE have it so much better than young Napoleon Bonaparte did in Brienne-le-Château, the next stop on the Via Francigena. After an overnight in Châlons, a train, a bus, and a short hike got me to the arched entrance of his military school, now a museum. The town is dominated by and named for the château, a mini-Versailles on a hill lording over the three thousand people who live below. The boy was just shy of his tenth birthday in 1779, a slender child with a thick Corsican accent, when he left home for Brienne's isolated military school. For the next five years, under strict Catholic rule, he would sleep on a straw mattress with a single blanket in an unheated room just large enough to hold the cot. Mass was mandatory every morning, as was evening prayer. His teachers were Benedictine monks, the same order that put me up for the night in Wisques. Napoleon resented their authority, developing an early

contempt for religious men with power. Despite his studies in the faith—
or more likely, because of them—it was here that he started to doubt the
divinity of Christ. It did not make logical sense to Napoleon that someone
could be both God and man, though he would later be given a title somewhat close to that. He studied history, math, Latin, practiced fencing and
gardening, and learned how to defend himself—a necessity.

"I was the poorest of my classmates," Napoleon wrote. "They had
pocket money. I never had any." One of the letters on display here is a note
to his father. "I am tired of exhibiting indigence and seeing the smiles of
insolent scholars who are only superior to me by reason of their fortune."
The other boys berated him for his accent and his looks, calling him
"straw nose." But his provincial tongue, his size, his relative poverty, his
loneliness—they shaped the man who would return to Brienne as Emperor of France in 1805, and spend the night in the château on the hill.
That would show them.

The wonder is that he ever made it off the island of Corsica, a conquered land, bony and hardscrabble. Napoleon worshipped his mother.
A Mediterranean beauty, Letizia Bonaparte was married at thirteen and
widowed at thirty-five. She came from a respectable family and joined
lesser island nobility in matrimony. But the baby-making wore her down.
She gave birth to thirteen children, each barely a year apart. Five would
die in infancy. "It's not poverty I'm afraid of," she told her son when he
was coming of age, "it's the shame." Living off a small pension and donations from friends and neighbors, she rarely left home except to attend
Mass. Her children were her life.

IN ONE WAY, my mother and Letizia Bonaparte were two of a kind, a
century and a half apart. In her late thirties, pregnant with her eighth
child, Joan Patricia Egan started to bleed and was rushed to the hospital.
It was very hush-hush and frightening around the house. Nobody would
tell us what was going on. We stopped fighting. We cried. We cleaned

our dinner plates. Was she going to die? Who would sing to us? Who would take us to the bookmobile to load up on Curious George? Who would make us feel wonderful when we felt friendless and alone? She lost the baby, a miscarriage in the third trimester. When she came home, my mother was pale and didn't talk much for weeks. She sleep-walked through her days in a nightgown and slippers. It was her fault, she said—her fault for losing the child. She felt she was a failure. She was ashamed.

Months later, the hemorrhaging returned—prolonged vaginal bleeding, leaving spots on a kitchen chair, though she was quick to clean them. We saw the blood and were afraid to ask questions. She smoked cigarettes and drank more than one glass of wine and could no longer find solace in a book at night. She was ordered back to the hospital. Her gynecologist said he would have to remove her uterus, a hysterectomy. Her baby-making days were over. No, my mother insisted. First, she would have to get permission from the priest for such a procedure. Father Schwemin said the decision was in the hands of God, being way *up there*. He passed her on to the bishop, though not before telling her that "the Lord may not be finished with you yet"—meaning, of course, that she was still duty bound to produce new humans. The highest spiritual authority in our diocese was not happy with her medical request. Give up your womb? It belongs to God, said the bishop. The operation could be seen as sinful. But she'd already brought seven kids into this world—wasn't that enough? Her life was at stake. This onetime fashion model, this artist, this lover of history and politics and music—she'd put aside her passions to be the mother of a big Catholic family. She'd abandoned her dreams of painting, of writing, of doing something creative outside the home, and never said a word of regret about it. For she did not regret the children, not one of them, on any day. She loved being a mother. She just didn't love being *only* a mother. But now, facing the prospect that her ability to bring life into this world might be taken as well, she was made to feel horrible.

"Now, Joan . . . ," said the bishop. "It's your decision. I'm not a doctor. I can only tell you how the church feels about this." She chose the hysterectomy. And life.

NAPOLEON'S MOTHER LIVED to see her son at the peak of his power—the Emperor of France crowning himself at the Cathedral of Notre-Dame in Paris, overseen by the pope. Letizia was given the title Madame Mother of His Majesty. He had the clergy right where he wanted them, better off than under secular fanatics, yes, but brought to their knees. Or more to the point, his knees. He took the crown from the pope's hands and placed it on his head, leaving no doubt about the balance of power. In the flush of his earlier victories, Napoleon had sent terms of submission to the Vatican. This son of a devout Corsican Catholic put the church on notice: the pope's days as a mover of armies were over. The Holy Roman Empire, once stretching from the Baltic Sea to the Mediterranean, had been broken apart, the pieces falling into nationalistic factions. What was left of it was "an old whore who has been violated by everyone for a long time," said Napoleon, words that everyone knew to be true. Yet something would happen between the moment when France's guns were pointed directly at the Vatican, and Napoleon's crowning at Notre-Dame.

"Religion is what keeps the poor from murdering the rich," said Bonaparte. But it was more than pragmatism that informed his thinking. As emperor, Napoleon ensured that his France would still be Christian, but would also tolerate Jews and those of other religions. He would not betray his mother's faith. Nor would he allow church to monopolize state. For some of his change of heart, you can credit Letizia, who outlived him. Other answers to the question of how Napoleon went from the spear's tip of a revolution fevered with atheism to a man known as the Restorer of Religion can be found, I hope, in following his boot prints on the southern side of the Alps.

But credit, also, must go to the Benedictine brothers who had control of him for five years at Brienne-le-Château. Napoleon came back to this town of his boyhood a third time, in 1814, and briefly set up headquarters in the château on the hill. France was under siege, the Grande Armée in tatters after the long retreat from Russia a year earlier, the territorial conquests gone. Throughout the wars, Napoleon's forces often billeted in the towns of the Via Francigena—Saint-Omer, Arras, Laon, Reims, Corbény. When he made a stand near Brienne in January, he was outnumbered, though he typically outwitted his Prussian and Russian enemies. But the end was near. By May, he would be exiled to Elba.

Today, the most prominent statue in town is of a skinny little boy in military academy uniform, hair slicked down, looking sad but not unsympathetic. The story of Napoleon's first battle, when he built a fort of ice in 1784 and routed the school bullies in a snowball fight, is given as much prominence as the clash of empires outside town. The cadet left school a few months after the snowball fight, a newly minted teenage agnostic. But the school never left him. "It is not Corsica but Brienne that is my native land, because it was there that I formulated my first opinions of mankind," he wrote. In his will, stitched together during his final exile on the lonely atoll of Saint Helena, Napoleon bequeathed Brienne a million francs.

THIRTEEN

WARS OF RELIGION

Somebody must be home at midafternoon in Wassy. It's blisteringly hot again today, and only a mad dog or an Irishman would be out in this open-air oven looking for revelation along a medieval pilgrim trail. I'd rather be napping, along with everyone else in this preternaturally somnolent town. I'd prefer to be in a splendid stupor after a long lunch of *salade niçoise* and chilled rosé. But *damn*—when you get a chance to knock on history's door you should take it. I've actually knocked on four doors, none of them labeled history, since I got here, and no one is answering the call of the ages. I can't even rouse a stray *chien*. You could squat in the middle of the main street, close your eyes, and feign sleep during the civic siesta, and not be bothered. I know, because I tried, in hopes that someone would bother me. Wassy—wake up! Your past is calling.

I found what I was looking for in Wassy, pronounced *Vassy*, a short detour from Brienne-le-Château. It's a barn, almost five hundred years old, with a small sign on the wall, *Musée Protestant de la Grange de Wassy*. Most of the beams are still intact and sun-cracked, the roof holding firm, but all of it is shuttered and crumbling behind a galvanized fence. It says,

Go away. I say, Open your doors. Is there someone who can let me in? The barn was a church, a deliberately informal house of worship for Christians who tried to bring their faith back to earth. They were Huguenots, French Protestants, butchered inside this barn. Entire families died in the middle of a service. The casual visitor knows at least that, because there's a plaque outside commemorating the Massacre of Wassy, March 1, 1562.

Any massacre is awful. A massacre in a church speaks to a potent kind of hatred. This one launched the French Wars of Religion—thirty-six years of violence, three million killed. I want to see where infants screamed when men with axes came for them. I want to look at the pulpit where a pastor was murdered in midprayer. I want to crouch in the corner where children cowered in their mothers' arms, as the swords came slashing. I'd like to see the charred roof where a fire took hold. Is that a perverse thing to do on a hot afternoon in rural France? Yes, by almost any measurement. But why do people go to Auschwitz? You see it, you touch it, you become a small part of it, you try to understand it.

FOUR CENTURIES BEFORE Catholic Christians started killing Protestant Christians, the keepers of the faith took up methodical slaying of believers in another religion—Islam, which had originated in Mecca at the start of the seventh century, and spread rapidly throughout the Mediterranean. After linking the cross with the crossbow, after finding that the marriage of church to state could be profitable and expansive for all involved, organized Christianity waged a series of wars in lands occupied by the imperial followers of the Prophet Muhammad. The emotional call was built around freeing the cradle of Christianity, the old city of Jerusalem. In 1095, Pope Urban II proclaimed a European-wide pilgrimage for war, and a holy war at that; it set the tone for the bloody expeditions that followed over the next two hundred years. *"Deus vult!"* the pope shouted in a fiery speech, God wills it. He guaranteed salvation to those who died. It was no longer a sin to take the life of a fellow human, so long as that human was a declared enemy of the church. Killing an infidel would carry you into everlasting life. "God has invented the Crusade as a new way for the knightly order and the vulgar masses to atone for their sins," said Urban. In that regard, the offer was democratic. And thus began the most murderous two centuries of a religion founded by a purveyor of peace.

In all, there were eight major "pray-and-slay expeditions," as the author Tim Moore called them. No sooner had armies flying the flag of Jesus set out in response to Urban's initial call to war than they took to butchering nonbelievers along the way to the Muslim-held lands. In settled communities of the Rhineland, places like Cologne and Mainz, thousands of Jews were massacred. It was the bloodiest epic of anti-Semitic violence until the Holocaust, nine centuries later. Even other Christians, those deemed heretical in the crumbling Byzantine Empire, were put to the sword. Jerusalem was eventually taken, then lost again. About one in twenty Christians died in the long marches, well before seeing any battle. In all, 1.7 million people were killed. The war-cheering monk Bernard of Clairvaux later issued an apology. He wasn't sorry about the many innocent lives taken, the orphans created, the villages torched, the property stolen. He was sorry that his side lost the Second Crusade, prompting many people to give up their faith.

Three centuries of relative peace followed the last of the drawn-out formal wars between two of the world's great faiths. The booty brought home to Rome had enriched the church. With its power and place in Europe secure, it grew more inflexible in its theological views, while meddling in the affairs of state from the smallest villages to the highest royal courts. But just as Catholicism was showing its corruption, venality, and age, a burst of ideas by independent thinkers looked like it might steer Christianity back to Christ.

In the Age of Discovery, as the printing press was bringing new voices to the masses, men like Erasmus became popular philosophers. The son of a priest and his lover, born in 1466, Erasmus promoted Christian humanism, which guided the Renaissance in northern Europe. His mind never took a break. "When I get a little money, I buy books," he said. "And if any is left over I buy food and clothes." He learned Greek in order to study the Gospel as it was written, and correct later Latin translations. And from that scholarship he determined that Christianity must be detached from war. Erasmus was a pacifist. In his writings, aimed at average people as well as the ruling elite, he argued that there was no such thing as a holy war. God did not take sides. Erasmus urged Christians to find their own way to the divine, to free themselves of clerical monopoly. Strip Christianity down to its core—love of fellow humans, mercy for the poor, striving for higher things. Erasmus was prolific. He influenced Martin Luther, that rebel Catholic monk, and later broke with him, while still keeping a toehold in the Catholic Church. He never left the faith.

Alas, his views could not prevail. The first Protestant in France to be executed for heresy by fellow Christians was a hermit from Normandy named Jean Vallière. On August 8, 1523, he was tied to a thatch in the Paris pig market and burned to death. The crowd cheered his agony. The monk's crime? He thought Martin Luther had some good ideas. France certainly practiced what it preached: One King. One God. One Law. But burning hermits could not suppress the dissidents. Forty years after that first execution in Paris, there were upward of two million Protestants in France—almost a tenth of the population. Those in power, encouraged by the Vatican, tried to limit them by decree and harassment. Huguenots could gather in prayer, but only out of sight, in the countryside, or underground.

So it was that the Catholic Duke of Guise was passing through Wassy on the first day of March 1562 when he discovered that Huguenots were praying in a barn inside the town walls. He summoned his soldiers and attacked. It was mass murder—by sword, club, primitive firearm, and arson fire, of children, women, anyone trapped inside. Sixty-three people were killed, and 140 wounded. The massacre prompted Protestants in other parts of the country to arm themselves and return the bloodshed. In all, there would be eight Wars of Religion in the following four decades.

The worst single atrocity was the Saint Bartholomew's Day Massacre in Paris, in August 1572. "Kill them all, kill them all, so that not one will be left to reproach me for it," said King Charles IX. It started when another Catholic duke murdered a Huguenot leader in his Paris bedroom. His body was thrown from a window, torn apart by a mob, the parts littered through the streets. Over the next two days, more than 50,000 Huguenots were slaughtered in a spasm of sectarian violence. The justification, as offered later, was that Catholics feared Protestant insurgency in France. But the apologists for this high crime went beyond that: the pope issued a medallion in honor of an event that cleansed the church of heretics. Huguenot hunting, as it was called, spread to the provinces. Protestants responded with attacks on priests, desecrations of churches, and massacres of their own. Many fled to Geneva and never returned.

The decades of murder between followers of Christ took an extraordinary toll on France: almost 15 percent of the population was killed in the Wars of Religion, roughly four times the total number of deaths in the Civil War, the bloodiest conflict in North America. If that happened in the United States today, on a similar scale, 48 million people would lose their lives. And speaking of the Civil War, let us not forget the motto of the Confederate States of America, the largest slave-holding nation on earth at the time of its brief existence: *Deo Vindice*—God on Our Side. The Wars of Religion in France would not end until the Edict of Nantes in 1598, guaranteeing substantial rights for Protestants. Still, those freedoms would be taken from them over the next two centuries, with forced conversions under threat of exile or execution.

A similar tragedy unfolded in Germany. In the Thirty Years War, beginning in 1618, Emperor Ferdinand II used violent coercion to force Catholicism back on people who had been inspired by reformed Christianity. This bloodbath would lead to the death of 20 percent of the population—at 7 million people, more than twice the total toll of the French. The Napoleonic Wars, which were fought by massive and well-trained armies over vast swaths of territory, did not cause as many military and civilian losses as a part of the overall population. Nor did World War I. A higher percentage of Europeans died in the intra-Christian wars than in the industrial carnage of the Great War. All the graveyards I saw in the Pas-de-Calais, rows of white crosses stretching to the horizon's end, could not match the ground turned to bury the dead of Europe's wars over God.

Only a tiny part of this history is inside the barn in Wassy. When I knock on a fifth door, on the same street as the massacre site, I finally get a response. A sleepy-eyed twenty-something, wearing nothing but saggy basketball shorts, comes to the door. I say *Pardonnez moi*, and ask in my ragged French if he knows anyone who could let me have a look inside the barn/museum. He yawns and scratches his belly, which is very tan. He yawns again and says, *"Un moment,"* disappears, and returns with a lit cigarette.

I repeat myself.

He says, in Dude-Slacker French, that he doesn't know what I'm talking about.

I point, and mumble something about the barn.

He shrugs, exhales smoke, and says, *"Je ne sais pas."*

I'm thinking, in heat-stressed English, "What the fuck do you mean you don't know what I'm talking about? You live next to the Wassy Barn. Site of the Wassy Massacre. The Wars of Religion started here, ass-pipe!" But I just repeat myself a third time.

He takes another pull on his cigarette, shrugs a *whatever*, then tells me to have a nice day in Dude-Slacker English. And he seems sincere.

So. I'm left melting on the street after my meltdown on his porch, my sunglasses smeared with sweat, reading the list of names of the dead on the wall of the Wassy Barn. De Bordes, Antoine. De Bordes, Nicole. A family. Jacquemard, Didier. Jacquemard, Jean. Siblings. A married couple. More children. A father and son. A mother and daughter. Nearby is a print of a gravure from 1568, showing scenes of the massacre. It was my own family's faith, attached to us for nearly as long as members of the Egan clan have walked the earth, the One True Church now calling me to Rome, behind these atrocities.

No one disputes this. But it took more than four hundred years for the faith to find its conscience on these crimes. In 1995, Pope John Paul II said he was sorry for the massacre of French Protestants—not just Wassy but all the murderous rampages of the Wars of Religion. He issued a formal Vatican apology, aimed specifically at France. Five years later, the pope made a more sweeping apology for two thousand years of violence and persecution—against Protestants throughout Europe, Jews, women, heretics, so-called Gypsies. From the altar of St. Peter's Basilica, the ailing pope, trembling with symptoms of Parkinson's disease, pleaded for forgiveness. It was the latest attempt to heal some historic wounds. He had already apologized for the Crusades, centuries of anti-Semitism, and the Inquisition.

In Arras, when I saw what twentieth-century German Christians had done to the cathedral of twentieth-century French Christians, I was disgusted by the destructive intensity. It was mindless, devoid of anything but dark-hearted malice. But at least there the fight was not over individual interpretations of Christianity. And the violence was mechanical—lobbing shell after shell at a faceless target on a hill. Here in Wassy, some man of faith, no doubt with a family of his own, believing himself to be in God's good graces, had to look into the terror-stricken face of a two-year-old before running a lance into the child's heart.

How this is any different from what Shiites do to Sunni today, I don't know. Certainly, not all wars are fought over religion. But this one in France—so named because of the sectarian nature of the conflict—was a particularly insane variant of organized violence in the name of God. Protestants believe in the risen Christ, as do Catholics. Protestants believe in the Trinity, as do Catholics. Protestants believe in the life-affirming power of the New Testament, as do Catholics. They differ over the control that the highest clerical authorities have over the souls of Christians. It's certainly not a small beef, but it's also not worth the loss of a single life. Faith does not fare well in this argument; organized religion, even less so.

I won't ask where was God in the Wassy Barn, going back to the first question I encountered on the Via Francigena, at Saint Martin's in Canterbury. God had been called to the barn at the start of the service. If God stuck around for what happened at the end, God would feel, like me, lost.

FOURTEEN

WANDERINGS

Red roofs and steeples, rolled hay and Gallo-Roman ruins. Paths of crushed white rock, leading to a forest or a listless town. Cyclists on cell phones, pedaling next to canals, on their way to a postcard. Deer browsing in predawn fields. Gray herons working platform nests in old trees, twigs stacked and twined in fine avian carpentry. Dogs barking with an accent and an attitude. Vines crawling over arched doorways, dripping grapes just starting to form into fruit. A dying village, its butchers gone and *boulangeries* buttoned up, its *école* shuttered after the children left and were not replaced by new ones, still has one live château on its fringe. And in front are shrubs pruned to a military butch cut, at the foot of a garden so formal the roses blush when they bloom.

There is nothing of real significance to see in the countryside that lies within the Haute-Marne, in the French heartland, and not enough time to take it all in. It is sixty-nine miles between Brienne-le-Château and Langres. In between is a part of Europe set to a different clock. The mornings are the best, everything new and slightly dewy. Just before dusk, clouds replace the white heat of the sky, thicken and bruise and threaten to break with pellets of rain, but never do. Thunder rolls over the countryside, noisy and menacing, like those dogs, but without a bite. I learn about hidden places to stay in towns that time has passed over. In Brienne is a *gîte-pèlerin* behind the big château, a traveler's bed going for ten euros a night. In Châteauvillain the *mairie* will give you a key to a simple flat, and let it go at that. If you come into one of these half-empty hamlets and cannot locate a place to stay, the *mairie* must put you up somewhere. Failing that, you go to what is usually the oldest building and knock. A pilgrim can always find a roof.

The River Aube flows to a town that hugs its banks. And there you get a *croque monsieur* and a beer and wonder what you were doing all your life without them. The homes are handsome and elderly, exuding domestic dignity. Clairvaux Abbey, once the largest monastery in the world, is just down another road. That is the place where Brother Bernard started his empire, in the hidden fold of a great forest in the twelfth century. I tour the part of it that's open to the public. Lay brothers, two hundred to a room, slept on stone floors marked with their scratches, tallies of wages owed. The Cistercians dug a pond in the shape of a cross and filled it with fish. They brooded in a square of scraggly grass, a sunless cloister enclosed by high walls. After the Revolution, the compound was seized and made into a prison—the largest in the Napoleonic era. If the Champagne shrine to Dom Pérignon represents an evolved use of monks, the prison built out of Bernard's fortress seems equally fitting as a logical end to his authoritarian ethos. The poor soul who inspired Hugo's *Les Misérables* was shackled there. So was Carlos the Jackal. Today, Clairvaux is filled with inmates still, the bulk of the old monastery serving as a maximum-security prison. I'm happy to leave it.

Among the curiosities along the way are dovecotes. I'd seen them in the English countryside, and here and there in rural France, but had no idea of their purpose. They are little outbuildings, usually brick or stone, with small windows and even smaller doors. Many are circular, topped by slate roofs. Dovecotes were shelters for domesticated pigeons—apartment buildings for birds. During the Revolution, dovecotes were torn down by rural mobs. The peasants hated them, complaining that the birds of the rich ravaged the fields of the poor—flying thieves, as they were known. The meat of young pigeons is quite tender, a delicacy. I once ordered the dish by accident. When I asked the waiter for an explanation of the *plat du jour*, he said, a *"leeetle birdie."* And when I asked him what kind of *leeetle birdie*, he said, "The kind that shit on tourists in *Par-ee.*"

Langres appears in the distance on an imposing rise, and is well fortified behind its ramparts. The town is some miles away when I first catch sight of it. I pass the second half of a day thinking about something an ex-priest said in Seattle, during that Search for Meaning festival in the dead of winter. He told us the human brain lacks the capacity to understand God. The divine is beyond us. Unfathomable. This, from a man who spent most of his life in deep theological thought and debate, and then became a psychiatrist, and now dabbles in Buddhism and other spiritual hybrids. It would take several hundred more years, or maybe several thousand, for people to evolve to the point where they could comprehend God, he said. At the end of his talk, I asked the ex-priest his age. He said he was seventy-eight. So, by his own calculations, he would die in a fog of ignorance.

I don't have another dozen lives to wait around. For now, I've got Langres, hometown of the philosopher Diderot, on the horizon. The low road leads to higher ground, a place that helped give flight to the Enlightenment. Diderot rejected God, after a long attempt to locate him in unlikely places. He tried to find sustenance for the soul by looking at much of what is venerated along the Via Francigena—much of what I've seen to date—as a fiction. But many others, in the big middle part of the trail just ahead of me, chose to lose the church but keep their faith in the founder. In the process, they nearly brought down Catholicism.

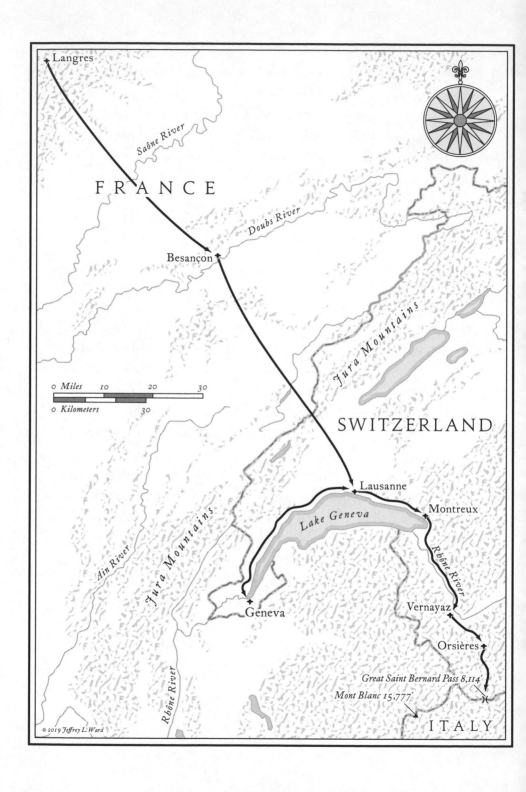

Langres

Saône River

FRANCE

Doubs River

Besançon

Jura Mountains

SWITZERLAND

Lausanne

Montreux

Lake Geneva

Ain River

Jura Mountains

Rhône River

Geneva

Vernayaz

Rhône River

Orsières

Great Saint Bernard Pass 8,114′

Mont Blanc 15,777′

ITALY

0 Miles · 10 · 20 · 30

0 Kilometers · 30

© 2019 Jeffrey L. Ward

II

Lost

LAND OF HERETICS AND HEROES

FIFTEEN

THE HOLLOWED HOUSE OF LIGHT

He was precocious, everyone saw that in Denis Diderot. He could talk as fast as he could think. The Jesuits found him brilliant but troublesome. Keep him in the church, they said, and one day he might be pope. Before he could shave, the hair on his head was cut in the tonsured bowl of a young seminarian, and off he went to an enclosure of theology. It could not hold him. Out of college, looking like a young Liam Neeson, he met Jean-Jacques Rousseau at a coffeehouse in Paris and argued with him, mostly productively, for fifteen years. Their ideas sailed across the Atlantic and landed in the heads of a band of brothers who would forge the first major country founded on Enlightenment thought, the United States of America. Diderot could unpack a mathematical equation. He wrote plays that filled theaters, and a book of philosophy that landed him in prison. He wanted to know all of it, to experience all of it, and then to share all of it. He spent almost thirty years assembling the world's knowledge for his *Encyclopédie*. And yet, in many quarters of France, he is best known—still—for a single offhand remark: "Man will never be free until the last king is strangled with the entrails of the last priest."

Langres, Diderot's home, is a town on a crown of civic high-mindedness. First planted by a pre-Roman tribe as a fortress in the clouds, it is undisturbed by time, or much of anything else except for a gendarme who followed me to my hotel out of boredom. Langres is just one existential question short of being Diderot Disneyland, which only the French could pull off. Is there any place in the States given over to a philosopher? And what a delicious geographic irony to have an ancient religious trail to Rome run right through a town that fostered so much thought to refute religion. You want Age of Reason? Langres is a City of Reason. Diderot's name is attached to a street, a pavilion, a statue, a college, and the House of Enlightenment—the Maison des Lumières Denis Diderot. But not the cheese. The regional *fromage*, soft and cylindrical like a large marshmallow, belongs to Langres, controlled under appellation-of-origin rules more detailed than the owner's manual of a Volvo.

I check into a former abbey, first mentioned in a scribe's aside in the year 834, the Hôtel Le Cheval Blanc. I'm greeted with a glass of champagne and a menu, for this ancient inn is a foodie destination, and the friendly owner has only a few seats left for tonight's dinner. I reserve a place at the table for later, and settle into a room with vaulted ceilings, a hint of faded frescoes, and a view to a countryside of forests, farms, and a large lake, well below the plateau.

Before there was the philosophy theme, or even that soft cheese, Langres existed because it was a natural place for self-defense. Its ramparts are intact, more than five miles of fortifications, giving Langres one of the largest continuous city walls in Europe—or so they say at the tourist office, where I get my pilgrim stamp and a fistful of Diderot brochures. And I did not know—though it is self-evident—that Langres has been consistently rated one of the most beautiful towns in France.

I skip the walls. They're impressive—twelve towers, seven gates, with expansive views fifteen hundred feet down. But I've seen enough mortared medieval flanks for the time being. Instead, I follow the Diderot trail to his statue, in Place Diderot. The placement is exquisite. Just be-hind him is the 870-year-old Langres cathedral, lasting symbol of his lifetime foe. And in front of him is the U-shaped compound that used to be the Jesuit institution he attended. It's now a school named for Diderot. He appears to be looking down on it, which, if you put him in the context of his eighteenth-century youth, would make sense.

To say that Diderot resisted conventional thought is a vast understate-ment. He created a body of *original* thought. And those ideas, refined in dozens of fat volumes, threatened the world order. Oh, for the pre-Twitter days, when it took something more than a word fart by a president who never opens a book to turn the world upside down. You read Diderot now and can't find anything that sounds subversive. He was a skeptic and a rationalist—basically, *prove it, and I'll believe it.* He despised supersti-tion and the charlatans who practiced it. He thought God should be freed from closed spaces. "Men have banished God from their company and have hidden him in a sanctuary; the walls of a temple shut him in, he has no existence beyond." Sounds like something a pilgrim would say. After he wrote those words, his book of essays was burned under orders from Paris. And after he wrote *Philosophical Thoughts*, his first original work, he was jailed for expanding on said thoughts.

"If you impose silence on me about religion and government, I shall have nothing to talk about," he said. He was allowed to continue talking.

He went from devout Catholic, to deist, to atheist. The middle stop would have found him at the same watering hole as American founders Thomas Jefferson, Benjamin Franklin, and Thomas Paine, who called Christianity a fable. Diderot's ruminations on liberty, tolerance, and ra-tional self-interest formed a big current of thought that flowed into the Enlightenment bible of the American Constitution. Deists believe in a single God who created the universe and then walked away. To a deist, prayer is meaningless. God does not interfere. God's design, power, and wisdom are seen in nature. Scripture is useless.

But perhaps because of the time he spent in prison for the crime of deep thinking, or because his sister, a nun, died at a young age in a convent, Diderot eventually rejected all religion. He died five years before the storming of the Bastille, and so he never lived to see the fresh-air part of the French Revolution, when his beliefs were written into a new set of civic commandments, the Rights of Man and of the Citizen.

AT DINNER, I'm seated outside on the terrace. In the spirit of Diderot's insatiable appetite, I decide to go for the full French experience. I've been eating at bistros and bars, mostly soups with baguettes, hearty stews, lots of roasted chicken and spring vegetables. On the menu tonight: frogs, in a sauce of onions and white wine. Not frog legs, but the whole slain amphibian. Sorry, Kermit. There's a duck terrine offering, with enough fat to narrow the carotid artery. It comes with "trumpets of death," as my English-translation menu explains. *Qu'est-ce que c'est* trumpets of death? Chanterelles, I'm told. Ah, yes. But maybe the translation mistake extends to the harvesting. Not worth the risk. Snail gratin—meh. I can't work up an appetite for something I've been throwing out of my garden and feeding to the crows. Emulsion of crustaceans. Sounds vaguely industrial. At last, I spot something recognizable: foie gras with porcini mushrooms. I feel a tinge of guilt, knowing how those goose livers were fattened. Would a true pilgrim eat foie gras? The question answers itself, *garçon*, and bring a half liter of the local red wine with it, *s'il vous plaît*. People aren't allowed to smoke indoors in this country anymore, thankfully. And another mainstay, the bidet, has disappeared in the places where I've stayed from Pas-de-Calais to the Haute-Marne. But food procured from mud or torture farms never goes out of style in France.

MORNING IN LANGRES reminds me of dawn in Laon—the crisp choreography of routine, the rituals of retail display an art form in itself. I've got another day here, which is much needed. While walking down a short hill on the path to Langres, just before the final climb to town, I slipped and tore something in my right leg. I heard a distinct popping sound, and felt a snap. I blame it on cramping and the heat, leaving me vulnerable to injury. Today, my quad is bruised and gnarly looking, and there's a little dip where one of the muscles used to be. I can walk, and it doesn't hurt unless I stretch, but I should not be carrying a pack fifteen to twenty miles a day. The sensible thing to do would be to take advantage of the remarkably efficient, world-class, and free medical care that is available in this advanced country. But I'm a guy, so I'll just ignore it until it's too late.

I'm at the House of Enlightenment when the big entrance gates swing open and have the place to myself for the first hour. The garden is formal and fussed over, too anal for my tastes. The three-story *maison*, built in the sixteenth century, is light and glorious in service of the faith of reason. It's a nice break, after spending so many hours in darkened Gothic churches full of body parts and paintings of mutilated saints. There are ten rooms, each a showcase of the Enlightenment, telling the story of a monumental thinker and his influence on the world. Diderot was the Leonardo da Vinci of France. He took as his life task "to observe nature, reflect on it, and experiment with it." One space shows his curious mind at work, his scribbles, drawings, letters, and notes-to-self. Another salon reveals his interest in theater, the plays he authored and critiqued, and in music as well. The purpose of art, he wrote, was "to make virtue attractive, vice odious, ridicule forceful."

His technical side gets a room of its own, his minor inventions, typographic designs, printing and binding, cutlery. And then there's his magnum opus, the *Encyclopédie*. Diderot was the coeditor. He sought out the best thinkers in Europe and had them explain the universe. All twenty-eight volumes of text and engraved plates are stacked and opened to many a random page in the *maison*. The frontispiece is a drawing of an orgiastic, pseudo-religious moment, with angelic, half-clad female figures representing truth, reason, and philosophy, their exposed breasts bathed in light. From asparagus to wax making, from chemistry to metaphysics, in 71,818 articles, here is the result of an attempt "to assemble the knowledge scattered over the face of the earth," he wrote.

It presents as a masterpiece, the Google of its age without the pop-ups. And yet, church and state found the *Encyclopédie* seditious. As Jefferson noted, clerics "dread the advance of science as witches do the approach of daylight." The first few volumes were condemned by the Vatican and temporarily banned by royal decree. What could possibly scare them? Let's have a look: under the letter A are listings for agriculture, astronomy, and—ah, here we go—atheism. The entry is a cogent argument against the existence of God, limited in that it's no more provable than the argument for the existence of God. The pope confined that volume to the Index of Prohibited Books, which was a thing until 1966, and also a surefire ticket to bestseller lists. In papal banishment, Diderot was in good company, joining Voltaire, Galileo, and John Milton. Also among the exiles were philosophers John Locke and Jean-Paul Sartre, the historian Edward Gibbon, the early Protestant theologian John Calvin. Further publications of the *Encyclopédie* were circulated quietly to avoid seizure by agents of the Crown. Benjamin Franklin, the publisher and polymath, was dazzled by the work and tried to get exclusive rights to sell the volumes in the American colonies. Diderot found a patron in Catherine the Great, the inquisitive empress of Russia. More significantly, his publication fed the young minds of the French Revolution.

I came home from my first year in college sounding like an evangelist for the Enlightenment. I was full of Rousseau, Diderot, and myself, the annoying nineteen-year-old who has just discovered philosophy. My dad rolled his eyes, sucked on a beer, and told me to save my breath—I might need it someday. My mother feigned interest. They were going through a rough patch, fighting a lot, mostly over money. My mom had to take a job, on her feet all day as a clerk at a department store, and then cleaning people's homes as well. The last job was humiliating, because the houses were those of her neighbors. Her faith had gotten stronger, though. She wondered if I might go to Mass with her on Sunday. Mass? With Father Schwemin? Is God still way *up there*? Oh, no, she said. Father Schwemin was gone. The church had changed. The Mass was in English. Nuns got rid of their veils and picked up electric guitars and tambourines. People attended Sunday service in short skirts and bell-bottoms. Hell was still around, but eternal damnation was downsized and deemphasized. Purgatory seemed to have disappeared altogether. Our parish had a new priest, to go along with the new church, finally built, just across the street from our house on Indian Trail Road. My mother had forgiven the diocese for making her feel terrible about getting her uterus removed. And she was clearly taken by this fresh face in a Roman collar, a priest so good with the kids. "He's young and funny and Irish," said my mom. "You're going to love Father Pat." It was the first time I'd hear a name that would haunt our family.

LIKE OUR NEW PRIEST, those who took the Age of Reason ideas to the barricades in Paris started off with so much promise. The Declaration of the Rights of Man could not be more commonsensical—and yet radical for its time. Liberty is "doing anything which does not harm others." People are to be "presumed innocent until declared culpable." And "the free communication of thoughts and of opinions is one of the most precious rights of man." Representative democracy took its first steps in France with those words, though women and people without property were excluded. But tyranny was never far behind.

In 1783, the French launched a hot air balloon, one of many inventions they gave the world. A duck, a sheep, and a rooster were on board. The flight lasted fifteen minutes. Such lofty things could not hold their minds for long. All the backed-up hatred toward religion came bursting to the front of the Revolution. You can understand why the French clipped church power at the beginning of their great upheaval, and why one of the first orders of the new National Assembly was to grant Protestants full religious freedom. You can also see why there was so much rage against the Vatican's reach. Intellectuals hated the church for its patent on piety. The poor hated it for the excess and hypocrisy in the highest clerical ranks, at a time when much of the country was starving. "The common people," said one archbishop in 1789, on the eve of the Revolution, "speak of nothing but tearing our hearts out and eating them." But none of that fury justifies the Terror that followed.

To eliminate the old order, the revolutionaries had to crush Catholicism. Churches and schools were nationalized, sold, or torn down. Monasteries and convents were dissolved. Clerics were hunted down and murdered—more than five thousand, by several estimates—some falling victim to traveling guillotines. During one massacre in Paris in 1793, priests were pulled from a prison and hacked to death, their heads put on spikes. During another killing at Nantes, men of faith were stripped naked, bound to a boat with holes punched in the bottom, and then drowned just offshore. These were "legal" executions, mind you, the kind of butchery that calls to mind the state crimes of ISIS or the Nazis. Extremists are alike in their self-righteous fury, and in how indiscriminate they are with their remedies.

I'd seen considerable evidence of this horror moment in French history, a time when mobs burned libraries simply because they housed the musings of men of faith, along the Via Francigena that was behind me. The holy ruins of the trail are a testament to the violent and lasting sweep of the Revolution—the shuttered, the vandalized, the destroyed, the vanished. In Arras, the town's first cathedral, dating to the year 1030, was torn down by the militants. The Jacobins then tried to replace that church with something called the Temple of Reason. They had the same design for spiritually neutering the Cathedral of Notre-Dame in Paris. "Dechristianization," it was called. For a brief time, one official religion was even replaced by another: the atheistic Cult of Reason. In service of this new faith, an ex-seminarian named Joseph Fouché ordered all crucifixes

removed from graveyards and declared that every cemetery bear this slogan: *Death is an eternal sleep.*

Eventually, religion was driven entirely out of public life, and the concept of *laïcité* was written into the constitution in 1905. It's used now to
keep Muslims from being veiled and fully clothed at a public beach, Jews
and Christians from displaying oversized symbols of their faith while on
secular ground. All of this backstory, to this American mind, shows the
pure genius of the First Amendment of the United States Constitution—
guaranteeing freedom to worship in any faith but banning "an establishment of religion" by the state. This was a product of European thought.
But it took the birthing of the United States to put the idea into practice.

To seek an understanding of how all things work, more than 250
years ago, was a monumental undertaking; Diderot's *Encyclopédie* was a
breakthrough for the ages. But now it's ho-hum. All knowledge is a few
clicks away, and yet the average American is arguably less well-read and
less well-informed than the French of Diderot's day, who had high literacy
rates. The philosopher from Langres thought that having the world's
knowledge in one place would set us free—truth, no longer monopolized.
Science and culture would liberate humanity. But it hasn't; just the opposite. The main social media platforms have been weaponized to sow confusion and turn people against one another. Mass murder has come with
misinformation. There's a community for every viper's pit of falsehoods
on the world wide web.

And who is left defending science, philosophy, and enlightened inquiry? The pope. Well, this pope. Not long before I left for the Via Francigena, the Vatican invited leading scientists to explain the Big Bang
theory, black holes, gravitational waves, and other subjects that would
have led to stake burning in another era. Science and theology are not at
odds with each other, said Pope Francis. To the contrary, the more the
universe is demystified, the better. "I encourage you to persevere in your

search for truth," he told a group of astronomers, who are not easily astonished. "For we ought never to fear truth, nor become trapped in our own preconceived ideas, but welcome new scientific discoveries with an attitude of humility." In a speech before a joint session of the Congress of the United States, the pope challenged those who don't believe the earth is warming because of human folly. It's become a major theme of the papacy of the man who took the name of the nature saint. "Whoever denies it, has to go to the scientists and ask them. They speak very clearly. Scientists are precise." So, it has come to this: the church that put Galileo under house arrest for promoting sound science is now urging all skeptics to put their faith in science.

Diderot died an atheist. He had a huge falling-out with Rousseau, who came to believe that secular progress was just a new form of enslavement, and would lead to imperialism. But as someone who spent his life in rigorous search for higher meaning, Diderot was restless until the very end. Could Pope Francis have won him over? Hard to say. They certainly would have enjoyed each other's company, as Francis seems to love nothing more than dialogue with nonbelievers. Diderot's main complaint against religion was that it fostered ignorance and barbarism. That's also the central argument of Christopher Hitchens, who's now been replaced on my Kindle rotation by voices from the other side, Augustine among them. Hitchens concluded that belief in God goes hand in hand with a delusional view about the origins of life and the cosmos. Faith cannot stand up to reason. But he died before Francis became head of the church. I would love to hear his take on a pope who embraces reason and promotes peer-reviewed science as a way to higher truth.

I step out of Diderot's Maison des Lumières into the even greater light of early summer. I walk away with an appreciation of the man, his genius, his persistence. But I feel a little empty. I can't . . . quite . . . put . . . my finger on it. Atheism, as it's been said, is like nonalcoholic beer. It's also human-centered, obsessed with self. The favorite atheist guide of modern Republican economic thought, Ayn Rand, believed that man "must exist for his own sake, neither sacrificing himself to others nor sacrificing others to himself. The pursuit of his own rational self-interest and of his own happiness is the highest moral purpose of his life." The motto that Fouché wanted emblazoned over every cemetery—*Death is an eternal sleep*—is a grim bookend to life. Diderot himself desperately wanted to believe that death was not the end. "Those people who are buried next to each other are perhaps not as crazy as one might think," he wrote in a letter to a longtime lover. "Oh, my Sophie, I could touch you, feel you, love you, look for you, unite myself with you, and combine myself with you when we are no longer here. . . . Allow myself this fantasy."

This temple of the Enlightenment in Langres is not soul-stirring, as was Erkembode's tomb in Saint-Omer or the Smiling Angel in Reims. There's also a whiff of condescension about the way the *maison* presents things: all was darkness until the Great Man of Reason came along and cleared everything up for the little people. Not true. Consider Erasmus— brilliant, humane, progressive, logical, and still a believer. Or even Dom Pérignon, observing nature, reflecting on it, and then experimenting with it to craft a most perfect thing. Diderot may have explained the universe, but surely he knew that wasn't enough. And when his followers tried to replace belief in God with belief in reason, that wasn't enough either. Robespierre himself, the dark knight of the Terror, called the Festivals of Reason staged in nationalized cathedrals "ridiculous farces." After the Revolution, a popular philosopher created the Religion of Humanity, with its own sacraments and priests. It floundered for lack of followers. "Of all the failures of the French Revolution, none would be so inevitable and so dismal as the campaign of 'dechristianization,'" wrote historian Simon Schama.

Predictably, I wander over to Saint Mammes Cathedral, which takes up an entire medieval block. The cloister was seized by the state; it's now attached to a public library and decorated with bland, consensus-driven municipal art. The church is dedicated to a boy saint from the third century, born in a Roman prison and tortured by the emperor. Mammes escaped, made his way to the mountains, and lived for a time off his legend. When captured, he was thrown to the lions. But lo, he tamed them and escaped again, this time with a beast as his companion. The Romans finally got him with a giant fork—a trident—in the gut. His relics are here in Langres, inside a gold box. And there's a statue of the child with the lion.

Diderot would disapprove of it all—the superstition, the box of seventeen-hundred-year-old bones, the dubious bonding of lion and lad. He despised myth. But there is something of Huck Finn in the kid who outwitted his tormentors and turned his predators into pals. To a ten-year-old boy sitting in church today, bored stiff by a clerical sermon, the tale of Mammes is electrifying. Religion is story, a narrative about a force much greater than us, enigmatic by nature. Most of us like to think that death is more than an eternal sleep. Until atheism can tell a story, it will always have trouble packing a house. But also, as Diderot said, "Only passions, great passions, can elevate the soul to great things."

SIXTEEN

UNITED EUROPE'S TICKING CLOCK

Without the Via Francigena, I would never have spent a day and a night in a city obsessed with time. Besançon is tucked into a fold that heralds the foothills of the Jura Mountains, with tall, orange-roofed stone houses sprouting chimneys that are distinct enough to be protected by law. The tidy sheen makes it feel like Switzerland, which is barely an hour away. But then you run into middle-aged men in tight red pants, a welcome assurance that you're still very much in France. A horseshoe bend of the River Doubs wraps around the old town, which is topped by a citadel built during the golden era of fortifications in the seventeenth century. A Gallic tribe from the Bronze Age, Julius Caesar, the Holy Roman Empire, Burgundy, Spain, Austria, and the Nazis all had control at one point. Now Besançon lives in contented obscurity, 120,000 people in the city proper, known for its watches, clocks, and gongs—all the ticking reminders of quantifiable time.

"Gorgeous city," I say to the young woman who stamps my pilgrim passport on a delicious morning, the heat finally starting to back off. "I'd never heard of Besançon."

"We're often overlooked."

"Do you get many visitors from the States?"

"No, none at all. Not that I can remember."

"None?"

"I beg your pardon: two. An American couple came through here last month. They might have been lost. Will you sign the guest book? Not even the French visit Besançon."

Pity. It's another gem on the road to Rome, though one apparently lacking in self-esteem. And the last chance to talk to myself for a while. My son, Casey, will join me in Lausanne. He doesn't really get why I'm on the V.F. But when I described the route, he perked up. He's always game to see someplace new.

Today I want to meet the Franciscans who live on a hill above town, to see the famed astronomical clock, and to stop by Victor Hugo's house. My hotel is an easy walk from anything I need for short-term happiness. Long term, well, maybe the Brothers of St. Francis can offer some advice on that, after eight hundred years of trying to live humble lives within the arms of nature. I stroll past storefronts displaying Besançon-made watches. Not just one storefront or two, but many. This does not count the retailers of sundials, clocks, and various things that chime or chirp on the hour. Nor the Museum of Time. Nor the Observatoire de Besançon, a 140-year-old institution that relies on the stars to certify the accuracy of your chronometer. Nor the glass-fronted workshop in Old Town, where you can watch a watchmaker make a watch.

The house where Hugo was born, in 1802, is just up a hill on Grande Rue, a stately, multistory *maison*. After he died, his coffin lay in state under the Arc de Triomphe, and two million people turned out to pay honor to a writer. Hugo is buried in the Panthéon, the great secular mausoleum in Paris, a fitting place for the playwright, poet, essayist, novelist, exile, politician, and man of sustained moral outrage whose name is attached to a street in nearly every town in France. Baby Hugo spent only six weeks here, which was long enough for Besançon to claim a substantial part of his legacy. Inside the house are quotes from his life's work and the themes that animated him. For all his prodigious output, Hugo was brilliant at capturing a complex truth in just a few words:

"He who opens a school door closes a prison."

"All the forces in the world are not so powerful as an idea whose time has come."

"It is nothing to die. It is frightful not to live."

"Death has revelations: the great sorrows which open the heart, open the mind as well. . . . As for me, I have faith. I believe in a future life. How could I do otherwise? My daughter was a soul. I saw this soul. I touched it."

This last quote is curious, since Hugo is said to have been an atheist. When he said that he touched the soul of his daughter, it was a reference to his child who drowned in the Seine at a young age. It seems he was more like Diderot, in constant search of self and God, advancing Enlightenment thought in the wreckage after the Revolution. He flirted for many years with Catholicism and Deism, telling a census taker that he was a "freethinker," never parked permanently in one theological slot. No one would ever look at the greatest cathedral in France the same way after Hugo wrote *The Hunchback of Notre-Dame*. And no one has created a purer soul than the bishop who takes in a thief in *Les Misérables*. I've found his observations about postrevolutionary Christian ruins to be spot on. But he was also a political visionary. And as I wheeze my way up the hill to view the Mother of All Clocks, I'm thinking about the fragile construct of modern Europe, which he prophesied.

In 1870, Hugo planted a tree outside the home where he lived in political exile, on the island of Guernsey off the coast of Normandy. By the time the sapling had grown into a mighty oak, Europe would be a unified political entity, Hugo hoped, all the nationalistic bile and religious hatred squeezed out of it. He presented this vision in a speech. "A day will come when you France, you Russia, you Italy, you England, you Germany, you all, nations of the continent, without losing your distinct qualities and your glorious individuality, will be brotherhood," he said. "A day will come when the only fields of battle will be markets opening up to trade. A day will come when the bullets and the bombs will be replaced by votes."

The oak tree still stands outside Hugo's Hauteville House. And the Day Has Come, indeed, when Europe is trying to be more than its parts. A French dignitary in 1949 envisioned a "great experiment" that would "put an end to war." That part has come true: never before have the major nations of the Continent gone so long without warring with one another. This, let us not forget, followed the near annihilation of the Old World in the past century. The European Union is a reasonable representation of Hugo's United States of Europe. "My revenge is fraternity," he said. The problem is that a common currency and a common market may not be enough to overcome uncommon political bonds.

Europe does not feel united. The small nations despise the large nations, particularly Germany. Britain is leaving in a fit of nationalism that has spread to other countries. Migrants are feared and loathed. Un-Christian Europe wants to hold on to its "Christian identity," in the phrase that threatens to disrupt many governments. Even the British atheist Richard Dawkins said he finds the bells of England's empty cathedrals soothing, a much better sound than the call to prayer of Islam. (He was told that atheists don't get to choose.) At the same time, the pope frets about a secular Europe facing "a vacuum of values." Too many people feel left behind, voiceless, their furniture-making shop or lace factory or nonpasteurized cheese a victim of the Eurocrats who sold them out to globalism. Spain and Greece suffer Depression-level unemployment, one in four out of work. Italy is a dead end for anyone under the age of thirty. A turn to autocrats and crackpots, in Poland and Hungary and Bavaria, in parts of Italy and France, not to mention the Russian menace, is evidence that the darker impulses of a continent long soaked in human blood have not been washed away by treaty.

But the alternative is worse. Far worse. What is that alternative? The history of Europe.

Besançon could have been another casualty of the grind of multistate capitalism. They make cuckoo clocks, *for Chrissake*! Who has time to craft a fine timepiece? You think of Geppetto-like laborers working half a year to make one thing by hand. And then you think of the Chinese, rolling out knockoffs on wages that couldn't pay for a French worker's vacation. This city is chockablock with big-windowed ateliers, designed to let in the maximum amount of daylight so people could see the tiny little pieces they were assembling.

But Besançon has found a way forward. At its peak, the watchmaking industry employed 20,000 people and cranked out apprentices from the École d'Horlogerie. It was a company town of time. What nearly killed the city was the rise of easy-to-make quartz watches in the 1970s. It's been revived by technology companies that welcomed the skills of former watchmakers. At the same time, there's been a renaissance of "artisan" timepieces.

The biggest timekeeper, the Astronomical Clock of Besançon, pulses away inside the Cathedral of Saint John, at the base of a mountain just beyond Hugo's house. It's a massive beast of brass, copper, steel, and gold, about eighteen feet high, with thirty thousand mechanical parts. The main faces are outside, on each of the four sides of the cathedral tower. Inside, over 70 dials and 122 indicators keep track of phases of the moon, sunrises and sunsets, tides in French ports, eclipses, and local time around the world. The calendar, built to take in leap years, is said to register up to ten thousand years. Considering that Europe didn't even have mechanical clocks until the fourteenth century, this has to rate as one of the supreme triumphs of timekeeping evolution. And yet, the big clock is still just a thing, not a hunchback roaming around Notre-Dame's crumbling bell towers. Here again is *chronos* time, measuring seconds, hours, days, months, seasons, and years, with no way to track the quality moments of *kairos*. It's lifeless. In an attempt to make the astronomical clock something more, the church says that one of the most complex horological devices in the world is really about the Resurrection of Christ. Come again? Every tick of every day, the guide inside the cathedral explains, represents fresh time since Jesus rose from the dead. Rejoice and take in a good-news moment! Well, O.K. I wasn't the only one scratching my head while exiting the cathedral. But I did wonder, not for the first time, how many beats of my own heart have passed while I was doing worthless shit.

Up the hill and above the river, the Franciscan friars run a little shelter for the poor and pilgrims. Testing my still-purpled thigh, I hike through a winding tunnel of green, on a part of the V.F. that is shockingly well signed—a by-product of the time-obsessives living below. Emerging from moss-draped woods, I come upon Chapelle des Buis, balanced on a knife ridge. The view below, of the chimney-studded homes, of Vauban's Citadel, of the oxbow of the River Doubs, requires more than a single deep breath to take in. The chapel, like the Franciscans themselves, is powerful in its simplicity. I grab a newsletter and read up on the latest good works of these men in cinnamon-colored robes held at the waist by a knotted rope. The Franciscans are happy to spread the news of their anniversary, the jubilee commemorating eight hundred years since a companion of the saint from Assisi founded an order in this country. Francis, the ex-noble in rags and friend of the dispossessed, has always had a large following among the devout. But he continues to fascinate nonbelievers as well.

"Come and meet Franciscan joy!" So they say in the newsletter.

Trying to do just that, I walk around the chapel to a small residence and idyllic garden. Trellises drip pink and peach-colored roses. Late-stage irises hold their papery blossoms. Tall geraniums, with the sturdy limbs of plants that have wintered over, sprout from pots placed between rows of vegetables. The only thing missing is the statue of Saint Francis, a hallmark of even the most secular gardens. It's a nice bit of irony. I knock on a door. No answer. It pushes open. Well, sure. In addition to having a sense of humor, the Franciscans would never lock a door. But I won't intrude. From a window overhead, I hear snoring. Nap time! I tiptoe away.

Later, I connect with Brother Alexis Mensah, one of five men in the Franciscan Fraternity of Besançon. I ask him what it's like to live by religious rules dating to the thirteenth century in a Europe that is so modern, secular, and paced by the demands of clocks set to the digital age.

"We are carriers of light in this world that is wandering in its own way," he said. "We are the past, the present, and we intend to inscribe ourselves in the future of this Europe." Though his words seem boldly aspirational for a faith that has been marginalized in France, he is without pretense. "We try to be simple people, living not by the grabbing of wealth, but in sharing, of perfect charity." I turn that phrase over in my mind: *perfect charity.* The duty to protect nature—creation, in his words—is stronger than ever. "Faced with a society of consumption and the scourges of global warming, we offer simplicity of life, proximity to the poorest and most neglected, and the preservation of our environment, which is undergoing suicidal exploitation."

The pilgrims who stay over, he said, arrive with GPSs blinking in their hands (guilty as charged), but leave with their phones turned off. "They know in advance the steps, the distances, what to expect," he said. "Spiritual research is not always the primary objective. What they usually seek is to find their way in the world and also to know their limit. . . . They are trying to find meaning in their lives." He has no way to register whether his tiny cell of ascetics has any impact, or can help those travelers with the search, except to say, "People are touched by the welcome, the life, the prayers, the fraternity of the brothers. That is all we have."

And more: a view that time should be measured by something greater than mechanical ticks, mindful of a Christ who said, "Who of you by worrying can add a single hour to his life?"

SEVENTEEN

THE BETRAYAL

The new priest was thirty-one years old when he arrived at our church on Indian Trail Road, there to take up duties as assistant pastor and director of youth activities. He had gone to the same Jesuit school as I, served in the army, and earned a master's degree in counseling after being ordained. Despite the impressive résumé, the Reverend Patrick G. O'Donnell insisted that everyone call him Father Pat. Likable, sociable, modern Father Pat. My mother raved about him. He exuded empathy; even if it was calculated, it was welcome after so many years of pastoral freeze. He visited our house often, and I can still see him sitting in the kitchen while my parents offered him food and drink. He had an overbite and dark bangs and was quick with a compliment. Our home was always open to him. He didn't have to knock.

My youngest brother was eleven years old when Father Pat moved in across the street, small for his age, the easiest child to raise, and also the most likable and the best athlete by family consensus. He and his friends, Tim and Mike and Randy, formed an inseparable band of boys. They explored the woods at the edge of town, built forts in the pine trees, rode their bikes with playing cards placed in the spokes to give off a cool sound, tossed a football until dark. They had the kind of childhood that a city like Spokane promised people: a great place to raise kids, it was said through the generations.

Father Pat had another thing going for him. He had access to a boat—a sleek cabin cruiser—and an off-road vehicle. Big toys. He offered to take the boys out four-wheeling and zipping along the water, something you could never imagine Father Schwemin doing. "He was a priest who was a Pied Piper with kids," said the pastor who served with him. And if the kids stayed late, they could overnight in a cabin on the lake. Father Pat had access to that as well. The parents trusted him. They had gone to Catholic schools, taken their wedding vows on Catholic altars, baptized their children in Catholic churches, and buried their dead in Catholic cemeteries. You always looked up to the priest. Think of the sacrifices Father Pat had made. Instead of working as a professional in a fancy office in Seattle, instead of raising a family of his own, he had taken vows of chastity and poverty to work with worshippers of Christ at the fringe of a town in eastern Washington State.

At breakfast, on the morning of August 29, 2002, my brother's friend Tim unfolded the Spokane newspaper to find a picture and page-one story about a priest who was accused of abusing dozens of boys, something the church had known about for years, the article asserted. By this time, Tim was a father of three children of his own, married for sixteen years.

"Look who's in the paper," he said, as his wife recalled in a story in the *Inlander.* "That's Father Pat. Read this."

She skimmed it.

"Read the rest of the article. Read it out loud!"

The account was about another parish, in a town of five hundred people in the wheat fields of the Palouse country south of Spokane. Father Pat was sent to that remote church after he'd been removed from several others. The story that followed him from parish to parish was always the same. The priest won the confidence of young boys, got their parents to trust him as well, and then betrayed their kids in the most horrific way. When his violations of children were reported to church higher-ups, Father Pat was admonished, but never punished or reported to civil authorities. They shuffled him off to another unsuspecting community. What was different about this episode in the little farm town was that one of Father Pat's victims, abused at the age of twelve, had recently killed himself. He left behind a suicide note with this line: "What happened to me destroyed me."

Tim's wife looked at her husband. He was stricken.

"Were you abused?" She had heard Tim talk about Father Pat a few years earlier, well after the boys had grown up, when a story first broke about sixth- and seventh-graders at Assumption of the Blessed Virgin Mary. Following gym practice, the priest would instruct the kids to strip off their clothes, line up naked in front of him on the stage, and wash their genitals with a bucket of water and soap he provided. Tim's family, like ours, lived within a Frisbee toss of the church. Tim's parents had served as Eucharistic ministers. His father was chairman of the lay council. His mother volunteered at school. They were Catholic to their core, the pillars of the parish.

"Did you get naked in front of Father Pat?" she asked Tim now.

"Yes."

"Did Father Pat touch you?"

"Yes."

He had said, in the years-ago conversation, that "nothing affected me," and that he was not a victim of this predator. Tim seldom lost his temper or let things get to him. He had a gentle, playful spirit. He was clearly upset now. Something in the latest story of the suicide victim, and that note, *"What happened to me destroyed me."* He put his cereal bowl aside and left the house in a hurry. Hours later, police arrived on the doorstep. Tim was dead. He'd lain down in front of a train.

My brother was devastated. "I lost my best friend." My brother was also one of those boys in the gym, told by the most trusted adult at school to clean his genitals in front of him. My brother was never touched. But once, Father Pat came by the house to check on him after he'd come home early from school, feeling sick. "He's in bed, but I don't think he's asleep," my mother said. The priest went into my brother's bedroom and talked nicely to him, the words of a man who'd spent his adult life grooming children. The priest reached under the blankets. My brother jumped up. "What are you doing?" The priest dashed out of the house.

My brother had not told our parents about that episode or the genital cleansing until the other stories made it into the press. But one of our best friends did try to get the word out on Father Pat. Rita Flynn was a mother of eleven, whose kids were all gorgeous, gregarious, and had ancient Gaelic names. Our families were very close. She was the most devout person I knew growing up, emanating goodness. She also had a master's degree in psychology from Loyola. Everyone adored her. When her eighth-grade boy told her about the naked cleaning in front of the priest, she took the story to the senior pastor at Assumption, the Reverend William Skylstad. He said he would talk to Father Pat about it, later reporting back to this mother that it would not happen again. He said he had "remonstrated" his fellow priest.

By this time, Father Pat had been abusing boys at our parish for two years. His crimes, unknown to all but a small circle of victims and clerical enablers, went much deeper than what happened in the gym. He took children to the lake cabin, which had a hot tub, told them to strip, and tried to fondle them. At that same cabin, Father Pat took a boy into his bedroom. My brother's friends remembered, much later, the horror of watching a door close as the child was led away. He also brought a twelve-year-old boy into his bed at the parish rectory, while Father Skylstad slept one floor above him. He took another boy on his boat, and let a second man rape him. The assailant shot himself after news of his abuse broke.

When these violations finally came to light, Patrick O'Donnell was revealed to be "a serial pedophile," as one court document put it, passed from parish to parish. A total of sixty-six people accused him of child molestation or rape. A third person had killed himself, after sexual assault by Father Pat, but before the dam of revelations burst. He got away with hurting so many children because he could count on the protection of the church. He'd been recommended for the priesthood even after abusing two students at St. Thomas Seminary in Kenmore, Washington. The faculty board noted that O'Donnell had "a special interest in youth," but had been "cautioned about an over interest." At his first posting, just days after his ordination as a priest, O'Donnell went after a boy. The incident was known to the diocese of Spokane. Still, he was named director of the Catholic youth ministry. He arrived at our church after several complaints of predatory abuse from the parish he had just left. But families at Assumption were not told that a sex offender had been placed in their midst, a man who would be welcomed into their homes, given the care of their children. Nor were the police informed. And by the time O'Donnell's past caught up with him, through civil litigation, the statute of limitations had run out on his crimes. He would never go to prison.

At one point, church leaders thought they could cure O'Donnell. They sent him to Seattle for "aversion" therapy. While there, he continued to destroy people; at least eight victims later came forth from the churches where he worked in Seattle. He also got a PhD in psychology, and a license to practice youth counseling. His dissertation was about how adults could gain the trust of children.

O'Donnell was removed from his ministry in 1986, after the allegations were too numerous for the church to ignore. In a court deposition, he said he couldn't remember the number, or even some of the names, of his many victims. "I felt sinful. I felt I wasn't a good person, wasn't a good priest," he said. "I feel very bad. And I'm sorry." A few years later, again under oath, he admitted molesting at least thirty children, but said it could be as high as sixty. "I'm terribly sorry," he said in 2008. "I don't expect forgiveness." He retired to live out his days in a small town on the shores of Puget Sound. The senior pastor at Assumption, the Reverend Skylstad, was promoted up the ranks, to chancellor, to bishop, and then to president of the United States Conference of Catholic Bishops. He retired in 2010. At each stage, he professed ignorance of O'Donnell's crimes.

The diocese was forced into bankruptcy, and nearly became the first to be liquidated in the United States since the Great Depression. The church sold some assets, raised money, and settled with 180 victims for $48 million. The money is small compensation, and small justice. It does not bring back the three lives that were taken, or restore the hundreds that were ruined, or end the generational ripples of sorrow still to come. Assumption was just one church, and Spokane just one town. But the pattern of abuse, the people who would never be able to repair themselves because of betrayal, happened in Boston, New York, Washington, Pittsburgh, Portland, Los Angeles, Tucson, Chicago, Milwaukee, anywhere that large numbers of Catholics lived, more than $2 billion in settlements. And it happened in Europe and South America and Africa and Australia. Apologies, high and low, have come and gone with the admissions. Wash. Rinse. Repeat.

Pope John Paul II, leader of the faith when it became clear that clerical abuse of children was thick in the ranks of Catholicism, was slow to take any action during his twenty-seven years as pontiff. He never ordered a deep inquiry into how church culture allowed so many criminals to avoid justice, the catastrophic failures in accountability. Since his death, he has been elevated to sainthood. Late in life, he sent an email to parishes worldwide. "Sexual abuse within the church is a profound contradiction of the teaching and virtues of Jesus Christ." No one would disagree with that, for nothing said by Jesus could ever justify what thousands of men who pledged their lives to him did to destroy countless children. And so I wonder whether the contradiction that the pope spoke of is so deeply woven into the ministry of men who take holy orders that nothing will ever change. I'm starting to doubt whether even the most reform-minded leader can do anything about this scourge. If not, why take another step in Rome's direction?

Though the church now has a policy of zero tolerance for offenders, Pope Francis admits that the institution is tardy. Sexual abuse is not a by-product of celibacy or the all-male culture that rules the church, he says. Instead, Francis blames "clericalism," the reflexive protection of Roman-collared guardians of the faith, the bishops and cardinals who moved monsters around within the system. "The conscience of the church arrived a little late," the pope told an audience at the Vatican. Too late for the lives broken at the church on Indian Trail Road and all the parishes in every corner of Catholicism.

My brother lost his best friend. I doubt if he will forgive the church, nor should he be expected to. He's fine, he says, and I have to believe him. I love him and want him to be happy and whole. He's tried to put his pain in perspective. The children of his friend are without a father be-cause of a priest in our parish, because clerics covered for one of their own. My mother was deeply shaken. She didn't like to talk about what happened at our church; her thinking was stuck in a cul-de-sac with no way out. She used to hope that one of her four boys would become a priest, and she continued to defend the vocation as a great and selfless calling. When I raged against the bastards who inflicted so much pain, when I said no institution that hosted this level of malignancy was wor-thy of her trust, she tried to explain her reluctance to break up with Ca-tholicism. Her loyalty was based on a connection to God, and could not be severed by the deeply flawed mortals who labored in God's name. She'd had several genuine spiritual experiences, times when she shivered at the proximity of the divine, which the church had helped her compre-hend. After O'Donnell's crimes were revealed, she stewed in denial for a long time, then flared in occasional bursts of anger, and ultimately ar-rived at some degree of forgiveness. She kept her faith, troubled though it was. My brother did not.

"I used to enjoy the structure and tradition of the Catholic Church," my brother said. "But I lost my wonder of what could be."

Wonder is a simple virtue. Like childhood, it's grounded in innocence, taken for granted until it's impossible to reclaim. One of the reasons I'm on the Via Francigena is to see whether I can maintain my wonder of what could be, while never forgetting what was.

EIGHTEEN

REFUGE AND REFORM

In the maze of Geneva's Old Town, the cobblestone paths go up and down, they narrow and twist and circle back to a center. It's easy to get lost, which seems a perfect metaphor for the people who flooded into this city of refuge because they were unmoored from a faith that was supposed to guide them from birth to the hereafter. At the heart of Geneva is a house of fourteen rooms above a vast lake filled with snowmelt from the Alps. The *maison*, built over the cloister of a great cathedral, is dedicated to a handful of ideas that overturned the Christian world five hundred years ago, almost to the day I arrive. The source of so much of the trouble is inside: a single, five-century-old certificate mounted to a wall. It's a "passport to paradise," so called, issued by the pope, signed by a bishop, and made out in the name of the buyer. The cost for this letter of celestial transport depended on the number of years you wished to knock off from purgatory, or whether you were purchasing for a deceased relative—one of the luckless souls stuck between heaven and hell. The average time in purgatory was pegged at nine thousand years, though it's unclear how the accountants of the faith came up with that number. What you bought was absolution; you paid protection money to stay out of hell or speed the flight to the highest level. Even a future sin could be forgiven for the right price. A coin box, decorated with an image of the devil tormenting those in a postdeath delay, was placed in churches by traveling indulgence hucksters. It was promoted with a slogan: "As soon as the coin in the coffer rings, a soul from purgatory springs."

The coins filled sacks, which loaded down mules, which made it up and over the Alps to Rome, to bribe the Turks menacing off the Adriatic shore, and to enrich a papal hierarchy that had embarked in the early sixteenth century on one of the most ambitious construction plans in history: building a city of sanctified marble. The centerpiece was St. Peter's Basilica. To encourage this industry, the pope allowed select clerics to keep half of what they collected—for themselves. In this way, bishops and cardinals were able to purchase palaces and stage sumptuous feasts off the meager earnings of people who gave up food for their children in order to get a shot at eternal salvation.

Martin Luther, the thirty-three-year-old Augustinian monk from a little German town, could find nothing in the Bible to justify this sordid trade in indulgences. Nor could he find anything in Scripture about purgatory. What was this waiting room, this halfway house, this place for people not saintly enough to make it to the next level or wicked enough for damnation? An ordained priest with a doctorate in theology, he was brilliant but prickly, conscience stricken at all times. Luther knew every verse of the Latin Bible—knew it well enough that he would soon go to the source, and translate it from the original Greek into the German vernacular of his people. He could not find a line connecting Jesus Christ to the shakedown scheme of the church he had given his life to. In 1517, Luther went public with 95 theses—formally titled "Disputation on the Power and Efficacy of Indulgences"—sending his remarks to a bishop and pinning them up on the bulletin board of the Castle Church in Wittenberg. He did not nail his protest note to the door, most scholars now believe, nor did he call for establishment of a new sect of Christianity in his name. But religion, remember, is nothing without story. And the founding narrative of the Protestant movement sounds so much better with a hammer that cracked the most powerful institution on earth.

THE WAY TO THE WRITTEN RELICS of the Reformation goes through the border town of Pontarlier, which is famous for the mind-altering drink of absinthe, into Switzerland through Sainte-Croix, Orbe, and ends in Lausanne—eighty-one miles along the Via Francigena from Besançon. Lausanne is the capital of Vaud, in the French-speaking part of this country. It's a city of 150,000 built on three hills, sloping to the crescent-shaped lake we know as Geneva but called by the Swiss and the French—who share it—Lac Léman. Back in the day, as in the Mesolithic era, people in animal skins reacted the way I did when I first saw the expansive bowl of mountain water, framed by the forested and glaciated enormity of the Alps, and decided that heaven could wait—for here it is. The Romans felt the same, as did the Celtic tribe of the Helvetii, various Germanic assemblies, Gauls, writers and artists from Britain and the United States, all the way up to the distinctly nonnationalistic Swiss who comprise the lucky present-day inhabitants.

I crossed no border station coming in from France. But I'm clearly in another world now, the land of pampered and entitled cows with bells, of spotless trains to everywhere, of a universal health care system so fantastic it makes you want to get sick just to try a free sample. The V.F. is well signed, marked in yellow posts. And the Swiss, being the Swiss, inform you not just of the distance to the next stop on the road to Rome, but how long it takes to walk there. These calculations will shame many travelers into attempting a brisk pace just to be average, while leaving others stranded after dark.

I met my son, Casey, in Lausanne; he flew in from Washington, D.C., through several connections. He'll be with me for six days. He's full of graduate school enthusiasms, his mind alive with the questions that many people stop asking after forty-hour weeks of study are replaced by forty-hour weeks of work. And just when I was starting to wonder why I let my kid learn the struggling profession of his old man, he said he met a cable news celebrity and was unimpressed. Skepticism, thy name is journalism. He has a million ideas for things to see, restaurants to try, places to swim, and mountain trails to hike. When I said, *Um*, our first stop really should be the International Museum of the Reformation in Geneva, he looked at me like I had just offered him an afternoon of advanced dental flossing.

I never told him the story of what happened in Spokane. Maybe he knows about it from one of his cousins. He grew up hearing me praise cerebral Jesuits who taught us to embrace the world and its contradictions. He was open-minded, even though he would probably say I romanticized my education. But he also came of age at a time when a global crisis of predatory priests dominated news about the Catholic Church. *Contradictions, my ass,* he used to say with a teenager's certainty. *Sounds like they're all hypocrites.* Well, you have a point, overstated though it is. *Religion is fable.* Yes, a story! Poetic. Universal. And I would start in about faith, which by its very nature can never be proven, and that the foundational narratives of most religious beliefs are perhaps more allegorical than factual.

We had this argument while he was growing up. His view is more nuanced now, and I'm trying to open him up even more with a gateway brief on behalf of Pope Francis. We didn't raise our kids to be Catholic, or even Christian. Maybe this was a reaction to the detached, binary tutorials of Father Schwemin. And after what happened to my brother and his friends, I stopped caring about whether one religion had a monopoly on morality. Why set our kids up for the inevitable letdown? But now, they have no idea why people genuflect at a certain time in church, or put ashes on their forehead on a late-winter day, or why an Orthodox Jew wears a yarmulke. Our plan was to give them the basics of the major religions—the mythology, the philosophy, and as many of the verifiable facts as possible—and let the free market of ideas settle the debate as they thought it through. It hasn't really worked. They have a reasonable person's skepticism toward the supernatural claims of religion. They can spot the cons masquerading as holy men and women of faith. But they lack literacy in the spiritual canon. And how can you understand the world, as the archbishop of Canterbury said, without understanding religion? It's one of my regrets as a parent. We didn't want to close the door on spiritual curiosity. Our kids should be open enough to allow themselves to be surprised, as Francis said, and not to foreclose on the idea that a great faith, though flawed, can contain great truths.

LAUSANNE WAS AFLAME with the Reformation in the first decades after Luther lit the fuse, and the city hosted a famous debate in 1536 on the merits of true Christianity. That was when Catholics and Protestants were still talking, and not yet slaughtering one another. But most of the action happened just down the lake at the city of Geneva, forty miles away. We took a slower, regional train and spent the hour with our faces pressed against the window. Vineyards! So glorious, on the steep slopes that meet the water, several thousand stone-terraced acres, not a vine out of place. And UNESCO-protected World Heritage vines at that, a legacy of the enological imperialism of monks in the eleventh century. Who'd have thought that Switzerland, surrounded by Europe's highest peaks, could make so much wine? Surely the juice is plonk. Not by any stretch, we soon learned. They make Oregon-worthy pinot noir, a fruity chasselas, and several dry whites from grapes I'd never heard of. Switzerland may be wasted on the Swiss, as the old line has it, but the wine is not. They drink most of what they produce, which is why you don't see a lot of *vin de Suisse* in American stores. Sunlight bounces off the lake and lights up the grapes, some of which are just starting to show early-summer gold.

We split up in Geneva, he for secular amusements, me to the Reformation shrines. The Protestant museum in Old Town, with the indulgence certificate, is packed with visitors. The docents show a trapdoor in a chimney, a hiding place for the Bible translated by Dr. Luther for the German people. There's a painting of a woman with a tiny Bible nestled in her hair. People were forced to hide the book, for it was a crime in many a city to be in possession of any holy book other than church-authorized Scripture. The only legal way to God was through a clerical filter. *Rome has spoken, the case is closed.*

Luther democratized Christianity. He wanted a better Roman Catholic religion, closer to its source and the needs of people who filled the pews. "Out of love for the faith and the desire to bring it to light," he wrote in the preamble to the 95 theses. As a young man, three years after he was ordained, Luther walked eight hundred miles to Rome. He was dismayed with what he saw—the indulgence racket, the profitable trade in phony relics, a debauched Vatican hierarchy. The church was the richest landowner on the Continent, and it was grooming Giovanni de' Medici, of the wealthy Florentine dynasty, to become the next Vicar of Christ. He was made an archbishop at the age of eight, a cardinal at thirteen, Pope Leo X at thirty-seven. "Since God has given us the Papacy," he said, "let us enjoy it."

Luther certainly wasn't the first to see hypocrisy in high holy places. The objections from the provinces of Christianity had been building for a long time, some coming from in-house dissidents like the brilliant Erasmus. But Luther was one of the first to *do* something about it. His concerns led him to a radical thought about the Word of God as messaged by its clerical carriers: "Who knows if this is really true?"

Back in the monastery, the Hermit of Wittenberg tried to find out. As he went into deep theological exploration, the corruption continued all around him. The lord of the nearby Castle Church had acquired a hoard of relics—a twig from the Burning Bush, a thumb from the grandmother of Jesus, a tooth from Saint Jerome, a straw from Bethlehem's manger, mother's milk from the Virgin Mary—and was charging a premium price for the right to feel the power. This went on as a despotic Dominican friar, Johann Tetzel, was shaking down the locals with his indulgence scheme. "I have here the passports to lead the human soul to the celestial joys of Paradise," he would proclaim. The rich could buy their way into postdeath comfort; the poor were out of luck, unless they scraped together money needed to stay alive. Luther's 95 theses were simply questions, an opening round of civilized argument, though his complaints came with real bite. "It is certain that when money clinks in the money chest, greed and avarice can be increased," he wrote, a clever play on the coin slogan. He dared to raise the issue that other clerics felt but feared putting to paper. "Why does the pope . . . build the basilica of Saint Peter, with the money of poor believers?"

His critique might have reached no further than the city walls without the help of another revolutionary. Johann Gutenberg grew up reading hand-scripted manuscripts in early-fifteenth-century Germany. As he was coming of age, craftsmen using block printing—pages produced by inking a piece of hard wood with letters cut into it—could turn out a book faster than a monk. But the process was tedious, with each new page having to come from a different block carved from scratch. Gutenberg drew on ideas for squeezing wine grapes to create a printing press. The Chinese had done something similar with clay lettering, much earlier, though the technology was unknown to Europeans. Gutenberg arranged metal type on a tray. The letters were inked. Hundreds of pages were printed. Then the characters were rearranged into fresh sentences for a new page—movable type, it was called. The Gutenberg Bible was completed in 1455, the first book ever printed. It had sharp, clear lettering, forty-two lines to a page, on paper and calfskin vellum, telling the story of creation up until the first days of Christianity. Two hundred copies were supposed to be printed of the first mass-produced book in Europe; the actual run was short of that. No longer would monks in tightly monitored scriptoria, or cardinals in a centralized church, or a tyrannical monarch, control the flow of ideas. The written word took flight just as the Renaissance was flourishing. Speech was freed.

The museum in Geneva has assembled a replica of Gutenberg's invention—"the most extraordinary act of divine grace," as Luther called it. Gutenberg, by the way, got his start selling "holy mirrors" used by pilgrims to capture the essence of a relic so they could take it home for healing. Had he not gone bust in a side business of the relic racket, he might never have crafted the invention that changed humanity. The curators also have on display one of the first 95 theses to be printed, and the tome which ensured that Luther's writings would be wildly popular: the Vatican's Index of Prohibited Books.

Rather than debate Luther's legitimate arguments, the church went ballistic. They would nail the pious little bastard to his own cross. "In three weeks I will throw the heretic into the fire!" said Brother Tetzel after the theses were published. Once the battle was joined, Luther never backed down. An obscure monk, without so much as a sword or a coin to his name, stood up to the mighty powers of church and state, the Vatican and the Holy Roman Empire. Tossing pebbles against a fortress, he nearly brought it down. What he had going for him was what Victor Hugo would later describe: the power of an idea whose time has come. "The Church of Rome, formerly the most holy of all churches, has become the most lawless den of thieves, the most shameless of brothels, the very kingdom of sin," Luther wrote the pope. Luther became a late-medieval celebrity; 300,000 copies of his writings were circulated between 1517 and 1520. In his lifetime, a third of all books published in German were penned by him.

He questioned celibacy; in this, he was surely on to something. "Men can go wrong with wine and women. Shall we then prohibit wine and abolish women?" He said the pope often erred. He said anyone could be his own priest. Excommunicated by the young Medici pope in 1521, he faced the Emperor Charles in Worms, Germany, a few months later for his civil punishment. But by then, peasants and lesser nobles had taken up his cause. The monk had started a movement, born partly out of rising Teutonic nationalism. "I cannot and will not retract anything, since it is neither safe nor right to go against my conscience," he said at his trial. The emperor was not moved; he branded Luther a "notorious heretic." Execution would surely follow. The trial of Martin Luther was "the greatest moment in the modern history of man," as Thomas Carlyle, the Victorian philosopher, called it. "It ranks with the 1066 Norman conquest and the 1215 signing of the Magna Carta and the 1492 landing of Columbus in the New World," wrote Eric Metaxas, a recent Luther biographer.

Luther fled, protected by his supporters. His notes from the underground were extraordinary: sermons and missives, but also something monumental, for it was during his time in exile that he translated that Bible into one that is still used today. He encouraged monasteries and convents to open their doors, and their occupants to live free lives. He married a nun on the run, Katharina von Bora, who was twenty-six years old when Luther was forty-one, and much more attractive than the jowly, raisin-eyed monk, judging by their portraits. He enjoyed having a woman next to him in bed, recalling the smell of the sheets, "a pair of pigtails lying beside" him. The Luthers had six children, and took in four orphans, the large clan residing in the former monastery in Wittenberg where all the heretical thought had been hatched. His ideas produced a much bigger family. In 1526, nine years after Luther first raised his voice, the rulers of nearly three hundred smaller German states opted for Lutheranism over the church of Rome. In 1536, Denmark officially adopted the new faith as the state religion. Norway soon followed.

Had Luther's public life ended there, his writings the basis of a church that now claims 72 million worshippers worldwide, his reputation would have been sterling. But like the institution he so skillfully attacked, Luther took a dark turn. When peasants who were inspired by his ideas on spiritual independence and human dignity revolted against their feudal lords, Luther cheered on the killing—*of his followers*. He was supposedly their champion, and yet he saw the Peasants' War as a mob uprising that must be crushed. "Let whoever can, stab, strike, strangle," he wrote. "If you die doing it, good for you!" The conflict left more than eighty thousand dead, among the poorest and most desolate members of German society.

With Jews, Luther was even more malevolent. He clearly hated Jews—"miserable, blind and senseless people"—and wrote some of the most repulsive things ever expressed by a respected man of God about them. His work not only fed the prevailing ignorance of medieval anti-Semitism, but it pushed that ancient animus to new levels. "They are nothing but thieves and robbers who daily eat no morsel and wear no thread of clothing which has not been stolen and pilfered from us by means of their accursed usury." Jews drank the blood of Christian children, a hoary lie, retold by Dr. Luther. Jews poisoned the wells of Christians. Jews were filth who "ate the shit" of Judas, "the vilest whores and rogues under the sun," he wrote in his infamous tract *On the Jews and Their Lies*. He urged people to burn down synagogues, to set fire to Jewish homes or cover them with dirt "so that not a single human being will see a stone or cinder, for ever and ever." How could this be the same monk—the great humanist—who had opened a big vein of common sense?

When King Henry II said, "Who will rid me of this meddlesome priest?" his words led to the murder of one man, Thomas Becket. But Luther's words were marshaled, four hundred years after he wrote them, by Nazis in his native land to justify the greatest crime in history—the murder of 6 million Jews. Certainly, Lutheranism was not the basis of Nazism. But when it was convenient, the Hitler cult found much to admire in his philosophy. At Nuremberg in 1946, one of Nazi Germany's leading ideologues said Martin Luther should be the one on trial.

I ask the museum director, Gabriel de Montmollin, about Luther's abhorrent side. There is very little on reformed Christianity's hatred of the Jews in this otherwise masterly showcase of the Protestant world.

Apologists for Luther say the hatred came near the end of his life, when he was old and cranky. He wrote 110 books or tracts throughout his time as the Reformer, and should not be judged by one invective. The director furrows his brow and seems to be in genuine anguish as we discuss this question. He knows better. Luther had a well-documented hatred of Jews going back to 1514—three years before writing 95 theses, more than thirty years before his death. "The Reformation, you know . . . it has some problems with memory," he says. Ah, problems with memory, the root of so much repetitive history.

Luther at one point tried to reach out to Jews. He thought his new Bible would show them the way. When they didn't convert, he got angrier and turned uglier. If they couldn't see the way, something must be deeply wrong with them. His written screed against Jews was sixty thousand words of aggressive loathing. Montmollin, who spends his days sifting through and explaining the original documents of Protestantism, has concluded there is no way to consider the good of Luther's revolution without taking into account the bad of his most odious exhortations. He feels the same way about his own faith, such as it is. "I'm interested in the *questions* of Christianity, not the answers."

THE QUESTIONS HAVE DRIVEN me as well. But looking for answers, and my intent to find a living faith along the Via Francigena, takes me a few doors away, to the Evangelical Lutheran Church of Geneva. It looks like a pleasant house, which it once was. An American in his late thirties, the Reverend Andy Willis, is the pilot of this 250-year-old ship of belief. Married, father of a preschool-age son, he is a product of St. Olaf College and Princeton's divinity school, with the Minnesota Nice manners of his native Midwest. He was a pastor in the West Bank of Palestine—yes, there is a Lutheran congregation in one of the world's most precarious spots—and ministered close to my home for three years, at a church in Olympia, Washington. This gives us an opportunity to discuss a true miracle: the time when the Seattle Seahawks came from twelve points down late in the fourth quarter, then picked up an onside kick and scored a touchdown in overtime, to beat the Green Bay Packers, sending our boys to the Super Bowl.

I was expecting white bread and mush from modern Lutherans, but see no such thing here. There are forty-four nationalities in his church; a third of the worshippers are from Africa, the fastest-growing region for the faith. And there are many young people with families. The church is often filled for Sunday service, which includes drums and guitar. The Jesus conjured up for this congregation would never have followed Martin Luther's call to slay peasants or burn down Jewish homes.

"Christ was born among the powerless," Willis likes to say. "He lived among the vulnerable. He died alongside criminals." For his Easter sermon, he was provocative and encouraging. "Sneaking life into a tomb— that's what Easter is all about! Easter is God whispering to us: 'Nothing can keep my love in a grave.'"

This is a forward-looking congregation, built on the best words of yesterday. "You can't be glib about the fact that for so much of the history of religion, humans have gotten this wrong," Willis says. During the five-hundredth anniversary of the founding act of Lutheranism, the Reformer's positive ideas still have a prominent place in the historic home of early-day Protestants. But his worst ideas are not completely forgotten. "I'm really wary of celebrating Luther too much, because he was a deeply flawed human being," says this Lutheran minister, a fascinating admission.

He admires the pope, and Francis has reciprocated to the faith of the renegade monk. The pope held a prayer service not long ago with global Lutheran leaders to commemorate the defiant act of a man his predecessors would have charred to a crisp. The pope said Luther was right about many things. "With gratitude, we acknowledge that the Reformation helped give greater centrality to sacred Scripture."

Now that they are free of state attachment, while being ridiculed or ignored by modern secularists, the two branches of Christianity find they have much in common.

But as with the encouraging reaction to the archbishop of Canterbury's surprising past, you have to wonder if it's too late—Christians, opening their hearts to one another despite doctrinal differences, just as Christianity is dying in so many parts of Europe. The newfound tolerance, the embracing across the lines, the forgiving and forgetting, the freedom to express ideas that once led to bloodshed and banishment—it's not unlike a deathbed conversion.

The Reverend Willis smiles at my analogy. He says the future of Christianity, what he hears from young congregants, is to be more meditative, more authentically spiritual, at a time when digital distractions have such a hold on us. "Our attention is a commodity," said Willis during one recent sermon on this topic. "We hand over our power to whatever is loudest. Nothing is left for the softest voices."

The pastor still struggles with his beliefs, which is one of the qualities that make him so likable. He's well educated, articulate. and soulful. And yet, he has to suspend reason and no small amount of logic to continue doing what he does every day. He's a man who seems at home with his own uncertainties. "The question of faith is chilling, frankly, but also very honest. I went through this in college, when you have to make a break with the shallow image of God. You have to take doubts seriously."

NINETEEN

A THEOCRACY ON THE LAKE

Before leaving Geneva, I have to visit a martyr. That would be Michael Servetus, medical doctor, theologian, mapmaker, a fugitive wanted by three countries and two religions. A Renaissance man before the term, he was one of the brilliant, gutsy early voices of reformed Christianity. He fled to Geneva for the same reasons that other persecuted men and women came here in the sixteenth century, transforming the little town that rose where the lake drains into the Rhône River to a home for breakaway thinkers. For a moment the doors were opened in a place living by words that now serve as a civic motto, words that adorn a prominent bas-relief: City of Refuge. Huguenots facing pogroms in Catholic France poured into Geneva. So did many others who challenged those who guarded the vault of theology. Four national languages are spoken in the twenty-six cantons of Switzerland—French, German, Italian, and an old Latin dialect, Romansh—but the lingua franca of Geneva is tolerance. Yes, the Swiss have long hidden the money of warlords, corporate criminals, Nazi thieves, and villains in Bond movies. But before that, they hid people of conscience. That is, until Michael Servetus showed up and begged another religious refugee, John Calvin, to protect him.

I'm waiting for an evening breeze and cooler temperatures before hiking up into the part of the city where I can spend some time with Servetus. He's not easy to find—the tribute to him is known locally as the "Lost Monument"—and not much talked about either. But then, people in Seattle seldom bring up the fact that the largest city in the world named for a Native American once passed a law making it illegal for a Native American to live there.

Casey and I load up on market cheese and fruit, and then settle into lakeside chairs for a sampling of those UNESCO-certified wines. We watch white swans make precision landings on the water, foreground for a tableau of lake, snow-crowned mountains, passing boats, and puffy clouds. He's impressed by Switzerland. So am I. In the villages and houses along the lake you still see a lot of what Hemingway called "the cuckoo clock style of architecture." But the stereotype of fondue-dipping, *Heidi*-loving, strangely indecipherable Swiss seems bogus to both of us. Every nationality under the sun is here, with more than just a representative sample; half the population of Geneva is resident foreign nationals. No one laughs at my French, though most quickly switch to English when I open my mouth. What is truly shocking are the prices. You need to take out a line of credit before coming to a mountain kingdom that boasts four of the six most expensive cities in the world. We burst out laughing the first time we ordered two coffees and a cookie in a nondescript café and did not get change back from the equivalent of a twenty. And that was the cheap place.

With the onset of early evening, we're back at a variant of one of our perennial arguments, er . . . discussions. Then he makes a confession. "I'm not an atheist, *Dad*." I reassure him, with the parental and Seinfeldian response: "Not that there's anything wrong with that." If he's now treading water in a pool of agnosticism, I hope he's thinking it through, and not just trying to please. I hope, also, that he's not parked there for life, waiting, say, for science to prove the case one way or the other—because that will never happen. Of late, science is moving closer to proving how life got started in the first place, something Darwin was dark about. A young MIT professor, Jeremy England, says that if you direct a strong enough light or heat source on inanimate clumps of atoms—poof, life will form. This thermodynamic theory has rattled traditional theologians—"God Is on the Ropes," was one headline—but it shouldn't. Where did the inanimate clumps of atoms come from? You could argue that it was God who put the ingredients in place for that life-burst of creation to happen. In fact, that's what I argue with Casey now.

"Sure, but there's no proof of that," he says. "Some would say it's 'lazy' to remain agnostic. I say it's intellectually honest. Which is more lazy: claiming you know without evidence, or waiting to be convinced?"

I remember a line I saw in the Jesuit residence where I worked off my high school tuition. It was a quote attributed to another Jesuit, the French philosopher Pierre Teilhard de Chardin, who died in 1955. He said, "We are not human beings having a spiritual experience. But spiritual beings having a human experience." But that's not the one I mention. Understandably, there were a lot of quotes by persuasive Jesuits spread all over the old school. The one I tell Casey is "Joy is the most infallible sign of the presence of God."

He thinks about it for a minute, and smiles. "What about alcohol?" We both laugh. "I'm just trying to keep *you* from getting too sure of your views," he says.

If joy indeed signaled proof of God, then John Calvin's Geneva must have been a godless place. Let us lace up our time-traveling shoes once again and wander back to Old Town, where we were earlier today, to see what became of the Reformation once it got established—free of Rome, free to make its own rules, free to show the world a more authentic, more tolerant face of Christianity. It can start fresh, returning the faith to its early beginnings. If only.

In Saint-Pierre Cathedral, less than a decade after the death of

Martin Luther, looms a small pastor with a long, pointy beard. John Calvin has tight-set eyes, a cap with earflaps, a vicious temper that makes children tremble. He's frail, thin, a whiff of a man, but inexhaustible in his certainties. City and church are one and the same in the Protestant Republic of Geneva. Calvin is in control, though he's subtle about the true extent of his power. Religious police, aided by spies, go house to house to ensure that proper dishes are set with the proper meal, that clothes are only cut from the approved colors, that music will not be made from forbidden instruments. Dancing is prohibited. So is flirting. So is card playing. So is naming your children after anyone but biblical figures. Fornication could result in execution. Same with a homosexual act.

All inhabitants have to denounce the Catholic Church. All have to attend sermons, up to seventeen a week. Bells, songs, pictures, statues, candles, books—strictly regulated. A woman cannot wear rouge, or certain types of shoes. A man cannot curse or hunt. Calvin's own sister-in-law is banished for adultery. In defense of "sure truth," as Calvin calls it, a heretic can be murdered by righteous citizens, with God's blessing. Geneva is a city of just over 10,000 people. And in Calvin's Geneva, 58 people will be put to death and 76 banished. The church-state execution that still resonates is that of Michael Servetus.

Not only is every part of life regulated, but it's also predestined. Where you end up, after death, has nothing to do with a life of earthly merit. We are all "totally depraved," Calvin preaches, though a few have been chosen at birth to make it to the highest level of the hereafter. Every minor act of being, from tripping over your husband's wooden shoes to eating an apple on Thursday, was part of a carefully crafted master plan, all of it drawn up and obviously known by God. My question for the Calvinists has always been: Why bother? Either go out with a bang, knowing you're doomed no matter what you do. Or go out with an even bigger bang, knowing it's the back nine of eternity for you, oh lucky soul. But no, those who were sure they won the predestination lottery lived dour lives under the glare of taut-faced authoritarians.

Calvin is the preeminent Protestant theologian of his day, succeeding Luther. If you laugh during one of his sermons, you can be whipped or put in jail. The same penalty applies if you refuse to call him "master" when you greet him on the street. If you question him in print, as did one worshipper who put up a poster accusing Calvin of hypocrisy, you can be tortured for a month, under threat of execution. Calvin left us a firsthand account of how he operated, in a sworn statement from 1545. A suicidal friend of his plunged a knife into his stomach. Calvin was called to the home. While the man bled, Calvin rebuked him, telling him he'd been seduced by the devil. He'd offended God, and must repent. "Then we prayed as the situation required, recognizing and confessing the error of his action," he wrote. Only after repeated assurances that the badly wounded neighbor had begged for forgiveness did Calvin allow him to be treated.

On this summer day in 1553 sits a fugitive, our man Servetus, in the pews of Saint-Pierre, packed with others who fled the intolerance of neighboring states. He's on the run from the Inquisition in Spain and the Catholic high command in France. The response of the Roman church to the Reformation was to ratchet up the torture chambers. Servetus broke out of jail a few days ago, crossed the border on his way to southern Italy. He comes to Geneva because the City of Refuge took in all those earlier dissenters. Most famously, it took in John Calvin when he was also forced out of France, and lived for a time under several aliases. Calvin came from aristocratic parents and was trained as a lawyer. He consumed Luther's writings, then went beyond the Reformer, traveling throughout Europe to promote his radical views. Scots, English, Dutch, Swiss, and many Germans were taken by him, starting religions that were exported to South Africa and America. Big pockets of New England would be colonized with Puritan thought that sprang from Calvin. When Calvin first came to Geneva he had a falling-out with other Protestants and fled. But upon his return in 1541, he found a tightly controlled community much more to his liking, and they fell under the spell of his busy mind. It was here that he put the underpinnings of his new brand of Christianity into practice.

Had Servetus just stuck with his profession, which was medicine, he would be a good-sized footnote in the history of health care. Dr. Servetus discovered that the blood of pulmonary circulation flows from the heart to the lungs—a very big deal, helping to pull medicine from the muck of medieval quackery. He also promoted the benefits of herbal tea and vitamins. All of those discussions, contained in Servetus's theological writings, were among the words of his to be burned in France. His inquiring brain found another error, or so he believed, in the teaching of the Trinity. The Reformation had invited creative thinkers to the banquet of re-examination, and Servetus pulled up a chair. Jesus was the Son of God, yes, but not one of three divine manifestations, he wrote in *On the Errors of the Trinity*. Errors? His head would soon be on a spike, the French bishops proclaimed. This was also too much for Protestants. Still, after transcribing such thoughts to print, Servetus managed to live a productive underground life for nearly twenty years. He started a correspondence with Calvin. Though he criticized him for predestination, he assumed they were two reformers cut from the same cloth.

After the sermon in Saint-Pierre, Calvin has Servetus arrested. *Arrested.* Any hope that a fellow exile would protect him is now dashed. Calvin is a bully with a pulpit. Beyond the pulpit, he's a strongman, "the bloodless figure of the dictator looming over all," Manchester called him. He makes nice to the poor, expanding charity and education. Geneva is well run and prosperous, with many bankers, clockmakers, and merchants among the newly arrived. Everything works. Life is predictable, safe, godly, and clean—if you comply. But Calvin does not suffer a heretic like Servetus, even if he is an enemy of his enemy, the Roman Catholic Church. Calvin, remember, is a heretic in the eyes of that same faith, the one he left behind. The seizure of Servetus after he tried to find refuge in the holy place of Saint-Pierre is predestined, in its way, for Calvin had written a friend: "If he comes here, if my authority is worth anything, I will never allow him to depart alive."

The trial is a sham. Servetus is denied a lawyer, after spending months in a lightless, rat-infested cell. He presents himself as a man of faith, a searcher; his crimes are ones of conscience, just like other giants of the Reformation. Can't they see that? His life is in the hands of the Geneva town council, all Protestants, though only one man's opinion matters. Calvin had already condemned Servetus in prosecutorial letters and notes around town. Servetus pleads with the council. He tells of his love of creation—how everything, even the devil, is God's work. They find him guilty, guilty, guilty of unorthodox thought. The sentence is death by immolation. But Calvin intervenes. He wants to show some mercy. Instead of burning Servetus at the stake, he suggests executing him by sword, until he bleeds out like a fish on the deck of a boat. It would be a less barbaric way to kill a man, he says—one of the few arguments he loses in Geneva. Two years later, he is given absolute supremacy over the city-state. He has more power, in this Swiss refuge, than the popes of Rome that Luther had attacked. It took just a single generation for the new spiritual boss to become as despotic as the old boss.

On October 27, 1553, a disheveled and sickly Servetus is dragged from his cell and bound to a pole next to a pile of green oak, twigs, and leaves. This esteemed doctor, this man of learning and character, is covered with sulfur. One of his books is tied to him. He asks the mob to pray for him and the executioner to make it quick. Dry kindling is placed over his hair and face. The fire is lit. It's slow to develop, the green wood hissing but not crackling to a clean flame. He shrieks in agony. More wood is put on the blaze. His screams are deafening. It takes thirty minutes to kill him. Across the border in France, Christian clerics of another kind burn his books and a scarecrow of him. "Michael Servetus has the singular distinction of being burned by the Catholics in effigy and the Protestants in actuality," wrote his biographer, Roland H. Bainton.

So the Reformation takes hold, from revolts launched by Luther, Calvin, and Henry VIII. In Scotland, the Calvin-inspired clergyman John Knox starts a faith that becomes the Presbyterian Church. The Protestant movement puts down roots in half of Europe, the British colonies of North America, and the Dutch-controlled lands of southern Africa. One of its offshoots, Puritanism, was known as "the haunting fear that someone, somewhere may be happy," in H. L. Mencken's lasting phrase. Geneva was the most censorious manifestation of that sentiment. Religion did what it often does once its members are no longer persecuted, once it's fused to power. What had started as a desire to be close to God's word, a movement to right the wrongs of a corrupt church, was now codified in a place where stray thoughts, expressed, could end in an executioner's pyre. For what had Servetus done to deserve having his life taken from him in such a horrifying way? What were his crimes? Specifically, per the trial: denying the Trinity and the significance of baptism at birth.

Calvin is immortalized, along with three other founding fathers of Protestantism, in the Wall of the Reformers—a pink granite bas-relief within the old city walls, more than three hundred feet long. It's impossible to miss. The figures at the center are fifteen feet high, imposing in the most dreadful way. Still, Geneva outgrew Calvin. It was long ago liberated from his theocracy. Today it is the diplomatic capital of the world, with its name lent to the accords that proscribe war crimes, with more professional peacemakers per capita than any other city on earth. It welcomed Victor Hugo, sheltered Voltaire, inspired Byron, Shelley, and Charlie Chaplin. Switzerland today has no state religion. The constitution grants full freedom of worship and specifically asserts a right to apostasy. In Geneva, Catholics outnumber Protestants by three to one. But the numbers of all Christians are declining, following the secular pull of Europe in general. One in four Swiss are "unaffiliated," the fastest-growing segment of belief. Like Casey, most of the people in this group identify as agnostic.

And Servetus? Let us now tighten the laces on the real-time boots and hike up the hill to have a look. My leg has improved, but I still feel a strain where the tendon was torn and muscle shriveled. The roads are twisty, traffic bound, and I hop on a bus for part of the way. I walk along the blank side of a hospital, look up beyond overgrown brush to find a statue of a man seated in deep thought. Two empty beer cans are at his feet. At the pedestal are words identifying the figure as Michael Servetus, Spanish physician.

Here is someone I knew nothing about until a detour on the Via Francigena took me to the magnificent city that holds his ashes. The sculpture was erected in 1903, on the 350th anniversary of the execution of Servetus—a way to atone for the crimes of Calvin's Geneva. As the commission that authorized the memorial explained, "We want to regret publicly this act and take advantage of this occasion to assert our unbreakable adhesion to freedom of conscience." This monument, then, can be seen as a tribute to the motto of the Reformation: After Darkness, Light.

But not for some time.

TWENTY

THE PERMANENT PRAYER
OF SAINT-MAURICE

The last morning in Lausanne is a struggle to get out of town. I'm clearly at cross-purposes with other visitors on the Swiss Riviera. They're after music and sun, beer in crafted steins and watches that cost more than a year at an American private college. I'm looking for ghosts, and O.K., God. But I still can't get myself to say that when people ask what brings me to Lake Geneva, because my explanation is too personal for strangers. Well, some strangers, the Swiss being among the more reticent. For all our mockery of ritzy Switzerland, some things are priceless. The lake air is free, as are the alpine views. Because this is a steeply vertical city, and the two rivers that flow through it are covered over, you have no idea where you are at any one time. We hop on the quiet and unassuming metro our final morning and get off somewhere in the center of the Old Town. It's like a Hieronymus Bosch painting, in that the dimensions are hallucinatory, a maze of bridges and underpasses, stairways and dead ends.

I duck into the cathedral, towering five hundred feet over the lake, while Casey goes in search of chocolates for his girlfriend. All I want is a pilgrim stamp. Get in and get out, five minutes max. Alas, my capacity for wonder is not yet sufficiently sated, and I stroll around in renewed appreciation of twelfth-century construction skills. The Notre-Dame Cathedral of Lausanne is the biggest space devoted to God in Switzerland. It has some charming quirks. Every night between ten p.m. and two a.m. a watchman walks 153 steps to the upper reaches of the tower and announces the top of the hour—to the bewilderment of besotted visitors staggering out of bars and clubs.

I notice an absence of relic boxes and graphic depictions of mutilated saints. That's because this is a Protestant cathedral, explains a woman named Anna who stamps my passport. It was taken over by Reformed Christians in 1536, nineteen years after Luther wrote his 95 theses, and they cleansed it of papist pigmentation. We chat for a while about pilgrims past and present. In the Middle Ages, the cathedral drew throngs of foreigners. Now, a small stream of V.F. sojourners trickle in. "They walk the Via Francigena because it's an adventure," says Anna. "And they want to get away from the material world."

When I tell Anna that I'm hoping to meet the pope at the end of my trail, she lights up.

"Would you like to see something?"

She shows me a picture from inside the Vatican. Pope Francis is embracing a little boy, whose smile projects the sugar-high radiance of a kid on Christmas Day. The child is her son, who has "a slight mental disability," she says. In Rome, she asked around, and with no inside connections or big names to drop, she and her boy were ushered in with a small audience to see the pope. She asked him to pray for her son.

"Can you see Francis's eyes? They're alive." She is so happy as she tells me this, and it's infectious. I'm not even jealous that she got in to see the pope while I'm still waiting for a reply. I'm just thrilled to be in the ripple of her joy.

ALMOST HALFWAY TO ROME. Since leaving Canterbury, I've covered 509 miles. St. Peter's Square is another 672. Just ahead is the toughest part—75 miles to one of the highest crossings in the Alps, Great Saint Bernard Pass, more than 8,000 feet above sea level. I want to hike the hardest section, above timberline, passing glacier-gouged boulders and milky little streams. The route climbs steadily, following the Rhône above Lake Geneva, through a progression of ever smaller villages, and then turns away from the river and up a valley that narrows and tightens as the tallest mountains on the western continent close in. Napoleon had the audacity to think he could march 51,000 men and 10,750 beasts of burden dragging disassembled cannons, hay, wine, and nearly two tons of cheese up and over the pass in the late spring of 1800. There was no road over Great Saint Bernard until 1905. He had to follow the ancient alpine trail, walking single file, trying to do with an army what no general had done since Charlemagne—and before that, Hannibal and his elephants.

Napoleon sent several thousand troops ahead to cache supplies and scout the route. He would try to take his forces over a pass that can get upward of thirty feet of snow a year. My doubts today are the same as his: weather being the main concern. Great Saint Bernard is still somewhat snowbound, several feet in the north-facing portions of the V.F. I've heard from people who were turned back by freezing squalls and zero visibility. Some decided to call the whole thing off. The traveler is also exposed to sudden thunderstorms in the higher elevations, with no place for cover. Weather of a different sort is making life perilous for people on the other side of the divide. Italy, like most of France, is experiencing a severe heat wave. The forests are dry, fields are brown, rivers are shriveling. And now wildfires are breaking out.

Montreux is our next stop, after a quick, dreamy train ride along the eastern end of the lake, passing the terraced Lavaux vineyards. The trees are cypress and palm. All of it is lined with peak-blossoming flowers, elegantly maintained Belle Époque *maisons*, and a lake as smooth as a fresh-made bed. We wait our turn to get close to the shrine that draws more people than anything else on Montreux's waterfront: the ten-foot-high statue of Freddie Mercury, the late front man of Queen, who had a home here. He has one hand pointing skyward, the other flinging his microphone. I'm trying to stay religiously meditative on this walk, but I've got a well-known lyric of Freddie's lodged in my head:

> *I see a little silhouetto of a man*
> *Scaramouche, Scaramouche . . .*

Now we follow the Rhône, which comes to life in the melting drips of a glacier at 7,244 feet and flows through Lake Geneva to Lyon, Avignon, and Arles before emptying into the Mediterranean. Our segment to Saint-Maurice is just twenty miles, but what a change it brings. Here the mountains are bunched in tight, and hold the weather, snagging clouds trying to sneak over the Alps. The snow is no mere mantle, but a heavy cloak wrapped around the upper third of the peaks. In an opening between spires, I catch a glimpse of the 10,400-foot eastern summit of Dents du Midi Mountain—named for the sharp teeth of the massif. We cross a bridge over the river and walk a short distance to the Abbey of Saint-Maurice, which claims to be the oldest continuously operating monastery in Europe. I've been looking forward to this since the flatlands of Flanders, and not just because I always feel more at home in the mountains.

"Within these walls prayer has never stopped."

That is the first astonishment of the abbey, which was founded in 515 by Sigismund, a Vandal king of Burgundy. A plea to God was started in Saint-Maurice fifteen hundred years ago; this single prayer has continued to this day—"a spiritual and cultural activity that is not found anywhere else in the Western Christian world," as the Augustinians explain in a short history. For a long time, more than nine hundred monks were on hand, divided into nine choirs, so that the prayer would go on without intermission, the chants relayed from one group to the other.

Today, Saint-Maurice lacks medieval-level monk power, but the chain has not been broken; it continues every day and every night. The abbey compound has been crushed by massive rockslides, buried in avalanches, and scorched by fire. Napoleon billeted some of his troops here, and the Reformation that swept through Germany and Switzerland stopped just outside the gates of the monastery, a firewall of traditional Christianity. Roofs have collapsed and been restored. Catacombs unearthed and cleaned for observation. The one consistency has been the permanent prayer, *laus perennis*, recited day after day, week after week, month after month, year after year, century after century, by a rotating band of monks known as the Sleepless Ones. Perhaps the permanent prayer gains force with the years, with each fresh rendition, like the Rhône gathering its tributaries. As we walk on floors built over the ruins of a shrine to the Roman god Mercury, I'm hoping to drop a request into the big river of prayer and see where it ends up.

When Sigismund set spiritual anchor here, he was fleeing an awful past. He killed his son; he had him strangled to death in 517 after the boy made fun of his father's second wife. Overwhelmed by guilt, he vowed to spend his remaining years in prayer and penance, living the monastic life on the banks of the Rhône under the shadow of the Dents du Midi. But he couldn't keep his violent side down for long, and soon took up arms against the advancing Franks. In defeat, he was found hiding in the abbey in a monk's habit. The invaders took him to Orléans, where he was killed by a son of the newly Christian Clovis—his faith also doing nothing to tamp down homicidal urges. Sigismund is a saint, though I'm not sure why. I learned this while reading up on the village of Saint-Maurice, but I have yet to share it with Casey. A story about a saint who killed his boy is not likely to influence my own son's agnosticism for the better.

The other astonishment, and a far more interesting-to-our-times figure, is the man who gave his name to this place. You can see a big portrait of him in the stairway of the residence of the monks who keep the prayer going. He's got amazing abs, huge upper arms, a red Roman cape, with a gold halo over his head. And he's black. Maurice is believed to be the "the first black saint," the historian Henry Louis Gates Jr. wrote. But he was not recognized as a holy man of color until many centuries after his death.

His story: Maurice was born a mere two centuries plus after the death of Christ, in the Egyptian community of Thebes. He was Christian, and a soldier in the Roman army. He rose through the ranks to become commander of the Theban Legion, which had a reputation as disciplined killers of their fellow men, in service to the Empire. Maurice was summoned from North Africa across the Mediterranean by the Emperor Maximian to put down a revolt in a strategic valley of the Swiss Alps. Before the attack, Maurice's men were told to pay tribute to Roman gods, per pagan tradition. They refused. And once word leaked out that their intended victims were a band of Christians, Maurice balked at the other command as well. He would not slaughter members of his faith, something that legions of Christians would do without blinking in the centuries that followed. Maurice is the conscience that was missing in so many other intra-Christian bloodbaths.

Punishment for this level of insubordination—a general defying the direct order of an emperor—was death. Maximian commanded that one soldier out of every ten be executed, a *decimation*, as the word came to us. This was followed by a second decimation, and a third, until the entire Theban Legion of more than six thousand men was wiped out. Maurice himself was beheaded on a slab in this valley, at the former Roman encampment, in the year 287.

Much of the story may be apocryphal. It wasn't passed on in the historic record until at least a century had gone by. But as with the legend of Clovis and the holy oil from the dove, the facts themselves may not matter so much as how the narrative of Maurice the martyr, answering to a higher cause, spread throughout the world, and still lives, larger than ever. For centuries, he was a white guy, and somewhat obscure. It wasn't until the thirteenth century that the leader of the Theban Legion was accurately depicted as dark-skinned. A statue of Maurice, wearing chain-mail armor and coat of arms, was erected in the cathedral of Magdeburg in Germany, in 1250—he became a patron saint of the Holy Roman emperors of that northern territory. There is no mistaking his race; the sculpture is said to be the first realistic depiction in stone of a black African in Europe. The Swiss resort town of St. Moritz was named for him about the same time. The Swiss Guard, protectors of the pope, honor Maurice as their guiding saint. The statue in Germany still stands. Maurice, however, fell back into obscurity at the height of the Atlantic slave trade, when people who looked like him were kidnapped and sold into human bondage by some of the leading Christian nations of Europe.

His modern comeback has much to do with the vibrancy and growth of Christianity in Africa, at a time when Christianity in Europe is dying off. If present trends hold, within twenty years Africa will have more Catholics than Europe. And let's be honest: Maurice's story is much more thrilling than that of the monastery's founder, Sigismund the Son Killer. Maurice has long been revered by Coptic Christians in Egypt. The Catholic church in the Ninth Ward of New Orleans, an area submerged by the waters of Hurricane Katrina, is named for Maurice—one of 598 houses of worship to bear his name. Our train to this site was full of dark-skinned schoolchildren from Germany and France making a pilgrimage to the place where the warrior from Thebes chose death rather than kill another Christian. Maurice is alive in one other sense: the permanent prayer was started in honor of his memory.

OUR NEXT TARGET is the cliff. High overhead in the near distance at the edge of town is a chapel and hermitage, dating to the seventh century, carved into what looks like a sheer vertical wall at the base of the big mountains. The trailhead has a warning sign for those who fear heights.

We start our way up the narrow path, 478 steps of stone, with a handrail on one side to cling to. The valley floor recedes. The mountains open up. Cars, houses, and the station below look like the set of a toy-train town. The last stretch is a strain, but worth every muscle ache. We level out at the most breathtaking spiritual lair on the Via Francigena—the Chapel of Our Lady of the Rock. It is carved into and mortared onto the mountain, defying time and gravity. It looks organic, an artful accident of geology, stones stacked against a much bigger stone anchoring the Alps, topped by a small bell tower. How did any of these pieces get up here? Casey is hesitant about going inside, assuming correctly that we'll find the usual reliquary holding body parts of some forgotten saint. But the small space in this nest of God is very moving, and he crosses the threshold to light a votive candle for his grandmother. The air is cool, a welcoming chill, like being in a well-furnished cave. Back outside, the view is one that belongs to raptors riding afternoon air currents.

Close to the chapel is a hermit's quarters, first used by a man named Amé, born in the year 560. He clambered up this rock and settled into a flat on the cliff "to pray, mourn his faults in this narrow place, and serve his redeemer with perfect submission," as a plaque at the base of his small statue explains. Saint Amé lived in sheepskin and walked barefoot. Friends from the valley brought him barley bread, water, and nuts. After he died in 627, he left something behind: those relics inside the chapel are his remains. People can still apply for solo residency on the rock. The last person to live here was a lapsed lawyer and ex-politician, Nicolas Buttet. He left just a few years ago, shucking his prior life to take priestly vows. "Once I spent nine days with only a jar of honey to eat," he wrote. And in a very curious twist, that former hermit on the ledge is now spiritual adviser to the archbishop of Canterbury, the ever-surprising Justin Welby.

We take our time walking down the 478 steps. We hate to give up the view. Back at the monastery, we rest in the long shadows of the cloister, framed by Roman arches dripping wisteria vines, a fountain in the middle. Next door, the latest iteration of the permanent prayer is under way in the basilica. It's a song in Latin. The plain and powerful voices are those of Augustinian monks, with a handful of young men among the older brothers—the Sleepless Ones doing their aural duty. Into the pool of these sweet male basso tones, linked through fifteen hundred years to Saint Maurice and his Theban Legion, to the pleas of all the pilgrims who've passed through this valley, I add my little prayer. It's a request, and somewhat selfish as these things often are, and also coming from a sense of helplessness. Things have only gotten worse for the person I love, on behalf of whom I seek intercession. Stall the cancer. Give my wife's sister a bit more time.

CASEY HEADS BACK to grad school for summer quarter, and I'm left with the great wall of the Alps. I miss him, and his original take on settled debates, before he even steps onto the train. My first dinner without him is particularly depressing. He's such a stimulant. What would Napoleon do? He would push on, push on, upward into the clouds, toward rock scrambles and narrow ledges. Thunderstorms are still in the alpine forecast, and fresh reports from a trickle of V.F. walkers I run into coming this way from Italy are terrifying. It's blue skies everywhere but *up there*, where the mountains brew their own weather. One couple tells me they waited almost a week to crest the divide at Great Saint Bernard. I spend a few days hiking uphill, building strength, inching forward and trying to swat away doubt.

I like to think I'm ready for the mountain ascent. My legs are strong but for the gimpy thigh. Feet blister-free. Endurance good, except at the very end of the day, when I'm flat with fatigue. In the mornings, I feel like the rusted and locked-up Tin Man—"oil can, oil can" needed to loosen the joints. But it gets better with caffeine and recuperative Swiss air. These afternoon t-storms are clangorous, deadly, and scare the crap out of me. REI has nothing to shield a hiker from a thunderbolt. The locals know enough to stay off the mountains, or where to find cover during the danger hours.

My goal is Martigny, a village ten miles up the valley. The walk is gradual, through fruit orchards and some grapevines. Just before town, I lose the Rhône. It cuts sharply to the left. I continue on straight, into a much narrower valley, the big walls blocking out the sun in the hours at the edge of the day. I'd hoped to stay in a pilgrim accommodation in Martigny, but no one answers the phone number I was given. I backtrack, settling for a B&B in the hamlet of Vernayaz, another thirty-minute walk. I get the little kid's room, with a too-small bed and books without words.

The next morning brings fog, visibility about fifty feet. It should lift. I'm aiming for another village, Orsières, eleven miles on the Chemin Napoléon, as they call this part of the route to Rome. I've learned since Calais that there is no single way on the Via Francigena. It's a blend of paths and pavement, nature trails and the old road of the Empire, shepherds' shortcuts and village connectors, moving in one direction—in this case up. For several hours, I don't see a hut, a hiker, a trail indicator, nothing but trees appearing spookily out of the mist. I wonder if, while daydreaming, I took a cow path the wrong way, something that will dead-end beneath one of the cliffs overshadowing me. By midday, I'm convinced that I'm lost. I feel a pang of real loneliness as well. I sit on wet grass and stew while noshing on a granola bar. I've had it in my pack for too long and it tastes like sawdust. The guidebook is not reassuring. "This is the worst section of the whole Via Francigena, all the way from Canterbury to Rome," writes Alison Raju, putting aside her understated and nonjudgmental prose. "You do need to be very careful if it is wet and windy, all the more so if you are alone."

I stagger on in a sunless soup of Swiss anxiety. When at last my fears get the best of me, I retreat to the B&B, arriving late, wet, despondent. Even a cheese plate and a snort of schnapps from the owner fail to cheer me. I'm back in the little kid's room. I strip off my wet clothes, take a shower, and lie on the dinosaur-print comforter, wondering what's next. At least there's adequate Wi-Fi, allowing me to access a glimmer of hope in my latest email from the Vatican. It came through the Jesuit back channel, an influential priest in Rome who writes many of the pope's speeches. He tells me that my letter has been personally delivered to Francis, that he held my request in his pontifical hands, and now "the Holy Father is considering your words."

Considering my words. Holy shit. Should I have rephrased them? Showed more piety? Groveled? I feel humbled, energized, but also guilty. With all the troubles in all the world, from religious genocide in Myanmar to refugee children staggering ashore on the Greek islands to a collapse in belief throughout Europe, why should the pope give a sniff about one pilgrim lumbering toward Rome? What can the Wizard of Christianity's Oz say that hasn't already been said? Why am I even troubling him with a handful of age-old, seemingly unanswerable questions?

And there's a larger issue about my motives. After what happened in our parish on Indian Trail Road, do I tell the pope that most of our family is not ready to forgive the church? That we feel deceived and heartbroken—like people in so many parts of the Catholic world? What hope is there that pope number 266 can do anything about these ingrained abominations that the other 265 could not?

I use the Wi-Fi to get a call through to my wife. She's in Los Angeles with her sister, trying to find an oncologist who can buy some time for a stage IV cancer patient. Fresh scans reveal fresh trouble spots—a radar of death. Margie has lost a ton of weight, and much of her hope. My wife pushes on, Napoleon to her own Great Saint Bernard Pass. It's so much easier to cross a mountain range. She will never give up, even as the returns on her initiatives are diminishing. Her sister weeps throughout the day, a wail in waves, a sound that people make when death seems near or pain is so deep you have no other way to react. And yet, she still teaches piano. She puts on makeup, fluffs her thinning hair, gets in a car, and drives to someone's house, challenging a child to play like Mozart. Or she teaches through a Skype link. I cannot possibly begin to describe my day after my wife tells me about the chemo, the nausea, the inability to hold anything down, the weakness, the doctors who can't mask their feelings of failure. My day is nothing. In the dark and despair, in the discomfort of the too-small bed, I thrash and think about the impassable col at Great Saint Bernard, the pope and his compromised faith, my sweet sister-in-law and the randomness of fortune and sorrow. For the first time on the Via Francigena, I have a sleepless night. And when the gray half-light of morning comes around, I know I'm done. I have to go back.

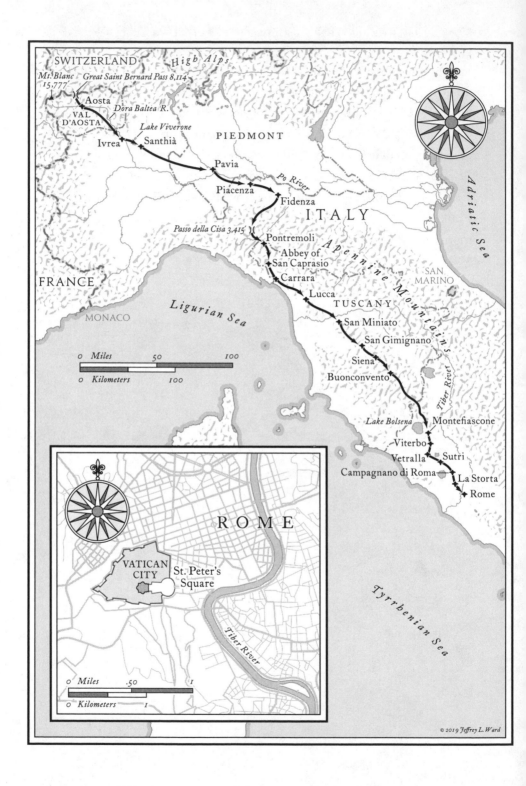

ANSWERS

LAND OF MIRACLES AND WONDER

* TWENTY-ONE *

A PILGRIM OVER THE ALPS

All summer the heat bears down on the southern half of the Via Francigena, one merciless day after the other. Rivers shrink and lakes dry and fish rot on hot clay that was once underwater but is now *terra cotta*. Trees lose their green and wither and catch fire. Sunflowers droop and crisp and turn away from the source of their former radiance. One day in the Umbrian town of Orvieto, it's 112 degrees Fahrenheit. In Rome, it's 104, and for the first time in more than a century, all 2,800 fountains are turned off. The aqueducts from the mountains, some dating to Julius Caesar's day, will soon run dry if this heat continues. The drought is "exceptional," the government says, the searing temperatures "unprecedented." Wildfires rage in the mountains and near the sea. In the afternoons, the sky is white with torpor. It's climate change, or maybe not. Italians agree on nothing, as always. But they settle on a name for this summer of swelter—Lucifer.

I went home, but my heart, head, and soul never left the V.F. I missed being a pilgrim. I missed days without digital distraction, days of discovery and setback, moving toward something. I missed a routine that was simple but never predictable. I finished more books by Augustine and another by one of his modern tormentors, the British atheist Richard Dawkins. I tore through volumes on the history of Jesus, from one claiming he was at heart an angry rebel who defied Jewish orthodoxy, to another saying he favored the wealthy and espoused a "prosperity gospel." I could find no consensus on anything but his death, the bare-bones historical record. I followed the weather on the V.F. and read Carlo's blog, as the English pilgrim tried to stay hydrated through doubt and drought. A better man than me, he. The soles of his boots were worn to a sheen, and it took him a long time to recover at the end of every brutal day's slog.

Margie didn't die. Nor did the cancer recede. Her days were filled with chemo, scans, radiation, waiting for results, uncertainty, and still she taught piano, because music made her something more than a patient. I can still see her playing "Forever Young," lifting Bob Dylan's words with her voice, when the cancer was just starting to eat her alive—though none of us knew it at the time. Over the last month, she seemed to strengthen a bit, and started to eat more, and then she weakened. My wife said I should get back on the trail. She said that if her sister stabilized, she would try to join me. Our daughter offered to meet me in the mountains of Italy. I didn't tell Margie about my request at Laon for a miracle, or the plea on her behalf that I slipped into the fifteen-hundred-year-old prayer-stream at the Abbey of Saint-Maurice. Because why? *My thoughts and prayers are with you?* No sentiment in America had been more devalued in so short a time. And yet, it was all I had.

I'M BACK in the Swiss village of Vernayaz, and this time I'm not stuck in the little kid's room. I would have a view of the mountains, if I could see anything. The window is smeared with the tears of the Alps. It's the first day of September, and what happened to Lucifer? Weather is drama in raw form, the surprises, the turns from one extreme to the other, the consoling calm after the tempestuous battering. Just as I arrive, the unbearable heat disappears, summer becomes late fall in a day. It's safe to go outside again. The pears in the upper Rhône Valley are big and the apples bigger, almost the size of cantaloupes, but the leaves and much of the fruit have heat blisters from Lucifer's breath. The forecast is dismal, a storm lasting several days: cold slashing rain, high winds, freezing temperatures, snow at Great Saint Bernard Pass, and below, down to the 6,000-foot level. Snow! Summer has three weeks to go.

Moonlight through the window wakes me. It's three a.m., or thereabouts. A clearing sky? A better forecast? A return of Lucifer? But it's just a passing—clouds racing by the silvery disc, flickering the light. I try to sleep and not bother about the weather, to get back into pilgrim mode. You command nothing. You're insignificant, a speck. Allow things to happen as they will. Do not hurry. Do not worry.

Dawn brings a decent breakfast of fruit and fresh zucchini bread, and goodbye to ground that is plumb. I will not be walking on flat surface until I reach the rich land in Piemonte where the Po drains northern Italy. Shouldering my possessions feels good, or at least right. Hello backpack, my old friend. It's heavier than it was in June. I'm carrying winter clothes—an old down coat, fleece, rain pants, cap and gloves, and a few emergency provisions that any pilgrim in distress can't do without. The legs feel fine. In Seattle, I finally went to see a doctor. He told me that the rupture left one of my quad muscles useless, balled up in the upper thigh. At some point, I might want surgery to reattach it. *At some point* are the only words I remember.

Today, I will try for Orsières, on the higher Napoleonic route, where I fell short two months ago. It's twelve miles of moderate uphill. Signs warn to stay out of the riverbed that parallels the path, La Dranse, a smaller stream than the Rhône. Don't be fooled by the water at low babble. In no time, it can become a flood, strong enough to dislodge boulders. The dam upriver is opened and shut, per the weather, a hydraulic punch in the waiting. I have new boots, lightweight Merrells, low-top leather with a great grip of the soles that give me the confidence of a mountain goat. I've studied the description in the guidebook to the point of memorization. I will not get lost. I will not blister. Saddled up and ready to go. Heidi ho!

I make it to Orsières just as the farmers' market is finishing up on this Saturday afternoon. Only one more village of any size stands between this town and the pass. I'm hungry enough to eat pinecones and wash them down with petrol. Lucky me, the bounty of an alpine harvest is there for the asking—huge, bright orange carrots, gourds that look as if they were raised on performance-enhancing drugs, and many herbal and medicinal teas from plants grown in the mountains. One man is selling honey-brown rounds of bread made from long-forgotten grains. A loaf is nearly the size of a basketball. I get a quarter round, pick up some soft cheese and a drool-down-your-cheek peach. I have not felt happier all summer.

Next morning, after staying in minimal comfort in minimal quarters, I'm ready for the summit. I'm walking before sunrise, which is 6:57 a.m., in the dreaded backwash of the season, when big blocks of precious daylight slip away every day without saying goodbye. The sky is muck, temperatures in the lower 40s. Bourg-Saint-Pierre is eight miles away, a four-hour walk uphill. I cross the river on a footbridge, keep a steady pace on switchbacks that rise in the forest and pass clusters of cabins, taking my time in the openings. The clouds part on a whim of unpredictability, providing views of green pastures and bone-white rock, all of it a tease. I meet only two other hikers, a couple who just finished a month of wandering in the Alps. Midway through the morning, the trail joins the road and enters a toy village of a few hundred people, named Liddes, with a café for coffee and calories. Fueled up, I'm back on the street that runs through the village when a kid in a van slows next to me, rolls down his window, and asks where I'm going. He's going there as well. I'm in Bourg-Saint-Pierre before noon.

Now, a decision: Do I press on to the pass, and put my Napoleonic misery behind me? Or find a place to sleep and start fresh at dawn? It's eight miles or so and 2,700 feet of vertical to the col. Even though I'm in the ancestral home of the jowly, selfless, oversized Saint Bernard dogs, I can't expect a canine rescue. That's not what the big guys do anymore, though they summer at the pass and winter just below me in Martigny. There's no cell phone coverage either. I feel strong, and the tug of Great Saint Bernard is irresistible. *Au revoir*, Bourg-Saint-Pierre.

It takes longer than it should to leave town. That's because the Bourg is a curious place with much to be curious about. The older, timber-framed, nonpainted houses—I'm guessing they've stood for five centuries or more—are built on stilts of stone. You can tell how much snow they get here by the entrances, some of which are six feet above the ground. The homes have a winter doorway and another for the warm season. The newer residences certainly look prosperous, in that Swiss, not-a-shingle-out-of-place way. But nobody is home. Anywhere. It feels like the entire town has left, or is hunkering down in their cellars, the shutters closed and locked. The place is clearly still inhabited, judging by the obsessive-compulsively stacked firewood outside most homes.

At the high end of town I find the V.F. sign and start to track up through the mountains. It's gradual, though fairly steep. I see farm buildings, huts, cabins, all of which look to be abandoned in keeping with the *Twilight Zone* vibe of the day. I'm following a path that roughly parallels what is known as the old road, since the new one is a tunnel that bypasses the mountain challenge altogether. "In bad visibility," the guidebook advises, "go to road instead." I can see to the next opening in the forest, maybe eighty yards, so I decide to stay on my chosen trail. After an hour and then some, the temperature starts to plunge. I'm wearing three layers: a long-sleeve, wick-away-the-moisture top, my down vest, and a raincoat, and still it's hard to stay warm. Hiking in the Pacific Northwest, you're always ready for a summer day to turn to January. The Cascade Mountains prepare you for anything. So I tell myself. I've been lost in a whiteout on Mount Rainier, and hypothermic next to a half-frozen alpine tarn in the Enchantment Lakes country. I can handle this. The rain had been slashing and horizontal. But now it's something new: wet snow. I keep my head down and move ahead, on ground that is increasingly slippery. I should stop and put my fleece on, but that would expose the other layers to the attack of precip. I'm not carrying a tent. If I fell, or snapped an ankle, I'd be prey to the storm.

The forest thins, the trees getting smaller as I approach timberline. Ahead, appearing in and out of the rage of clouds, are waterworks of some kind from the dam that backs up La Dranse. The image disappears so quickly that I question my direction. Did I let my mind slip from the task at hand? Did I miss a step? Julius Caesar, Hannibal, Napoleon, innumerable medieval pilgrims and primitives from the Bronze Age trod this very path, with much less sophisticated gear. Their footwear had to suck. Napoleon's men carried packs weighing sixty to seventy pounds, driven onward by drumbeats. Bonaparte rode a mule, bringing up the rear, not a white horse as depicted in the famous Jacques-Louis David painting.

My feet feel clammy; the rain has found a way inside because I'm not wearing gaiters. The pack deflects water but it's off kilter, and the cover flaps like an errant kite. When I planned this trip, I envisioned the top tier of the Via Francigena as a heavenly walk through alpine meadows, a wildflower show at the peak of its ostentation, marmots whistling in chorus, with maybe a glimpse of Mont Blanc, the highest peak in the Alps, showing some part of its albino essence. It's a mere ten miles away. I didn't envision a struggle in a place that has the colorless feel of an anxious dream. The winds lash and whirl. They are almost strong enough to knock me down. Wet snow, zero visibility, body temperature dropping. It makes no sense to continue on today. In defeat, I turn around.

BACK AT BOURG-SAINT-PIERRE, there's no letup from this mountain rage. The town is still lifeless. If only I could find an unlocked door, a public place. What did Napoleon do? He pillaged, his troops raiding wine cellars and pantries, though vowing to reimburse. "We are struggling against ice, snow, storms and avalanches," he wrote in 1800. This town still has a promissory note from Napoleon. And when French president François Mitterrand paid a visit nearly two hundred years later, residents reminded him of the outstanding bill—for twenty thousand bottles of wine, a half ton of cheese. I'm drawn to the church, because surely its doors will be open. Only one church has been closed to me during this entire journey, the cathedral in Calais. The *église* of Saint-Pierre was built over the foundation of a tenth-century house of worship. Out front is a little graveyard in a tiny terrace, topped by a large crucifix twice my size. What a pitiful sight: the left arm of Jesus has broken off, lopped at the shoulder. It hangs downward, held to the cross by a nail through the hand. The arm-severed Christ is jarring, appearing as it does in this storm, and so sad. It's the only time I've ever seen Jesus with an amputated limb.

The door pushes open. Reprieve. Instead of wet, horizontal snow, it's soft light through stained glass and an escape from the elements. I hear a repetitive sound from outside: the creak of the swinging arm of Jesus. I remove my wet coat and set it on the back of a pew, take off my hat, gloves, and shoes. My fingers are white and there's no feeling in my toes. I walk up a staircase to a choir loft, to study the stained glass. It's an image of the same saint my high school was named for—Aloysius Gonzaga, the original Zag. It's not that I recognize him, this Italian son of Renaissance aristocrats, like me one of seven kids, but his name is emblazoned in the colored glass. He could have been a prince, but he renounced his inheritance and title to become a Jesuit and work with the poor. When a plague hit Rome, he nursed the sick, which cost him his life after he caught the disease. Dead at twenty-three, he's now the patron saint of students and, more recently, people with AIDS and their caregivers.

I sit in the pew and try to read the Bible in French, which is futile. I switch to my dog-eared V.F. guidebook, looking for pilgrim refuges nearby. There's something here I missed: a bus passes through Bourg-Saint-Pierre late in the day, on the way to the pass. I lace up my boots, wrap myself in the half-dry shell of Patagonia's fine rain gear, and step outside. The arm of Christ still swings in the wind. He looks forlorn, a stark image of the message of his death, the message of Gonzaga's death as well—sacrifice.

Late in the afternoon, a bus stops on the road through the Bourg. The driver looks at me as just another wet, pathetic casualty of overreaching ambition. I hop on, happy to be moving again. We pass from rain to sleet to blizzard of heavy snow, above timberline, above the dam, past slabs of glacier-cut talus and heather. We slow at hairpin turns but never stop until there is no more road going up, until we crest the Alps and arrive at Great Saint Bernard Pass, at 8,114 feet, and a refuge of stone and lore. Italy is 300 yards away. Rome is another 594 miles.

TWENTY-TWO

MONASTERY IN THE SKY

A bell summons us to supper in the dining room of a hospice that's been welcoming followers of Sigeric's trail for ten centuries. Outside, snow blows sideways, a river of white, lapping at the four-story spiritual sanctuary. Droopy-eyed Saint Bernard dogs, looking world-weary but not the least bit put off by the weather, pull their two-legged leashmates through the first white stuff of the season. The place is nearly full, people scampering about in shorts and flip-flops as they dry their clothes. Earlier, I was greeted by an older man in a black robe who spoke good English to my Italian. He gave me a small room with a view of the blizzard and told me the rules, which boiled down to *respect this place, it's been here forever and seen it all.* Oh, and the showers are set to a timer, so be quick.

Saint Bernard has been a safe space since well before that term took on its current meaning, shelter from the storm. Charles Dickens spent the night here in 1846. Napoleon was given two glasses of wine and a slice of rye bread by the monks when he arrived in 1800. I was told I could get the same across the street, at a small bar in a newer hostel, or wait for dinner here at the inn of the Augustinians.

The dogs have the run of this pass, staying in a well-tended kennel, with a museum devoted to their service. They've been bred for size and tolerance of cold, and along the way, they picked up personality traits that make them a delight to be around. They're comically huge, weighing as much as I do, 170 pounds, with a tongue that looks like a pink sirloin steak, if meat could drool. Their equally huge paws act like snowshoes, allowing them to romp through a drift. They're smart, sensitive, and sociable. They hate to be alone or to miss out on a party. They're low maintenance, aside from prodigious food requirements. They don't like hot weather or confined spaces. Over the years, Saint Bernards have rescued more than twenty-five hundred people, using their exceptional sense of smell to find lost souls in the snow. As selfless and likable as they are, they lead relatively short lives, eight to ten years. They no longer carry casks of brandy around their necks—it's doubtful they ever did. Nor are they used anymore for rescues, most of which are done by helicopter. The dogs are just too heavy. In that sense, the Saint Bernards of Great Saint Bernard are living relics.

The hospice and the dogs are named for Bernard of Menthon, a bishop from the Italian side of the pass. Like Gonzaga, he was born into wealth and nobility, but balked at following the family path to prosperity. He jumped out the window of a castle rather than go through with an arranged marriage. After that, Bernard gave up a life of privilege to serve pilgrims and pagans in the land that reaches up to the sky, between the Valais on the Swiss side and the Val d'Aosta on the Italian. It was not just snowdrifts of forty feet that threatened people trying to walk over the mountains to Rome, but thieves and hostile Saracens, as raiding bands of Muslims were known. Bernard established this place about the year 1050, the start of an unbroken tradition of rescue and refuge.

At a communal dinner table, I meet a cyclist and his son, their faces sandpapered by the elements; three millennial-age women, exuding the spirit of a generation that isn't afraid to try anything and post far too many pictures of it along the way; two French mountain climbers; a woman in her thirties from New York; and a psychologist from the Italian seaport of Piombino named Stefano. He is seventy-three and has been making a pilgrimage to the mountainous part of the V.F. every year for the past two decades. I try to block out the old joke about meeting shrinks—after you say *Hello*, he says, *I wonder what you meant by that*. Stefano is radiant with good cheer, as is everyone at the table. We're all stranded, which nobody is complaining about. Where were these people on the trail below? Not on it, as it turns out. Most are starting their camino at the highest point of the V.F.

A soup course of *zuppa di zucca*, steam rising from the gold of liquefied pumpkin, gets us started. Carafes of wine, a Valais pinot noir made by monks, is passed around, and is wonderful as well. It's good to be speaking Italian with Stefano, rolling the *rrrrr*s and punctuating the points with my hands. When our kids were very young, our family moved to Italy while I was on a book leave; we lived there long enough to fall in love with the language, the landscape, and the people. I can stay in most conversations, though my jokes often fall flat.

Stefano says he returns to the alpine monastery because it helps him see things clearly. He takes long hikes by himself, meditative strolls among the pyramidal peaks that neighbor Mont Blanc. The silence, the distance and space, is everything that the clutter of cities below are not. "I always discover something new about myself," he says. I mention a story I'd read about Pope Francis just a day or so ago, that he saw a therapist for six months when he was a forty-two-year-old priest. His analyst was Jewish, all the better to avoid the clutter of doctrine. "I needed to clarify some things," the pope explained.

"He should have come to Saint Bernard," says Stefano. "When I leave, I never look at the world in the same way."

The main course is a pork tenderloin with carrots and bell peppers, served with polenta. Everyone is ravenous. The woman from New York is taking a break from a management job in high-end retail. She flies 50,000 miles a year and doesn't have the spare time to keep a houseplant alive, let alone nurture something so esoteric as her soul. She's exhausted on weekends, too worn for anything but sleep. She hasn't read a book off her professional topic in years. She's lost touch with her friends. Downtime scares her. "I'm such a cliché," she says. When someone suggested that she disappear, she thought it was rude at first, and then brilliant. Her research led her to the Via Francigena. She plans to walk for a week, unplugged. By dessert, a panna cotta with mountain berries, we all feel like family. Such is the fast fellowship that comes from being willfully stranded at a high pass in the Alps. We wish one another a hearty *buon cammino*, clear plates, and retire.

I stay back and ask the man in the black robe if I can talk to him about this place and his life. He's happy to oblige me.

When my sister lost her son—murdered at the age of seventeen by a teenager with a gun—she asked me to do a eulogy at the funeral Mass. I hadn't been to church in many years. My sister, like my mother, held on to her faith. After I arrived at my sibling's parish in Spokane, I walked past the open casket of her only son. It brought me to immediate and uncontrollable tears. It had been just a few months since we'd played a game of touch football together at Thanksgiving. In the waning sunlight of November, my nephew slipped past me for a touchdown and did a cartwheel in the end zone. Now here he was—beautiful and lifeless. I kept my eyes down, to prevent people from seeing my tears, and there I caught sight of the sandals of a brown-robed Franciscan, the priest who would say the Mass. I forget his name. But his words at the service were comforting and stayed with me. More important, they stayed with my sister. The priest could not explain why her boy would be taken from her at such an age, or how a person who believed in a just God could find a place for an anvil of grief. But over time, he said, my sister would understand. She took that to heart, and in her search she eventually stopped questioning; she felt that God was protecting her son from some unknown evil to come. From that service on, I've tried to keep my suspicions

in check whenever I meet a priest. I assume that the crimes of other clerics are not theirs.

Over tea, the man in the black robe formally introduces himself as
Father John of Flavigny, a community of Benedictine monks in France,
the same order that put me up in Wisques. He has bright eyes behind
rimless glasses, with sprigs of short hair. He never intended to become a
priest, he says with a burst of laughter. "God, no!" He was going to be a
doctor. In his final year of medical school, he went on a spiritual retreat—
a last diversion before jumping into the ardors of medicine. What happened next surprised him.

"They introduced me to the Ignatian Method. Do you know what
that is?"

"I've heard of it from the Jesuits. It's based on their founder, Ignatius.
That's all I know."

He explains the method, also called the pedagogical paradigm. It's a
spiritual exercise, more than 450 years old, that involves going through
several steps to develop the conscience and give you the tools to be a better
person. John tackled this as only a medical student who'd mastered organic chemistry could.

"'Argue with yourself,' they told me. Use contemplation. Repetition.
Knock down your assumptions. So I drew up an argument, for and
against my mission in life. I did it in a very intellectual, straightforward
way. And the conclusion was: join a monastery."

He laughs again. This time, I join him. It's damn funny, actually: a
guy on his way to one of the most admired and remunerative professions
in the world decides to put everything on hold to take up a life of poverty
and meditation with other ascetics in a cloister. And give up women as
well. His family, who lives near the Basque country, was perplexed.

"It took me six years to become a priest."

"Regrets?"

"No. I received much more and I can give much more." That was forty years ago. He started coming to Saint Bernard because he got mired in doubt, and like the future pope, he needed clarification. In Father John's case, he became deeply depressed in 1989.

"They sent me to Saint Bernard to rest. There are times when I felt . . . boxed in at the monastery. Here there is breathing room. It does wonders for me. I've been coming back every year. Will you join us for Mass tomorrow?"

I dodge his question with another of my own. "Do you believe in miracles?"

Here this man of science, someone who knows more about the mechanics and biology of life than 95 percent of the general public, answers without hesitation.

"Oh, yes. Absolutely."

"Incorruptibles? The bodies of saints that never decay?"

"Yes, of course."

"How can you believe these things? You're a person steeped in logic, reason, the scientific method."

"That is exactly right. I wouldn't believe in miracles if I hadn't seen them happen. And I have. At Lourdes. It's very well documented."

"Do you have doubts?"

"About miracles? No. About my faith? Yes. Doubts are allowed by God. Reason can help you come to faith. It's a bit like training for sports. If you only ride a bicycle with the wind at your back, that's not going to help you. You need to ride your bike against the wind."

I ask him what it's like to walk around secular Europe in the robe and collar of a Catholic priest.

"That depends on where you are. I'm mostly well received. But even in Rome, some of the monks would only go to town in civilian clothes, because they were afraid. I've only had five or six people yell at me. It's nothing. Will I see you at Mass?"

"I can't say." He finishes his tea and stifles a yawn. I have one last question for Father John of Flavigny.

"What's the best way to make a pilgrimage? For someone on the Via Francigena, give me some advice."

"I don't recommend the rosary."

"Agreed."

"Keep your ears open. You know what the first word of the holy rule of Saint Benedict is? Listen."

TWENTY-THREE

MOUNTAIN MYTHS

First light comes with music from within the old walls, a wonderful way to wake. When I pull back the blinds I'm nearly knocked down by the sun. The great glory that had been hidden by the storm reveals itself: diamond-cut peaks frosted in fresh snow, tufts of glazed grass, a bluebird day in the making. A small lake holds the color of the sky, and a light wind ripples the water like keys on a player piano. I take a quick breakfast of eggs and pastry, and pack for a long day. It's just a degree or two above freezing, but already the snow is turning to slush on the road. I slip out quietly, relieved not to bump into Father John of Flavigny. His Mass is at ten-thirty, too late for my start, an excuse he would probably find lame.

It's all downhill from here—more than 6,000 vertical feet to Aosta. A few Saint Bernards are out, slobbering and sloshing. I'd love to be hiking with one today, a canine guide better than most humans. Less than five minutes into my walk past snow-glazed fireweed and thistle, I rejoice at a sign near the end of the lake: *Italie*, the French word coupled with that flag emblem the color of a pizza Margherita.

My companion this morning is Oscar Wilde again. We parted

company in Calais; it's good to have him back, as witty a pilgrim who ever rambled his way to Rome. Wilde came to this country while a student at Oxford, twenty-three years old, his brilliance just starting to blossom, and returned in the last months of his short life, looking to resolve his questions about faith. Early on, he penned a sonnet to Italy, which I found in one of the guidebooks, that reads in part:

> I reached the Alps: the soul within me burned
> Italia, my Italia, at thy name:
> And when from out the mountain's heart I came
> And saw the land for which my life had yearned
> I laughed as one who some great prize had earned.

He went to Genoa, Brindisi, Ravenna, and Rome, where he couldn't get enough of the pope and young Italian men, a not entirely unusual combination. He visited the grave of Keats, one of his heroes, writing a sonnet for him. Catholicism fascinated this Irishman, the ritual and mystery, the incalculable dimensions of the soul. His genius announced itself with the publication of his first volume of poems, in 1881, followed by his parable of vanity, *The Picture of Dorian Gray*, in 1891. He became the toast of London theater with *The Importance of Being Earnest*, in 1895.

He came by his way with words, he always said, from his mother, the poet of Irish sedition: Lady Jane Francesca Wilde. She was lucky to escape a lifetime sentence in prison for her fiery call to arms against British occupation of her homeland during the Great Hunger.

The soul of Oscar Wilde was the only thing not taken from him during the hard time of hard labor he spent behind bars, convicted of sodomy under section 11 of Britain's Criminal Law Amendment Act. He spent many days in jail reading Saint Augustine, Dante, and the New Testament, forming a number of conclusions.

"The only difference between a saint and a sinner is that every saint has a past, and every sinner has a future."

Out of prison, he was Europe's best-known convict, a verse-loving vagabond, though unable to make a living speaking, or even to summon original thoughts to paper.

He broke off with his longtime lover, and then took up with him again for a time in Paris. His health fell apart. He couldn't scrape two francs together. His clothes, a source of his inimitable flamboyance, were threadbare; he even accepted hand-me-downs. In Rome in 1900, he lived a shambolic existence, sickly, pale, and destitute, having lost the paltry stipend he'd been getting from his ex-wife, who died that April. Still, he was enthralled to be in "the city of soul," he wrote, and was determined to find some fresh air for a deflated life-force. On Easter Sunday morning, he went to St. Peter's Square, jostling with the crowd to get a glimpse of the pope. He made it to "the front ranks of the pilgrims in the Vatican," he wrote a friend, "and got the blessing of the Holy Father." In the evening, he went to vespers for a round of prayer, followed by time spent with a Roman infatuation named Armando.

Every day thereafter, he was back at St. Peter's. "I do nothing but see the pope," he wrote. "I have been blessed many times, once in the private chapel of the Vatican." He was, adamantly, not a Catholic. "No one could be more 'black' than I am." In May, he made his way back to Paris, his final home in exile. On his deathbed, he summoned an Irish priest, Father Cuthbert Dunne, and was baptized into the Catholic Church and received last rites. He died at the age of forty-six.

Were he walking with me now down the switchbacks of the Italian Alps, Wilde would be gratified by how well he's been treated over the last few years. Not only was he granted the general pardon by Queen Elizabeth II in 2017, but the Vatican has embraced him as well. Yes, the Vatican! The church's head of protocol recently printed an anthology of Wilde's sayings, including, curiously, this line: "The only way to get rid of temptation is to yield to it."

Wilde was praised in *L'Osservatore Romano* for his "lucid analysis of the modern world," and for being "a lover of the ephemeral." It was mentioned only in passing that he was also a lover of other men, an act the church has long considered "intrinsically disordered" and "contrary to the natural law," per the catechism. The law that he was convicted of breaking likely had its roots in Christian canon law. And just as likely, Wilde grasped the irony of his trying to share a faith that would have nothing of his kind. The Catholic stance was reaffirmed in a letter from the Congregation for the Doctrine of the Faith in 1986. Gay sex constitutes a "moral disorder," the enforcers of dogma wrote. They did not cite any words from Christ to back this claim, for there are none. But now— what's a thinking Catholic supposed to believe? Pope Francis seemed to let the whole thing drop with his famous "Who am I to judge?" shrug. And then he went even further, telling a gay victim of clerical abuse, after ministering with him for a week, "You have to be happy with who you are." He added: "God made you this way and loves you this way, and the pope loves you this way."

In the village of Saint-Oyen, I say goodbye to Wilde and take up with a young woman full of another kind of wit and wisdom, spiffy in hiking half pants and a not unfashionable floppy hat—Sophie Egan. I haven't seen my daughter for months, and I almost squeeze the wind out of her. She had a rough time getting here, a canceled flight from the West Coast to the East, followed by a domino of delays, Euro trains, and buses of varying degrees of discomfort. But here she is now, looking crisp, and not complaining. She's heavily sunscreened, loaded down with water from a two-liter container and lots of little boutique snacks, her hair in pigtails. We talk a manic streak in the shade of Saint-Oyen's church, founded in the fifth century—a spurt of *oh my gods*, and *can you believes*, and *wait, that's not the best parts* until we realize that we have many days to catch up and should start to move.

I'm a bit slow to this pony's pace, and happy for her to blaze the way. In the splendor of an alpine morning, with yesterday's storm a mere vapor trail in the faraway sky, I behold the image of my child toddling off to play on the front lawn, her diaper swishing below her. Then I see a little girl in a kindergarten musical, playing a penguin while trying to hide her broken arm in a cast, an impression that fades to a fresh-minted college graduate, tassel flipped triumphantly to the side, black gown rippling in a breeze. You think you're done then. You think you've lost all influence. You hope that the best of what you tried to give is imprinted for life and the worst long forgotten. But you're not done—you're a father and she's the human you helped to bring into this world, always. Is there a parent who greets a child after a long absence and doesn't see time compressed, your life and hers? I need only to catch a glimpse of the braid of her hair ahead of me on the Via Francigena to remember the two-foot girl giddy to climb Mount Daddy, me pulling her up from the knees to the chest and shoulders. We introduced our kids to the wild at an early age, bribing them with Skittles to get up the trail, promising to protect them from every horsefly and mosquito in the Cascade range. Lucky for us, and them, it took.

For scenery, today is a sensory overload. We're surrounded by the highest peaks of the Alps: Blanc, the apex of Western Europe at 15,777 feet; Rosa a close second, 15,203 feet; the pyramidal exclamation of the Matterhorn, which the Italians call Cervino, 14,692 feet, and Gran Paradiso, the 13,323-foot centerpiece of Italy's first national park. The recent heavy rains have shocked the Val d'Aosta back into vibrant greenery, as if it got a high-voltage jolt of hydration from nature's defibrillator. Here the V.F. parallels a canal system, narrow waterways built in the fourteenth century. These concrete veins bring life to all parts of the lower valley. The water runs clear and fast. Flowers, fronting homes on mountain perches, spill from hollowed logs cut lengthwise to hold garden soil. The trail zigs and zags between clusters of fir trees and the rock huts of shepherds and alpinists. Some of the oldest of these stone shelters are abandoned refuges for pilgrims.

I love the roofs of storm-washed slate, glistening black with the water still on them, and nimble cows with bells on the way to giving up milk for cheese. The mountains are medicinal on days like this—head-clearing and lung-freshening. You can see why so many sanatoriums sprang up in the nineteenth century, offering sunlight and clean air for tubercular patients, and inspiration for Thomas Mann's *The Magic Mountain*. And you can see why, long before the Alps became a playground, before Mont Blanc was first climbed in 1786, those who lived at lower elevations thought that the highest ground was sacred, and only the gods could reside there. Most people don't go to the mountains to find religion, but religion finds you there, in the storms, the clearings and ordering of nature.

Sophie has an undergraduate degree in European history and a master's in public health, so I expect her to answer the most arcane questions about distant monarchs, in addition to wonkish explanations for why the American health-care system is so bad when compared with Europeans'. For starters, I'm curious about the people whose territory we're walking through—descendants of the House of Savoy. The signs in the Val d'Aosta are bilingual—French and Italian—and just as precise in detail as those on the Swiss side. V.F. postings give a time estimate to the next village. We're striding along at better than five kilometers an hour. But it's downhill, so hold your applause. The toes pound, the pack feels like part of me. We shed layers of clothing with every drop of a thousand feet or so. First to go is the raincoat. Then the fleece. Long pants are starting to irritate. Savoy?

"The last royal family of Italy, I think."

I've been wandering within the historic boundaries of Savoy since Lake Geneva, a district that takes in parts of Switzerland, France, and Italy. It was the feudal territory of a family dynasty, established in 1003, that hung around long enough to become the oldest surviving royal house in Europe. Savoy managed to avoid the violent fevers of the Catholic Church and the pious excesses of the Reformation. It made peace and bought separation from the German kingdoms to the north, and even welcomed the Enlightenment imperialism of Napoleon. The puzzle pieces of Italy, emerging from city-states and the domains of European powers, did not combine into a single modern nation-state until 1861. The Savoy line was intact, and its head was enthroned as a largely ceremonial monarch. Italy's last king, Victor Emmanuel III, reigned until 1946, when the war-ravaged Italians voted to end their connection to royalty, closing out the House of Savoy.

The valley feels very different from other parts of old Savoy in one way: the exuberance of the people. Italy has embraced the Via Francigena as none of the other three nations have. This country never threw off its Catholicism; monarchs with their own religious agendas were scarce, and Protestants still are. The faith seems stitched to the land; no small space is without a roadside grotto or devotional statue in the courtyard behind gates. People go out of their way to wave, and wish a sincere-sounding *buon giorno* or *buon cammino*. We pause to chat with a woman who looks about sixty, her hair tied back, her face deeply tanned, walking with a Labrador. She cannot believe we are American because she sees so few Yanks on the trail. Her family has been in the Val d'Aosta for centuries. She's rhapsodic, in almost musical Italian and equally fluid hand gestures, about the countryside we are walking through. She says we are blessed to be seeing it for the first time—the impression that makes many fall in love. When we ask if there is a place to get a late lunch nearby, she offers to lead us to her home. We can't accept, because of the many miles still ahead. She switches to English.

"Then you must do this for me. You walk another kilometer. You turn left at a little pond. You drop down. You go past—I don't know for sure, three or five or maybe seven houses—and then drop down again. There's a place there that has the best food in the valley. I am sure of this, and I've lived here all my life. And they are open today. *Capito?*"

"Grazie mille."

She then gives each of us a prolonged hug. A hug! Not once in England, nor anywhere in the Pas-de-Calais, in the Marne or Champagne or the Jura Mountains, along Lake Geneva or in the Alps, has a stranger tried to hug me.

"And then you must do one more thing for me," she says. "You are pilgrims, so this won't be difficult. When you get to Rome, if you get to Rome, say a prayer for me when you see the pope. I am not Catholic. Not for a long time. I like this pope. Will you promise me a prayer to the Holy Father?" I do, and she kisses me on the cheek. I've known her for maybe fifteen minutes. *Benvenuto in Italia!*

We find the *locanda* just as she described—five houses after the little pond, folded into the mountainside. Though we arrive sweaty, stinky, and disheveled into a well-kept inn and eatery with stickers on the window showing off guidebook gushing, we are not disrespected. We ask for liters of *acqua fredda, non gassata*, and whatever is best to eat. A dish of tomato water—not a paste or a sauce, but the pure distillation of *pomodori* in high season—over handmade, saucer-shaped tortelli is regenerative. We follow that with a plate of steamed vegetables, down a couple of espressos with biscotti, and try to push away, back uphill, past the pond, to rejoin the Via Francigena.

Our hike today is about twenty miles, with another two to three allocated for getting lost and diverted. For most of the way, it's a gradual descent, on a path cushioned with alpine mulch, but then the drops get more precipitous, coming in gulps. We take gravity for granted until it's dominant, holding us in its grip. The toes of my feet are starting to feel the effects of down-pounding, and I suspect I'll have a blue nail or two by day's end. Soph is carrying a pack that feels a bit heavier than mine, but she's hoofing it like one of the ibexes of the Alps. She's practically prancing.

This is a walk through a fairy tale, in more ways than one. A curiosity of these mountains is a little man in a pointed hat and a wooden staff, holding the head of another man, bearded and bloodied where it has been severed at the neck. He looks like a Hobbit sneaking away from an execution. This is Saint Grat, the patron holy man of the Val d'Aosta. You see him in fresco form, in oil paintings, and most often as a wooden statuette in many of the churches and grottoes of the high country. Originally Gratus from Greece, he came to Rome in the fifth century, and while in the formerly pagan expanse of the Pantheon, he had a vision of God calling him to preach the Gospel to people of mountainous northern Italy. After working these meadows, he got another divine command: to retrieve the head of John the Baptist. Off to the Holy Land he went, finding the skull in Herod's palace, smuggling it out of Jerusalem, and offering it up to the pope, as bells rang out. Thus, the depiction of Grat and the saint's head. This story grosses out Sophie, and is somewhat incomprehensible as well.

"You don't believe this, do you, Dad?"

"No, most of it is bullshit. There was a man named Grat who was bishop of Aosta in the fifth century. There's a record of that."

The rest of little Grat's tale is almost entirely made up. But why, then, is his feast day of September 7 still such a big deal in the Val d'Aosta, with many workers getting the day off? Why the ubiquitous iconography? Why the rituals around his relics, which reside in a gold encasement at the finest church in Aosta? Why celebrate the coming of spring with the invocation of his name, the wishing away of biting insects and predatory animals with the same? The lives of the saints seldom hold up to fact-checking. But the saints are approachable. They're . . . just like us! Or they were, until they rose to meet an impossible challenge, or sacrificed profoundly on behalf of a fellow human. Only a pope can name a saint, through a lengthy trial process, though that wasn't always the case. In the early days, as when Grat roamed the land, the acclaim of friends and family could be enough to get certification that said soul has crossed into heaven, joining those lesser-known folks who lived lives of anonymous virtue.

Myths help us understand our experience, give shape to shapeless events, order to our fears and desires, narrative to chaos. The huge step that *Homo sapiens* took away from Neanderthals in the Cognitive Revolution of 70,000 years ago was made possible by the ability of our species to collectively imagine things, as Yuval Noah Harari argues in his book on human origins. Is it wrong to pass on the fictional story of a good man risking his life to bring back the head of a slain man for a higher purpose? All religion is informed by myth, as are most cultural bonds, from *Ulysses* to *Game of Thrones*. "Mythology is not a lie," said Joseph Campbell. "Mythology is poetry, it's metaphysical. It has been well said that myth is the penultimate truth—penultimate because the ultimate cannot be put into words."

None of this makes the image of Grat walking around with the head of John the Baptist any less weird to Sophie.

"Are Catholics required to believe this stuff?" She asks this without a hint of cynicism. But again, her question is a result of my negligence as a parent, leaving our kids somewhat spiritually illiterate.

"You can take what you want from each of these saints, or take nothing at all. Italians pray to saints more than they pray to God, though you're not supposed to worship them—that would be idolatry. It's nice to have a supporting cast, don't you think?"

GLIMPSES OF AOSTA, still way down the valley, appear through a forest that gives way to orchards and homes with gardens of oversized produce. I've never seen squash so big outside of Alaska, and everyone has piles of them, stacked like firewood. Rows of wooden trellises hold lipstick-red tomatoes. This region is stocked with castles and clock towers as well, nary a high point without a well-tended fortress or a copse of turrets. I drink freely from little fountains that bubble up outside these residences, ignoring to my peril the *non potabile* signs in front of some of them. I'm sweating heavily, and can't resist the cold mountain water. I had taped my heels, as usual, but did nothing to protect my toes. Big mistake. And when I broke in these new boots at home, I didn't think of trying them out on a prolonged downhill hike. I feel rubbing and squishing with each step, but we're close enough to the end that it's not worth a medical stop. At one orchard with a view back at the fresh snow on the roof of Europe, we pause to pluck a pair of apples from a tree. Sophie pleads with me to tend to my feet, but I choose to suck it up.

After another couple of hours, I stop to take off my shoes. I'm in a lot of pain, and have trouble moving. The toes on my right foot are a throbbing mess of bubbled blisters. Why, why, why didn't I listen to her? The best I can do is wrap them in tape and treat the skin later with antiseptic and cushions. This leaves me with one last Oscar Wildeism to carry forward at day's end: "Experience is simply the name we give our mistakes."

Near sunset, we breach Aosta's city boundaries, the broken twenty-foot-high walls built to surround a classic Roman rectangular urban design, with forum, temple, and stadium in the middle, guard towers in the corners, four main gates. Aosta is a little mountain kingdom of 35,000 people that is Shangri-La to a pair of tired hikers, built at the confluence of two rivers. We cross the smaller of the streams and stagger over to the most prominent landmark in this 2,100-year-old town: the Arch of Augustus. It was erected in 25 BC, after Augustus had enslaved an indigenous tribe of Latin Celts, the Salassi. It's a single arch, Corinthian columned, on a pedestal of stones moved into place by my conquered Celtic ancestors. The monument is a tribute to the man who reigned for forty years, and did more than any other Roman ruler to expand the Empire's roads, rules, and religions. We plop ourselves down on the lawn and take in the last light on the flanks of the arch. I don't think I will get up again. *Hail, Augustus, and the city of thy name!*

The emperor does not need mythic enhancement. Born in 63 BC, a great-nephew to Uncle Julius Caesar, he was a superb man of war, with a first-rate mind and a nose that could smell the slightest whiff of deadly intrigue from any of the Seven Hills of Rome. After his conquests of rivals foreign and domestic—most notably, the besting of Antony and his lover Cleopatra—he took the name Augustus the Exalted One, the first

Roman emperor. He turned Rome from a republic into an empire, but he offered his subjects citizenship, even for freed slaves. He had the eighth month of the calendar named for him, following the lead of Julius, who claimed the month before. He restored the massive temple to the god Jupiter Optimus Maximus, the largest in the capital. And making use of a blend of water, quicklime, sand, and volcanic ash—concrete—to go with marble and tufa, he oversaw construction of the Eternal City. His territorial legacy would remain in some form for the next 1,500 years. He ushered in Pax Romana, the two centuries of stability, expansion, and rule over a third of the world's inhabitants. At its peak, the Empire collected taxes from nearly 100 million people. On his deathbed in AD 14, a very old man of seventy-five by classical standards, he is said to have uttered words that served as a proper tribute: "I found a Rome of clay, I leave it to you of marble." Postmortem, the Roman Senate declared him a god.

Augustus passed on to divine status in a year when a great empire was in ascendancy. He was unaware of a teenage boy growing up in hardscrabble Nazareth at that same time, in a carpenter's house at the southeastern fringe of the Roman realm. Today, nobody worships a deity named Augustus, or Jupiter for that matter. But as I lay exhausted on grass beneath the Arch of Augustus, I see that boy now as a dying man nailed to a cross, holding the monument together. You can't miss the crucifix at the gate of a town that Augustus oriented toward the deities who lived above the mountains—the gate into one of the oldest outposts of the Via Francigena. We end our day on a part of the trail where all roads now lead to Rome. But what waits at the end is something that has outlasted every empire of the last two millennia, a force that is, by design, not of this world.

It's a trait we humans have developed over our spiritual evolution, and no small skill, to fuse one god to another, to borrow the better bits of fading mythologies and weave them into a story that fits our times. Rome's Pantheon, built by slaves a century after the death of Augustus to honor all the gods of the Empire, stands today as it did 1,900 years ago, though now it is dedicated to "Saint Mary and the Martyrs"—the first pagan temple to be transformed into a Christian church. To throw out the old entirely would be saying our ancestors were wrong, and to realize that future generations will say the same thing about us. So we keep the best parts, and believe little lies in service of a larger truth, or so we hope.

TWENTY-FOUR

PROVING THE EXISTENCE OF GOD

O n the main, cobbled street of Aosta is a residence, barely a quarter mile from the emperor's arch, at 66 Via Sant'Anselmo—three stories of weathered beige concrete and stone, connected to other similar-sized buildings in the quiet *centro storico* of the old outpost of the Roman frontier. At this address in the year 1033, a boy was born into a wealthy and well-connected family. He was sent to good Benedictine schools and grew into a budding scholar of theology, language, and history. At fifteen, he had a dream in which he spoke to God, and God spoke back. He tried to join a monastery, but his parents restrained him. His father wanted him to be a politician. His mother, a noble Burgundian, thought he might take up something in the courts of Europe. He rejected both overtures. And so, like many children who chafe at a life that is set for them before they've had a chance to chart their own way, he left home just past his twentieth birthday and started to wander.

For three years this young man, Anselmo, traveled around Europe. It was a time of relative peace and stability, allowing an increase in literacy and scholarship. Mostly he wanted to argue about the existence of God, going back to his conversation in the dream. In the abbeys of the late Dark

Ages, Anselmo found plenty of people willing to engage him. It was in Normandy, in the village of Bec at the far northwestern coast of France, that he finally put down his walking stick and took up residence at a monastery staffed with some of the brightest minds in Europe. Anselmo was determined to show, through reason and deduction, that God existed. Even with the church at the height of its control over all elements of European society—its reach felt in law, in schools, in civil courts, governments, family structure, royal families—some matters of the soul were not entirely settled. Sure, Pontifex Maximus in Rome had proclaimed the great issues to *be* settled. But Anselmo, and many like-minded Christians, believed people should not just accept the reality of a creator because others told them to, under threat of damnation, or because of Scripture.

The argument that Anselmo developed was simple, though complex enough to engage philosophers to this day. His motto was Faith Seeking Understanding. In his *Proslogion*, he made his plea for spiritual wisdom:

"I do not even try, Lord, to rise up to your heights, because my intellect does not measure up to that task; but I do want to understand in some small measure your truth, which my heart believes in and loves. Nor do I seek to understand so that I can believe, but rather I believe so that I can understand."

He presented his formula, also known as *Discourse on the Existence of God*, in 1077. Here's the short version:

1. God is defined as the greatest possible thing that can be imagined.
2. This concept of a "being than which no greater can be conceived" exists in the mind as an idea.
3. Even if you believe that God doesn't exist in reality, the fact of being able to imagine such a formulation proves . . .
4. The existence of God.

Anselmo's theory was something even a fool could grasp, said the suffer-no-fools theologian. His argument for God's existence, he said, was self-evident to him, and should be to anyone who gave it a deep thought. Two centuries later, Saint Thomas Aquinas expanded on this foundation, putting forth five proofs of the divine. The most convincing of those was the idea that creation needed a first mover—"everything that is moved is moved by something"—and that had to be God. This contention has drawn the best minds of modern times as well.

People long ago figured out that the earth is not the center of the universe, but rather a tiny planet in a distant galaxy in a vast universe—putting biblical literalists to shame. In the seventeenth century, an Irish archbishop, James Ussher, had famously calculated that the earth was created in the year 4004 BC—at six p.m. The consensus now is that the universe began almost 14 billion years ago with the Big Bang. Our own solar system formed 4.5 billion years ago. Primitive life showed up 3.5 billion years ago, and cells evolved into more complex organisms 2.5 billion years past. Early mammals similar to us arrived 100 million years ago; 70,000 years ago, *Homo sapiens* moved out of caves and the savannah to form cultures. Recorded history is a mere 10,000 years old.

"The one remaining area that religion can now lay claim to is the origin of the universe," wrote the cosmologist Stephen Hawking, just before he died. He asked, as did Aquinas and Anselmo, what triggered the whole process—that is, energy and space combusting into matter, ultimately leading to the particles of nature that make up humans. Hawking cited Albert Einstein's general theory of relativity: space and time are not absolutes, but dynamic quantities. "Time didn't exist before the Big Bang so there is no time for God to make the universe in," he wrote. Hawking concluded that "the simplest explanation is that there is no God." But he couldn't prove that.

So we are back with Anselmo and proof by deduction. After the Normans, those descendants of Viking raiders living in the northwest part of France, conquered England, Anselmo was asked to move across the Channel and become the archbishop of Canterbury. His position of power allowed him to promote the question that had obsessed him. It stirred a number of well-argued responses, including one from the fool. Gaunilo, a monk and contemporary of Anselmo, wrote *Book on Behalf of the Fool Who Says in His Heart There Is No God*. Others pointed to an obvious fallacy: one can imagine, say, a frog the size of a castle, and just because that image exists in the mind does not prove the existence of a frog the size of a castle.

Some of these same questions followed Napoleon as he marched out of Aosta, a few years before he was crowned Emperor of France. At the start of the Revolution, Napoleon supported purging church authority. He went along, for a time, with the new societal order built on logic and reason, a pretentious new calendar, the supremacy of ideas backed by terror. After waltzing into Milan, he assembled two hundred priests for theological debate. He told them he was favorably disposed toward their faith, perhaps an influence of his mother. Or it could have been convenience; Napoleon said he was open to whatever religion of the country he was conquering.

"No man is considered just and virtuous who does not know whence he came and whither he is going," he said. Well, did he believe in God? "Simple reason," he said, is not enough for belief, ruling out conversion by Anselmo's principle. Yet "without religion, one walks continuously in darkness." He didn't want to walk in darkness, nor would those millions of people newly under Napoleonic rule have to. But he remained a skeptic until his death.

He was not persuaded by the bottom-line argument of another Frenchman, the seventeenth-century philosopher Blaise Pascal. Suppose belief was a bet, he wrote in "Pascal's Wager"—an early advancement in probability theory. If you bet against a God and lost, you missed out on the joys of life-affirming faith and risked eternal damnation. If you bet on God's existence and won, you gave up very little in life and got the much greater reward in the afterlife. There was more upside in belief.

I took up this issue of finding God through logic on the advice of Father John of Flavigny. He told me that during his wrestling-with-the-soul-and-mind period, while still a medical student, he found Anselmo's proof compelling. In Aosta, after the long hike down the mountains, though I could hardly move, Sophie persuaded me to rally. And then, at a twilight dinner outside, surrounded by an amphitheater of alpenglow, we found ourselves within a few feet of 66 Via Sant'Anselmo—birthplace of the wandering ontologist. I owed it to serendipity, or the convergence of hints, to engage Anselmo's argument further.

Mildly self-medicated with an Aostan wine and a dish of eggplant and melted fontina from the cows we had seen earlier in the day, I attempted to explain Anselmo's theory. I played the advocate. Sophie poked the same holes in the argument as did I while thinking about it earlier, which shouldn't surprise anyone given how much DNA we share. She asked whether being on the V.F. had changed my mind on these things.

"I mean, you still believe in God, right, Dad?"

I tried to explain, as Anselmo had pleaded with the fool, as Napoleon argued with the atheists of the Revolution, as Hawking engaged his readers from his final days in a motorized chair, that thinking people owe it to themselves to ask the questions that tormented the man from Aosta. This stop on the Via Francigena settled for me one part of the questioning. Pope Francis said God is not someone who waved a "powerful magic wand," to effect creation and all that followed; he's not a magician. But nor can God be deduced by an exercise of the mind. *Damn.*

TWENTY-FIVE

A FAREWELL TO AUGUSTINE

The spirit was willing, but the feet were not. The expedition to break-fast, one flight of stairs and a shuffle to a small buffet counter, con-vinced me that I was not going anywhere with these toes. This filled me with self-loathing. What kind of wuss was I? Anselmo, Labre, and Fran-cis of Assisi—these guys crisscrossed a continent in slippers. Joan of Arc crushed the English on foot and horse. A Roman legionnaire was ex-pected to march twenty-two miles in five hours, in fifty pounds of armor and supplies—every day. I had the finest melding of technology, leather, and craftsmanship, and still I was stalled. So I made cutouts just larger than Cheerios, placed them on antiseptic-lubricated blisters, and mum-mified my toes. If I stayed hydrated, and kept off the pavement, I'd have a fighting chance. We caught the train to Ivrea, sixty miles away, moving out of the mountains and into Piemonte with the best protected feet in northern Italy.

Ivrea, established in 100 BC, hosts one of the strangest festivals in the world. In the dead of winter, the town imports 500,000 pounds of oranges from Sicily. Then, two sides spend three days in open warfare, drenching the city and each other in hurled citrus, ending on Fat Tuesday—forty days before Easter. The food fight goes back to the twelfth century, centering around the story of a miller's daughter who refused to allow a local duke to rape her on her wedding night. This was the custom, similar to droit du seigneur in France. But in Ivrea the story took a twist: the heroine fought back, beheading the entitled bastard who was trying to force himself on her. Now, every year leading up to the Battle of the Oranges, a young woman is chosen to play the role of the miller's daughter. Her forces fire oranges at the duke's guard, who dash around town in medieval carriages. The orange war is part of Italy's Catholic heritage, in that Carnival is a Christian-tolerated bacchanal leading up to the Lenten penance. Ivrea has a very low crime rate, so perhaps the soft violence is merely war by other means, as they say about international soccer.

OUR GOAL FOR THE NEXT few days is to make it to Santhià—about twenty-two miles away, with an overnight somewhere in the middle. To get there by train from Ivrea would involve rerouting through Milan or Turin, a real detour off the V.F. The only choice from here is to hoof it. We fortify ourselves with cappuccini and follow the well-signed route out of town, up a long gradual hill, past a small lake and the stately homes of Piemonte. The mountains are still in view through a morning haze. I feel the downward pull of the Po, which flows from the Alps to the Adriatic, bringing water of life to Italy's breadbasket. We just left the Dora Baltea, the stream we followed from Aosta to Ivrea. It heads south to join the big river. We angle toward the east, parallel to the Po but about ten miles above it. I feel something else as well: mosquitoes. We're approaching the rice fields of the Vercelli plain, and it's both muggy and buggy. They like Sophie's youthful blood more than mine.

In a few days, I plan to shake myself of Saint Augustine. Not that any Catholic, lapsed or otherwise, is ever rid of him. He's a founding father and doctor of the faith, inescapable. He steered the church he had once shunned over to his complicated worldview. And the written words from his prolific output are still marshaled in debates about the nature of faith and the duty of those who believe. In Pavia, farther down the V.F., is a cathedral that holds his remains, among the most sanctified relics in Christianity. That seems like a fitting place to part. But before I do, I want to engage him one last time and see if I can't come to some resolution. He's a nag; he knows how to get under my skin, skillful fourth-century polemicist that he is, particularly that line about great travelers who "pass over the mystery of themselves without a thought." The only way to be rid of him is to give him a full airing.

Augustine influenced Anselmo, Calvin, Luther, people from across the theological spectrum. But he's such a contradictory character. He wasn't even baptized until he'd lived a full life, by the longevity standards of the late Roman Empire. He was thirty-three years old in 387 when he renounced his former self and formally joined the Catholic Church. Remember, this was after getting his fill of life's sensual pleasures, including food and sex, art and sex, philosophy and sex, theater and sex. "My sin was this," he wrote, "I looked for pleasure, beauty and truth not in Him but in myself and his other creatures, and the search led me to pain, confusion and error." The young Augustine was "inflamed with desire for a surfeit of Hell's pleasures."

His initial "error" in his search was embracing a philosophy of dualism—the idea that everything is either good or bad, spiritual or material. Surely he could see the flaw in that. For life is not black or white, but with many shades. The spirit-lifting forest we walked through in the Alps was aflame with fire and terror just a month earlier, when Lucifer raged. Each of us is capable of acts of compassion, just as we can turn intolerant and cold on the same day.

As he moved toward Christianity, Augustine tightened his focus on the issue that bothered those worshippers back at Saint Martin's in Canterbury, and continues to bother me. It's a question he was determined to answer: How can an all-knowing, all-loving God allow so much evil to exist? Augustine doesn't mention the evil done in God's name, but it's part of the same scheme. You can see why people shun a supposedly beneficent creator who presided over the slaughter of the Wars of Religion, the African slave trade, the butchery of the Great War, Stalin's mass executions, genocide in Germany and Uganda and Cambodia. And why did upward of 90 percent of the native populations of Australia and the Americas die for no other reason than they lacked immunity to the diseases of European Christians advancing on their shores? What higher power dreamed up these towering crimes against innocent humanity? Augustine's response was to give God a pass. It's us. God foresees it, then allows our choices to unfold. You can be part of the inevitable bad thing, or opt for good. God knows the outcome, either way. You do not. For many Christians, this explanation is enough.

Sophie is not in my morning ruminations. She has gone ahead, scouting for a place to eat lunch. Her reconnaissance leads to a small bar on the quiet main street of Bollengo, a village without much movement on this humid day. A woman runs the counter, cooks the food, refills the wineglasses of two silent older men who might as well be statuary. We sit outside in the shade and rest. I bring Sophie into the Augustinian conversation and she gives me a quizzical look. My daughter, unlike me, never rushes to judgment. She's also in a bit of pain herself. Her pack has been pressing into her shoulders.

After a half hour or so, an enormous plate of pappardelle is brought to our table. The wide ribbons of pasta are silky with ragù and furry with fresh-grated Parmigiano. Steam rises from the pile. The owner brings us chilled watermelon slices. It's damn near impossible to get back out under the hot sun again after such a repast. The sensible thing would be to take a siesta, as most living creatures in Italy are doing just now. The imperative is to push on. As we pass a little church at the edge of town, I stop and take off my pack. After rummaging around, I find my old down coat, my weather-resistant pants, a fleece.

"What are you doing?"

"Dropping weight."

I leave my little donation in the church, feeling at least four pounds lighter, and a pound more righteous. I'm like those wagon train settlers on the Oregon Trail who rid themselves of furniture, books, and other heirlooms as they made their way west and struggled to get over the mountains. Arriving at the Columbia River and a new life, they had shed a sizable amount of their material past.

"Hold on," says Sophie. "I have something for you."

She produces a bag of chocolate caffeine bombs—"cold brew coffee bites." I take a handful. It doesn't take long for the stimulant to kick in. I want to jump, sprint, dance, skip along the Via Francigena. And look at the sky now, with just a beard of clouds near the foothills, and here's an abandoned villa, must be five centuries old, *huh, Soph*, and *OMG, the grapes*, a perfect pitch of purple! I switch to Italian and talk another blue streak, throwing my hands out ahead of me and rolling them over, clearing rhetorical brush. I sound like Vince Vaughn in manic mode.

"Basta, Babbo," says Soph.

With the rucksack readjustment, and the jolt from the coffee bites, we're both in less pain as we struggle through the hardest part of the day. The route finally leaves pavement for a grass-and-stone byway through vineyards. We are walking along the best place on the planet to grow nebbiolo, the black grape used to make barolo—the wine of kings and the king of wines. Harvest, *la vendemmia*, is just days away, for the grapes are ripe. We nibble at little bunches of juice-fat fruit. The vines are thought to be indigenous to Piemonte, and the winemaking dates to early Roman times. The name stems from the word *nebbia*, the fog that hugs this land on harvest mornings.

Just off the trail, surrounded by rows of wrinkled and thick-armed vines, is an open-air chapel of some sort: a Romanesque ruin without its roof. We go inside, looking back through the intact entrance arch framing the countryside. The floor is grass, wildflowers, and runaway vines. The frescoes inside what is left of the vault are still visible. The overall picture is stunning, with the open sky in the background, all of it wrapped in rows of nebbiolo. Sophie warns me not to get too comfortable.

The farmers keep dogs, and they are active, even in this heat. Signs along the way warn: *Attenti al cane!* Back on the trail, we ignore the yaps until a pair of growling guards are in our face. The dogs move ahead to block the path, directly in front of us, ready to pounce. We can go no farther. We're boxed in by ten-foot rock walls on either side of us. We cry out for an owner to call the dogs off. Ten minutes into our standoff, a woman appears out of the vines, apologizes, and summons one animal. The other, the more ferocious-looking one, remains. It moves closer, a menace of barks.

"*È un vagabondo,*" says the woman.

"*Vagabondo?*"

"*Sì, sì, mi dispiace.*"

It's not hers. She's sorry. Sophie stands, trembling while trying to hold her ground, her hands down to show no aggression. The dog leaps at her, just missing. I shout and stomp. The dog comes again, and this time tries to bite her just above the heel. I kick at the stray. Sophie backpedals, checks her leg. The skin has not been broken, but she's got some scratches.

"Walk fast," I tell her. "Straight ahead. Don't look at him."

We do this, and the vagabond starts to trail off, still barking, no doubt feeling victorious. Sophie says she's O.K. But she's clearly upset.

It takes forever to crest Piverone. My blistered toes are begging for relief, a pulse of pain with every step. On another day, in another mood, this hilltop hamlet would be charming. Now it's a gauntlet. We walk under an arched clock tower on a road barely wide enough for a mule. We have not run into another person since the dog owner. But in the post-siesta part of late afternoon, we stride past three elderly women sitting on a bench in the shade. The look they give us is . . . how to describe? Not quite disgust or sympathy, but more like, well, here it is, from the mouth of one:

"Pazzi."

"What did you say?" I stop in my tracks, glare, my sweat dripping on their feet.

"Pazzi."

"You think we're crazy? *Non siamo pazzi. Siamo pellegrini."*

"Ah, pellegrini. A Roma?"

"Sì, sì."

"Bravo, signore! Brava, signorina!"

Now they couldn't be nicer, answering our questions about how far it is to overnight accommodations: another five kilometers to the lake and a hotel.

Lake, hotel—a thought-bubble carrot for incentive to carry on. A few blocks later, when I sit and remove my boot and sock, what I see is a shock: a bloody mess of skin, gauze, blood, and pus. My makeshift medical dressing has slipped and is mangled together, exposing fresh skin, and causing blistered skin to bleed. I strip it off and wash my toes under a public fountain, one of the relief valves of the Via Francigena.

"I'm done," I tell Sophie.

"No!"

"I'm sorry. I can't go any farther."

She brightens. "Uber!" God bless millennials.

Would that violate the pilgrim spirit? I'm sure there's an app for enlightenment, but I still think you should have to earn it. My goal has been to follow the entirety of the Via Francigena, but not by any single conveyance. So long as I stay on the ground, tracing Sigeric's route to Rome. I imagine, after a long day in the year 990, that if a fresh horse came along, and Sigeric was just few kilometers shy of an inn, he would hop on.

I power up my phone, see that I've got two bars, and go to the Uber app. The little radar circles and searches, circles and searches. There is nothing nearby. The closest car is Milan, or thereabouts—a hundred kilometers away. We're stuck. Sophie has another idea. She searches her phone, tells me to wait, wait, wait. She finds a *farmacia* on Google Maps, about fifteen minutes away.

"Hold on, Dad. I'll go fast."

She returns with Euro-power ibuprofen, 500 milligrams a pop, antiseptic, fresh gauze, blister lubricant, tape, and a bottle of barbera from a second stop along the way. Her act of kindness nearly brings me to tears as I limp toward our destination.

LAKE VIVERONE IS A PANE of Piemonte freshwater, sailboats at anchor in the foreground, mountains in the distance. Immersing for a swim, just at sunset, is a baptism all over again. The hotel is old-school, the kind of meals-and-a-bed place favored by German pensioners. And in fact, it's packed with Germans of a certain age, who waited until the less-crowded month of September to go on holiday. At dinner outside the waiter opens time in a bottle, our barbera from a winery a few miles away. We eat four kinds of bruschetta, pork in a pesto sauce, lake trout in a butter cream (common in this dairy-loving part of the north), and a mountainous plate of grilled squash topped with pine nuts.

I have a question about the dog that went after Sophie: Was that little act of aggression predestined, and known by God, per Augustine's view? Well, yes, by logic and extension of his argument. As an omniscient being, God knew the dog would nip at Sophie's heels. O.K. Fine. Predestined and known by God. Though not an act of evil, it certainly wasn't a good thing for the *vagabondo* to go after Sophie. What if the scratch had been deep, and the dog had some disease? She suffered, albeit mildly, for what reason? There was no free will involved. The attacking dog was no fault of her own. She didn't make the wrong choice. She made no choice at all. She was a victim of a random small cruelty known by God. Augustine asserts that God is blameless for evil because evil is a consequence of human choice. But Sophie was not presented with options. My sister-in-law's

cancer is not punishment for doing the wrong thing. The millions of indigenous people who fell to the disease of foreigners invading their homeland did not select one fork in the road of free will, and face genocidal
carnage for doing so. The philosophy of *shit happens* cannot, then, hold
God blameless, if he sees it all unspooling in advance.

And in other abominations where free will is not involved—the black
plagues of medieval Europe, the body tortures of typhus or AIDS, the
slow-motion erasure of the memory of love through Alzheimer's—what
moral equation is at work there? Augustine would argue that illness and
accidents are all tests on the way to salvation. Some make it through.
Many do not. "Oh, Lord, you teach us by inflicting pain," he wrote. God
allows evil to exist because good comes from it. I find this argument un-
settling and not very convincing, but that's been the explanation since the
old theologian went to his grave in the year 430, leaving behind volumes
of ruminations, which scholars of the faith have whittled into truths.

WE RISE IN DARKNESS. First light over Lake Viverone is worth an early
wake-up. As the sun touches the evaporating mist off the still water, we're
the only people at the breakfast buffet. I soooooo want to walk today.
Movement is a pilgrim's oxygen. It takes me almost thirty minutes, with
Sophie's help, to dress the toes on my right foot. She winces when I wince,
backing off with the tape application because she doesn't want to hurt me.

"Your feet are gross."

"That's not helpful."

What good is a master's degree in public health if you can't improve
the health of one member of the public? When she's done, I shoulder my
pack and try to move forward. I take a few steps, but it's painful. To hike
the nine miles to Santhià would be risking infection. The hotel has a
driver for hire.

Santhià is named for Saint Agatha, another of the virgin martyrs of
the faith, who died sometime in the mid-third century. Like the miller's

daughter from Ivrea, she put up a fight when harassed by a sexual tormentor. Agatha was from Sicily, a gorgeous and well-spoken woman by mythic lore, and a Christian just before the Empire adopted the religion as its own. The Roman governor had his eye on her. When she resisted his advances, he ordered her imprisoned in a brothel—ostensibly, for the crime of being Christian. There, she continued to fight off predators. This infuriated the spurned governor. He had her tortured; his method of cruelty was specific to his initial intentions: both of Agatha's breasts were cut off. Badly wounded, she was thrown in prison and left to die. In her cell, an apparition appeared. Her wounds were made whole, her breasts returned. This further angered the governor. He had her stretched out on the rack and prodded with burning metal hooks. Still, she would not die. He ordered that she be rolled naked over hot coals. That's what finally killed her—getting grilled alive. Agatha is held in such prominence that her name is in the Eucharistic prayer of the Mass, the centerpiece of Catholic ritual. She's one of the seven most prominent women in the church canon, the patron saint of breast cancer survivors and victims of sexual assault.

In Santhià, inside the church named for Agatha, is a frescoed apse that tells her story. It's a thousand-year-old church in an otherwise forgettable town, and I have to go in. I'm enthralled by Agatha, as represented in the illustrated narrative over the altar. Agatha is a #MeToo saint, one of the first to the cause, more than seventeen hundred years ago. If you want to pray to her, you are told to say these words: "Help heal all those who are survivors of sexual assault, and protect those who are in danger." When Sophie asks what's inside, I tell her it's one of the better tributes to the tortured.

Santhià has train service, a sleepy local line. Also, they love the V.F. Along the route are life-sized cutouts of the yellow-robed pilgrim with his bindle and staff. People stop and ask if we want our pictures taken. Restaurants offer *pellegrino* specials. A man in the doorway of a *forno* beckons us inside to try the day's baked treats. We order two pieces of focaccia topped with tomatoes for lunch on the train. The baker insists we try something he calls *pane con farina di canapa.* Neither of us has heard of it. *Canapa?* He ducks under the counter and fetches a jar of the *canapa* pesto used on the bread: the label is a marijuana leaf. After putting up minimal resistance, we each try a sample.

PAVIA IS A REVELATION. I didn't know what to expect. A university town, set on the banks of the Ticino just before it flows into the Po, it presents the rarest of sights in an Italian town: young people. Residents are aging in place throughout Italy, a nation with one of the lowest birthrates in the world, and one that keeps breaking records in its bend toward depopulation. Nearly one in four citizens is older than sixty-five. And with its broken economy, it's no place for people just out of college. Pavia defies the trend. It's medieval and modern, solemn and talkative, a hive of Italy's tomorrow. We duck into the University of Pavia for iced coffee in the shade of stone first stacked to frame studious purpose in 1361. The open-air corridors, the tight courtyards, the library with a large globe from the sixteenth century showing a vague nothingness in the part of North America where I live. Who wouldn't be inclined to knuckle under to Dante in such a setting? After asking around, we check into a hotel off the main piazza.

At dusk we're out in the swift current of young Pavians taking their early *passeggiata.* I crave a smooth surface and can't venture too far. You never think twice about walking on rounded stones until your feet are hamburger.

Because we're in Arborio rice country, Sophie insists that we dine on risotto tonight. Across the square of the church of Santa Maria del Carmine, we sit outside at a family-run osteria featuring *risotto ai funghi—* the rice from the Po Valley, the mushrooms from a forest up north. The last light is lovely, slowly crawling up the Gothic brick façade of the church, brushing over the big rose window.

We are just blocks from Augustine's final resting place. How would the best mind of Christianity have viewed this evening? He said everything made by God is beautiful and good because God is beautiful and good. But then he drew up a long list of prohibitions regarding these beautiful and good things. He went into a fit of self-flagellation over being "much attracted to theatre," his fondness for "food and drink" and "beauty of a lower order." He loathed his restless early inquisitiveness—"this futile curiosity masquerading under the name science and learning." He never reconciled pleasure with piety. And in seeing love of good things of this earth as bad, he retreated to a sanctimonious form of his old dualism.

As the night comes on, the small square fills with people. They arrive on bikes, in wheelchairs, the youngest on the shoulders of parents, the oldest helped along by their grandchildren. It's a buzzing crowd of all ages. We assume it must be a holiday event, reenactment of a miracle or rare military victory in a city battered by Charlemagne and Napoleon, the onetime capital of the Kingdom of the Lombards. But no—the church of Santa Maria del Carmine is celebrating something else, something simple. As we linger over dessert of poached pears, a spotlight is cast upon the flanks of the church. The gathering hushes to low murmurs, then silence. A woman walks up the steps of the church, takes a microphone.

"Buona sera, Pavia!"

The crowd roars. The woman soars. She is Antonella Ruggiero, as I discover from a poster, a star of some renown in Italy. She has the voice of an angel—neither fallen nor beatified, just a sweet, perfect tone. For the next hour, she sings, and people in the square are lost in the power of a human instrument put to its highest use.

When I left Canterbury in the spring, I wasn't sure what I would find on the Via Francigena. No pilgrim ever is. There are moments and days that you can't anticipate, and moments and days when there is clarity on some things. I know this now, as I did in Aosta—some bit of clarity. It follows me into the morning, when I wake with whatever is the opposite of a hangover. I hobble my way to the Basilica of San Pietro in Ciel d'Oro, named for the interior ceiling of gold. After Augustine's death in 430, his North African home of Hippo was besieged by Germanic Vandals. His remains were spirited off to Sardinia for safekeeping. When Muslim Saracens raided the island in the early eighth century, the bones were moved again, to Pavia.

And so here they are, inside a golden urn encased in glass, in a marble ark of ninety-five statues and fifty bas-reliefs depicting highlights of his long life. It's on a raised crypt, the dominant feature of a heavily frescoed and ornamented basilica. For almost thirteen hundred years, what was left of Augustine's mortal life has been a holy destination for popes, kings, and sojourners of the spirit. It's a good thing that this stack of brittle bones, little more than *ossobuco* without the marrow, is not what we remember of the great Doctor of the Faith. He asked the right questions. But some of his answers do not fit in a world that is so much more than sorrow and penance, more than denial, more than predestined awfulness or salvation, a world capable of producing joy and wonder in its everyday details. And those joys and wonders are not forbidden fruits— otherwise why would they be so abundant? To reject the "pleasure, beauty, and truth" that can be found in creation, as Augustine said he had to do in order to understand the divine, is not an argument for God. It's an argument against God.

TWENTY-SIX

A SERIES OF UNFORTUNATE EVENTS IN A SMALL CAR

We walk the few blocks from the old power corridor of Pavia, where the Holy Roman Emperor was crowned by the pope a thousand years ago, past storefronts selling cheap cigarettes and three-packs of underpants. The distance from the city's high mark, when all of Western Christianity looked to its cathedral, to the grittiness of workaday modern life is short. For me, hope crashes in just a few steps. I will not be moving on my own this morning and perhaps for many days to come. I apologize to Sophie and curse my fate and right foot. We have another mountain range still to cross, castle grounds to explore, saints to meet. Reluctantly, I decide to rent a car. After nearly a half day of hassles with an Avis outlet determined not to do any business, I get a Cinquecento—the classic, boxy, durable Fiat. Mule of cars.

We make it to Piacenza, less than forty miles away, in a blur. My, my, my, the Via Francigena passes by so quickly in a compact *macchina*. There is not enough time for anything to make an impression, to be startled by what comes around the bend, to experience the deep relief of finding another red-and-white V.F. road post or an informative fellow traveler, to feel the weather on your face. It's all *turn here, stop there, and don't slow down in the roundabout, you effing idiot.* And getting into a garage parking space the size of a birdcage is no small challenge. Nothing very pilgrim about any of it. You're not on a journey. You're not special. Nobody is going to wave to you, unless it's with a middle finger, or offer you a cold drink, or invite you in for focaccia, or tell you about their own experience with God, or call out *Bravo, pellegrino!* If you get lost, good luck. That's what Siri is for. If your car breaks down, hah! It's a Cinquecento, what did you expect. I don't mind the insane drivers. The rule is to get within six inches of the car ahead of you—that's six inches, even if you're moving at eighty miles an hour. I exaggerate. Ten inches. You menace that car until it gives up and lets you pass, even on a blind curve. There's a speed limit, sure, a posted one. The real limit is infinity.

I like one thing: the Autogrills along the highway. These may seem like interchangeable big-brand pit stops within the closed universe of Italian toll roads. In truth, each one is an oasis of steaming cappuccini and fresh-baked cornetti. You can get a big chunk of perfectly aged Parmigiano Reggiano from one bin, a wine sold nowhere else in the world from another. You line up at the bar, inhale your caffeine, and newly fortified, get back on the autostrada. The only disconcerting thing is the sight of bleary-eyed truck drivers downing their *caffè corretto*—the espresso corrected with a liberal shot of high-alcohol grappa.

We have a couple of errands in Piacenza, a city of 100,000 along the plain of the heaving Po. The ground is flat and the air is heavy. We're in Emilia-Romagna now, in a community that was once among the richest in the world. The great families built palaces and villas under the mostly tolerant thumb of a half-dozen conquerors, the same armies that marched through Pavia. To live under so many rulers from so many different sovereigns breeds a person who shrugs at nationalism, a person for whom the changing of one flag for another is little different from the change of seasons. The consistency, the thread that ties these northern Italian towns together, is the Via Francigena. It brought a lifeline of pilgrims, beginning not long after Sigeric wrote up his journey. At one point, Piacenza had more than thirty hostels for leg-sore seekers of the spirit.

Before we can sample Piacenza's *centro storico*, we need something from the industrial outer ring. I will not walk without a change in shoes. I'm looking for footwear that is open-air and nonrestrictive, allowing my blisters to heal. Good sandals would do. We find nothing at the *supermercato*, nothing at the normally reliable Coop. But a low-slung gathering of sad-looking stores is promising. At a chain outlet, I ask for *"sandali, per favore,"* like Jesus wore, preferably cheap. I'm out of luck. It's September, and the shoe selection has changed for the upcoming colder months. There is not a single pair of sandals in this entire mall, maybe in all of Piacenza. In another part of the store, Sophie finds a contender among the pajamas and bathrobes. A clerk eyes me trying on a pair of something with leather crossing over the top, open-toed. She rushes over to scold me, frowning, wagging her finger as if I'm a shoplifter caught in the act. In rapid-fire Italian, too fast for me to get most of it, the saleswoman tells me I do *not* want to make that purchase. Sophie translates.

"Those shoes are for old men."

"Old men . . ."

"You should not buy them."

"My toes are butchered. I need something like this. I don't care about fashion."

"You should care. What kind of man are you?"

"Well—"

"Don't you have any pride in yourself?"

"I'm in a triage situation."

"You are—let me guess, American?"

"Yes. You could tell?"

"No Italian man would ever be seen in . . . *those.*"

"Are they infectious? Faulty?"

"You put them on when you step outside the shower. They are

bathroom slippers. Never wear them anywhere but your bathroom. God would strike me dead if I let a man do that."

"Why?"

"Because it would make you look like a homeless man wandering around in his bathrobe, a crazy person talking to himself. *Un uomo pazzo!* The Carabinieri would be suspicious."

Maybe this attitude is a holdover from Mussolini's Fascists, who urged Italian men not to wear slippers because it would "feminize" them. I tell the clerk to wrap the shower shoes in a paper bag, and then I'll meet her at the counter after they're hidden, so no one can associate my purchase with her. Italians take great pride in making a *bella figura*; even being an accomplice to a violation of pride of appearance is a misdemeanor. In the car, I slide into new footwear. My toes can breathe.

We have to see Eataly in Italy, the market that sells the idealized projection of their cuisine and culture in the place from which it came. Nearby, we stop at the Italian idea of *our* food, something called the Old Wild West Steak House. It has chuck wagons out front, and life-shortening pallets of beef, fries, and big-gulp sodas inside. It's not a fair representation, of course. Even small American towns have Thai, Mexican, Chinese, or Indian food, and a decent diner with someone who will call you honey while pouring a bottomless coffee. You can walk a block in a big city and pass two dozen savory enticements from our immigrant citizenry, the food that makes America great. But what gets exported is cowboy swill from a dead era.

Piacenza's Eataly is two levels of homage to fruit, cheese, wine, bread, and pasta so beautifully presented you would think they are World Cup trophies. It's a big change from all the skeletal relics we've been looking at in church crypts. Eataly was started in 2007 by Oscar Farinetti, who opened the first of thirty-five stores in an old vermouth factory in Turin. He came out of northern Italy's Slow Food movement—dedicated to food that is "good, clean and fair," served in a way that it was meant to be eaten. His idea combined a school, a store, a gathering place, and a brand, all in one place. It would be the village on market day, capsulized and remade. The latest extension is a theme park in Bologna—a fortress of food, more than twenty acres, with stalls that stretch for half a mile, calling itself the world's largest "agri-food park."

I know this because my daughter is on somewhat of a food pilgrimage, in contrast to my search for the eternal verities of the Via Francigena. For every church I drag her into, she forces me to sample an unusual pasta from Parma or a fresh pesto from Portofino. She works at the Culinary Institute of America, trying to get companies and institutions to change the way they offer food, for the better. We have our concerns about Eataly. Sophie hates to see what is a typical market street in a typical town—a block with a *macelleria*, an *enoteca*, a *frutta e verdure*, and a *pasticceria*—commodified for mass duplication. But as we debate the merits of Eataly in Italy, I notice people are staring at me. Two little kids point and snicker. It's the shower shoes!

TIME TO CHECK IN with the pope. It's been a month of Sundays since I heard anything from the Vatican. The pontiff's handlers haven't closed out the chance of my asking the Holy Father a couple of questions, not just yet. He continues to embrace random pilgrims, taking the scarf of a walker to wear as his own, welcoming others in for a chat. "Pilgrimage is a symbol of life," he said early on in his papacy. "It makes us think of life as walking, as a path. If a person does not walk, but instead stays still, this is not useful." Francis has been making headlines. He pleaded with leaders of Europe not to turn away the migrants washing up on the Continent's shores, a message that is unpopular at this moment. He brought children from those desperation journeys into the gold-accented center of global Catholic power, had them face the cameras, and dared us to look into the eyes of the innocents, to consider what Christ would do. Our hearts are not hard, he insists.

The number of sex crimes by the clergy seems epidemic. The pope says all the right things; he's learned to speak the language of this trauma. "It is a sin that shames us," he wrote in a letter to bishops. "The sin of what happened, the sin of failing to help, the sin of covering up and denial, the sin of abuse of power." Clerical abuse, the pope said in a preface to a new book, is "an absolute monstrosity," leaving behind many victims. Some of those victims, he notes, took their own lives.

Francis praised a Swiss man, Daniel Pittet, who endured four years of rape and torment when he was a boy. "Forgiveness does not heal the wounds or wipe away the misery" of the monster who hurt him, Pittet wrote, but has "allowed me to burst the chains that bound me to him and prevented me from living." Francis is begging for forgiveness, a way to unbind many others of their chains. He will host a global summit on clergy abuse. Those who lost their childhoods, who fell into depression, rage, suicidal thoughts—the living victims—are invited. But beyond an airing of pain and a promise of new vigilance, something as shattering as the Reformation may be required for real change to happen. Francis himself may not survive as pope. Just how deep is the well of mercy for a church that keeps finding criminals among its men of God?

I also catch up with Carlo, through his blog. He's far into the Italian leg of a journey that began when he left his home in London about a week ahead of me. But he's starting to falter. He fell and hurt his hip in the Val d'Aosta. He's lost twenty-five pounds. He feels sick, weakened by the long walk. His feet are killing him. He's been vomiting. "I'm not well," he writes one day. "I hope to finish and not be hospitalized," he notes on another. And yet, though his body is complaining, though he has his doubts about finishing—as do I—the pilgrimage is bringing him closer to accomplishing some of the things he set out to do. He's been thinking about his late parents, what they meant to him, his place in the world they brought him into. And the other goal, to try to comprehend "the nature of God, or gods." He hasn't resolved this, but he has a better understanding than he did when he set out from England.

———

I'M READY TO LEAVE the haze and humidity of the Po Valley. Ahead, almost sixty miles out, is a different climate and a different world—the long backbone of the Apennines. Sophie doesn't drive a stick shift. I'm the solo pilot. But I want to look around, taking slower roads up to the mountain pass. The solution is the robo-voice on our phone GPS. She's someone who never took a single lesson in Italian. Her pronunciation is criminal. Cinque—properly pronounced *cheen*-kway—comes out of her auto-voice as "sin-cue." Via Benedetto Antelami is rendered as a street named for Ant-hill-of-my. It takes barely half an hour to get to Fidenza, but once we pass through the Roman portals of this lost-in-time town, we are lost on roads barely wider than a pushcart.

Sophie tells me to calm down, take a breath, and we'll try to translate the robot's atrocious accent. Our goal is the *duomo* of San Donnino, a prime pilgrim stop for centuries. I catch glimpses of its Romanesque towers, but that's followed by more inadvertent turns down wrong roads, and we lose sight of it. San Donnino was another headless martyr. A convert to Christianity in the late third century, he was decapitated by the Romans along the right bank of the river near this town. The saint picked up his head and crossed over the water to the other bank. Charlemagne, while passing through, found the remains when his horse died on the spot, miracle on miracle. Now it's the site of the cathedral that Google Maps is incapable of leading us to.

At one point, following the bot's directions, we end up in a medieval dead end—the thick, blank side of an ancient and unmovable edifice in front of us, towering stone walls on either side. We're stuck. All I can do is slowly back up, and hope I don't run over somebody's cat. I have only a few inches or so on either side of the car, even after pulling in the mirrors. Approaching the turnout, I'm sweating the slow retreat over the cobblestones. Then—*arrgghhhh*, the wail of metal on stone, the side of my

Cinquecento scraping against a much more durable object. I lean out to check. Shit! The crunch has left an ugly scar on the car from the front fender to the rear.

Fidenza is almost worth the anguish. After we find the church and park the battered Fiat, I go inside to talk with a parish volunteer, who stamps my *credenziali*. He explains the art on the façade. The life story of the martyred saint is told in carved detail, ending with a pair of angels carrying Donnino's severed head off to heaven. On another wall is a crowd of characters in bas-relief. They're Via Francigena pilgrims, walking single file, circa eleventh century. The medieval travelers are dressed in tunics, their feet in simple sandals, hauling their loads on their backs— a bindle on a stick. A dog is atop a horse, and at the head of the procession is a man with a sword, the protector.

A cynical historian would say these people were illiterate peasants— rubes getting fleeced by relic dealers and hoax peddlers on a dubious journey of the soul. They're walking to Rome, a once-in-a-lifetime odyssey to stay out of hell, following the imperatives of a pope whose primary motive is to fill the coffers of the church. Certainly, there is some truth to that. But I cannot look at distant wanderers along the same trail I'm now following and fail to feel some connection with them, knowing what the cynics could not. In jubilee years, such as 1300, two million people walked to Rome. Any day could be their last. About half were robbed—and many killed—along the way. They seldom had an idea what was beyond the next river or mountain range. I have a car with access to a map of every square mile on earth, and also, a blistered foot and scrapes along the side of a fast-moving vehicle. Who from the medieval days wouldn't trade places with me? And among these silent pilgrims, the stony sojourners in the statuary of Fidenza's cathedral, is an encouragement. The most prominent of the bas-reliefs is a depiction of Saint Peter, the fisherman whom Christ entrusted with building a faith. He was not fluid in Greek, was unlearned in theological law, and could be stubborn and skeptical—a pragmatic man of labor. The fingers of Peter, the mariner who met Christ at the Sea of Galilee, point in a southerly direction. His other hand holds a scroll with these words in Latin: I show you the way to Rome.

THE CINQUECENTO WHEEZES as we make our way up the Apennine foothills, ascending the third mountain range of the Via Francigena, after the Juras and the Alps. We took a right turn just before Parma, leaving the Po's flatland for cleaner, crisper air. I'm pissed about banging up the car. I ordered all the insurance, but still, it's weighing on me. It shouldn't. Twenty years ago, when we lived in the heart of the Chianti Classico region, I came around a sharp turn in the hills and collided with a deer that sprang onto the roadway. Blood, flesh, and fur splattered all over the front windshield. The fender was badly mangled. The kids were freaked. I took the car back to the rental agency in Florence and showed two men what had happened. I spoke no Italian and relied on a book for basic translations.

"I've been hit by venison," I said, in a quickly cobbled attempt at a sentence. "What can I do?"

The men started to laugh. One of them clapped me on the shoulder and explained. I should sauté up a little garlic in olive oil, maybe throw in some mushrooms, and open a bottle of good Chianti. It goes well with venison.

We follow the trickling remnants of the Taro, as the V.F. does, gaining altitude. The river is depressingly dry, most of its wide, rock-strewn channel exposed and bleached by the sun. We pass pine forests, the first change in ecology in some time, thick chestnut trees, and a small town, Berceto, with a large trove of treasures and illustrated manuscripts on display in the nine-hundred-year-old church. Grateful pilgrims, happy to be alive at this perilous point in their journey, left behind little offerings in Berceto. Robbers lurked in the forest, lying in wait to ambush those struggling to get to the pass. In response, the woods were cleared on either side of the V.F., as wide as the arrows of predatory archers could fly.

Passo della Cisa, at 3,415 feet above sea level, is the high point, a welcoming nub along the spine of Italy. From here on, every drop of rainfall is pulled toward the Ligurian Sea. We park the car, and I walk gingerly in my shower shoes toward a stairway above the pass that rises to a chapel of glacial stone and slate. Popcorn clouds are low and white on the horizon, the green and marbled Apennines spread out below. At the crest just ahead, a large, carved wooden portal is an invitation to carry on, to take those next steps to the next destination. *Porta Toscana della Francigena*, the gateway to northern Tuscany. It's many steps to the top, and I take them slowly, as was intended by design.

I think of the butterfly effect of not properly taping my toes in the Alps. It is said that the fluttering of a monarch's wings in one continent can set off atmospheric events in another, a chain reaction, starting with the slight pressure on surrounding molecules and ending with the convulsion of heavy air that leads to a hurricane. It's a theory. Had I taken the right precaution, I would never have needed the car, never have gotten lost in the Dark Age warren of Fidenza, never have scraped the side. I'd be walking, as I'm struggling to do now, beneath the portal to Tuscany. It's impossible not to see a message here: Take the time and care to let the Via Francigena reveal itself, respect the pace, and have one ear attuned to the elements, another to the groans of your body. What did Father John of Flavigny say? Listen.

TWENTY-SEVEN

THE WAY OUT OF A LABYRINTH

The drop from the pass leads to the first sniff of Mediterranean air. Hairpin turns reverse through the forest, in and out of early-fall canopy, down, down until we pick up the River Magra, another pallid stream sucked dry by Lucifer's heat. We're in the Lunigiana, northern Tuscany. It should come with its own glorious soundtrack. We drop anchor at the base of a well-fortified town, Pontremoli, where pilgrims once coiled behind castle walls and burrowed into darkened sleeping quarters. Here, they could atone for their sins, forgive their enemies, write up a last will in anticipation of not making it home. They already would have made arrangements for spouses to remarry. Pontremoli means Trembling Bridge; the span we cross on foot lives up to it, as twisty in places as a piece of licorice. Yet it stands.

Also upright, for going on nine hundred years, is a column inside Saint Peter's in the town proper. The church was nearly destroyed by aerial bombing during World War II. A labyrinth, one of the oldest in Italy, is carved onto this pillar of resistant sandstone. Ah, the mysteries of the Catholic Church, embedded like so many clues along one of the oldest religious highways in the world. Who knows how many weary eyes have stared into that circular maze, wondering if they would ever get to the center? And why did it withstand the destruction, when nearly everything around it crumbled?

I trace a way in with my fingers, going to the left as you're supposed to do. I'd seen a similar one in Piacenza, with this inscription: "The labyrinth represents the world, wide for those who enter, but very tight for those who want to get out." I think of it as an abstract road sign, truth in the telling that many dead ends and false starts still lie ahead. And here it is, just as we cross a milestone: only 300 miles to Rome.

Every other shop window is a tease for testaroli, the oldest pasta in Europe, its origins dating perhaps to the Neolithic age. Sophie is salivating at a chance to experience the best food relic on the Via Francigena. But before lunch, we clamber up a narrow path to the thousand-year-old castle, an immense hulk looming over the valley. At the entrance is a large room for the ancient ones who turned this ground when Rome was but a shepherd's path. They left behind statues the size of tombstones, flat on the front, depicting men and women who appear to be a species unknown to the family of hominids. The bodies are legless, the heads are somewhat oval, like footballs, or—excuse the pop cultural reference—Stewie, the wry toddler with the British accent in *Family Guy*.

These figures are a mystery, which adds to the aura of a stretch of the Via Francigena stocked with riddles. The male type holds a dagger and has no penis. The woman has breasts barely larger than chocolate chips. Hundreds of these Stele Statues were scattered around the valley in farm fields, or buried beneath the sea. Now they have a rightful place here, on display as native Italians, not unlike our Anasazi in the American Southwest.

I have a question, which the museum caretaker cannot answer: Were the souls of these pre-Christians doomed? The teaching on the "unlearned," as theologians put it, is a muddle. Augustine said they were condemned, having had the misfortune of being born before Christ, and that the only way into heaven was through professed love of the Lord.

This is clearly not something he thought through. Or if he did, he settled on a conclusion of cruelty. But as with other punitive theories put forth by Augustine, his view was later soldered into church doctrine. Another long-held idea put our pagan ancestors in a holding pattern in something akin to purgatory, the delayed-flight lounge from which they were finally freed by the risen Jesus. The most humane of the suppositions says that people who lived good lives, even if they worshipped a tree trunk, would have desired baptism had it been available, and therefore can be granted a pass into heaven. God saves all people—not only Christians. That seems to be the current view of the church, post the 1960s reforms of Vatican II.

More than any place I've seen on the trail, even Laon in France, this three-thousand-year-old town has managed to lock time into place. Here it's the year 1226, when Frederick II came storming through. Rather than rape and pillage, this Holy Roman Emperor declared Pontremoli a free city. Wine, property rights, and a clean conscience for all! Every August, his arrival is reenacted before thousands of people who come to wear scratchy tunics, eat testaroli, and try to figure out how to operate a catapult. Pontremoli has lost half its population over the last eighty years. Our longing for all things medieval is what keeps it alive.

Frederick II is fascinating, another enigma. In church history, he served a term as the Antichrist for his constant challenges to the imperial curia. But he was also known as *Stupor Mundi*—the Wonder of the World. Instead of shedding blood while in the Holy Land during one of the Crusades, he peacefully divided Jerusalem, made alliances with Muslims, and enlisted "infidels" as personal bodyguards. Christian and Islamic sacred places would be under the care of their respective faiths. To the Knights Templar, this was traitorous; they tried to assassinate him under papal orders. In Sicily, he similarly reached out to an oppressed people, employing Jews in his inner circle. Another sin. One of his greatest reforms was getting rid of trial by ordeal, in which people were subjected to life-ending horrors as a way to prove guilt or innocence. So, a woman accused of adultery would be weighted down with stones and thrown in a river. If she floated back to the surface, she was set free. If a face survived a plunge into a vat of boiling oil, God was revealing his verdict. But as Frederick knew, gravity and 300 degrees were immutable laws. Today, Pope Francis would embrace Frederick for his reaching across religious lines and his progressive sense of justice. In his era, he was excommunicated four times by three popes.

Lunch is at a trattoria on a cliff overlooking the halfhearted river. Everyone is eating testaroli, a workaday meal for five euros. We'll have what they're having. The pasta is made from a spongy flatcake—a batter of water, flour, salt, and a pinch of rosemary cooked on a *testo*, a hot skillet or terra-cotta. The big round is cut into diamond-shaped slices and smothered with a rich pesto sauce, topped by a dash of pecorino. The porous surface soaks up the Ligurian flavors—pine nuts, basil, garlic. Like the best Italian food, testaroli is simple, without fuss, the taste true to its ingredients. Our waiter tells us that only three farmers in this part of Italy grow the coarse grain used to make testaroli. The food was a staple of the Etruscans, and fuel for those fashioners of half-moon heads on stone. Through the centuries, through many overlords who introduced strange food, peasants never stopped eating it. And now testaroli is enjoying a renaissance, as people look to the attics of time for different flavor experiences.

DOWN THE VALLEY twenty miles is another labyrinth, this on a wall inside one of the oldest monasteries on the V.F., the Abbey of San Caprasio, founded in 884. The place still serves as a hostel. A welcoming priest, Father Giovanni Perini, invites us to have a look around. The artifacts from those who came this way over the centuries are the best I've seen. I'm taken by the shoes of pilgrims, like moccasins, remarkably thin-soled, and a cloak of someone who arrived not long after Sigeric left. A single lace binds the footwear. There's a leather pouch, a walking stick, a rucksack, and a hollowed-out gourd to hold water. The sash at the beltline of the cloak is a rope.

I ask Father Perini what kind of pilgrim stops over at his outpost.

"They're highly educated, for the most part. Women more than men. Many are not Catholic. They're searching for something."

"What would that be?"

"It's not always clear."

The priest is about fifty years old and looks a bit like Jerry Seinfeld, with a brow of furrowed world-weariness. He opens his top shirt button and removes his Roman collar. It's hot, inside and out. A homeless man with long fingernails and a bird's nest of hair wanders in; he's given a drink and some food. This is a place of hospitality, without vetting. Father Perini pours cold water for us. He glances at a beeping cell phone and lets it go.

"They want to talk about their marriages. Their jobs. Their families. A woman who came through here last week told me walking the trail helped her make a big decision in her life. I don't know what that was, but she said it was a big decision. My sense is that people who do the whole Via end up with a major change in how they live."

"What sort of change? They become more spiritual?"

"Not necessarily. They learn how to think clearly."

"It's not like they forgot."

"I can speak only about my country, and here's the problem for Italians. Thirty years ago, everyone took a siesta in the afternoon. Rest. Relax. Sleep a little. Now everyone works, works, works all the time. It's all about work and money, work and money. *Lavoro e soldi! Lavoro e soldi!* People don't have time to think. Then they start walking on the Via Francigena. Now they have time. More time than ever in their life. They are not used to having time to think. They are out of practice. A lot of people on the Via, they won't even go into a church. They say that they're walking to practice mindfulness." He stifles a chuckle. "Mindfulness. They used to call it living."

He invites us to observe the labyrinth. It's traditional for pilgrims to follow the path with their fingers while praying. Chiseled in one corner of the maze are words attributed to Saint Paul: *Sic currite ut comprehendatis*—so run to comprehend. It's a reminder that life is short, that there are far greater things than *lavoro e soldi*, so get on with the real search.

THE TRAIL TURNS SOUTHEAST near the coast, clinging to the base of the Apuan Alps, a side range. The sea is just ahead, turquoise and white-capped. The more diverting image is inland, in mountains of gleaming white. It's not snow, but marble flanks that reflect the late-afternoon sunlight. These are the rock beds that provided the stone for the Pantheon and Trajan's triumphal column in Rome, producing more marble than any other place on earth. Michelangelo came to these quarries overlooking the town of Carrara, a mile above the Mediterranean, at the height of the Renaissance. Carrara smells of white dust and decay, an old company town with a story. It barely stirs but for the buzz of cutting machines in the distance. The flanks overhead resemble ice blocks of a fresh-cleaved glacier.

Most people look on this scene and see industry and maybe a kitchen remodel. Those who know their history are reminded that Rome's luster was built on slave labor, all the broken human backs it took to move a mountainside. But it's also the terroir of genius. Michelangelo's brilliance was seeing emotion in hard rock, a moment in marble. Every block of stone "has a statue inside it, and it is the task of the sculptor to discover it," he said. His slabs were slid downhill, lowered by cable to the water, then hauled by barge up the Po to the master's studio in Florence. He fashioned the *David*, the most exquisite human form ever sculpted, from Carrara rock. But my favorite is the *Pietà*, cut from a shank he called the "most perfect" he had ever worked on. In his hands, a marble chunk was transformed into a grieving mother holding a dead child, all life gone from the body of the slain Christ. Jesus is never more human than in his mortality. He's not God. He's not King of the Jews, or the Messiah. He's Mary's boy, flesh without soul, gone. The *Pietà* captures a duty that no mother ever wants—to put a son into a tomb, the same thing my sister went through. It is the only piece ever signed by Michelangelo. He was twenty-four when he sculpted it.

Along the shore, Carrara's most valuable export is loaded onto ships, a million tons a year, for bathrooms in Las Vegas and showrooms in Saudi Arabia. We pass through this industrial stretch, the mountains to our left. The land softens and smooths before it flattens at the place where the Etruscans planted a city along the River Serchio. The exit to Lucca comes at the end of a long day. I'm tired. Sophie has some kick left in her. But as we pass through Lucca's walls, under the V.F.-signed Porta San Donato, I'm a new man. Lucca is its own labyrinth, and all the dead ends are alluring. The way to see it is to throw aside any map and follow the most curious thing just ahead of you.

Every city along the Via Francigena seems to have some trace of its old defensive walls. Lucca's redbrick ramparts rose five hundred years ago to resist the Florentines, who never came. What was built for war would force Lucca inward, to make every square foot of the limited urban plat work as part of the whole. Lucca stands out because the walls are intact, encircling an entire city of nearly 90,000 people. Inside, the design of the Roman colony, its street plan, forum, square, and theater, are lively and much used, as intended. Remember what Churchill said: We shape our buildings, and thereafter, they shape us. Odoacer, the barbarian who crowned himself King of Italy after forcing the last Roman emperor of the West to abdicate, sacked this place. You would never know. Napoleon installed his sister Élisa Bonaparte, as the "Princess of Lucca." By most accounts, she was a devoted and civic-minded ruler, helping to transform the top of the walls into a tree-shaded promenade.

I have just enough time to get a V.F. stamp at the fantastically frescoed church of San Frediano, named for the Irish monk who ended his years of roaming around Europe here. "Wandering is an ineradicable habit of the Irish race," wrote a fellow monk. Well, that explains it. Frediano tried to live a hermit's life nearby. He was lured out of seclusion by a flood that threatened to destroy Lucca. On his command, the Serchio jumped its channel and spared the city, something no Irishman has done since. He lived to nearly ninety, an almost impossible feat in the sixth century, and a tribute to the healthful air of Lucca. The breath of the sea blows in one way, another breeze comes down from the mountains. They used to call Lucca the city of a hundred churches, but the count is now down to barely a dozen that are open for worship. The one I have to see is the Cathedral of San Martino—not for the building, but for its legendary labyrinth. I get there just as the light is starting to fade. I'll be back.

In the evening, streets that were empty upon our arrival are full, shops doing a lively business, young and old, well dressed in a city compact enough that word would soon get around if you ever made less than a *bella figura*. We're lucky to have friends, Paolo and Paola Pacini, who invite us to their apartment in a Renaissance tower for drinks, and then make sure we eat at La Buca di Sant'Antonio. We have the full attention of their friend the chef. It's one of those nights when you wish you had multiple stomachs, like the ruminants we saw wandering the Alps. The restaurant is in the basement of an old horse stable, and has been serving food longer than the United States has been a country. The red wine is from the hills outside the walls, made of grapes we never see beyond Tuscany. For starters, we try little pies of leeks and ricotta, a liver pâté, and trout carpaccio. Then chestnut gnocchi. They serve baby goat from a spit, guinea fowl smothered in muscat grapes, and other dishes that I will replay slowly in my mind next time I'm stuck in a TSA line at the airport. Dessert is the house cannoli. Can we get it to go?

This is Sophie's last night, and it saddens me. There's an improving chance that my wife, Joni, will join me for the last hundred miles to

Rome. Margie lives from scan to scan, the Groundhog Day loop through chemo, hope, and test results. If Joni can get away in the brief recovery period after Margie takes her latest dose of poison, it would do her good. I don't use the word "miracle" because it seems too facile, but Margie has asked me to pray for her. She also wondered about the religion of our children. Joni told her it was complicated. "It *is* complicated," Margie replied. "Until you need it."

I'm curious if being on the Via Francigena has changed Sophie.

"I wish I could go all the way to Rome with you."

"But has it changed your thinking in any way?"

"It's helped my thinking."

"How so?"

"The process of elimination. I'm definitely not an atheist. It feels too extreme. And also because it sets it all up so negatively, like casting doubt on everyone I know and love who does have God as the central organizing feature of their belief system."

"So you believe in God?"

"Sorry, Dad. I can't tell you honestly that I do believe."

"Agnostic? Like your brother?"

"I know agnostic is also a little lazy, since it spares you the trouble of really thinking hard about the bigger 'it'—the question of how we got here, the origins of life."

"What do you believe?"

"I believe in molecules in motion, in the Big Bang, in evolutionary biology."

"So do I. So does Pope Francis. The Vatican held that poor wretch Galileo under house arrest for staring into the cosmos and stating the obvious. But this pope says the more science the better."

"And certainly there are things that can't be explained by science. But I guess I'm wired by reason and logic."

"The Jesuits would love you."

"I don't like labels. I don't have a text or Bible I consult. But I know what I believe in. I value family, friends, love, community, lifelong learning, continuous self-improvement, reflection, creative expression, empathy, care of the natural world and all the creatures who inhabit it."

"You're going to be fine."

TO THE WALLS, to walk off the feast. Of course we take the cannoli, if only to be able to say the line. This is a *passeggiata* to remember. The night air is settled and warm enough for us to be coatless. The city is aglow; to the north, you can discern the outline of the mountains with a half-moon on the rise. We're forty feet above Lucca's floor, on a foundation that is a hundred feet wide at the base. The Guinigi Tower, with its trees growing from the top, stands out. I don't recognize any other landmarks. I did not keep track of where we started, nor am I sure where we will end. It's impossible to get lost. Wherever we drop down we are in Lucca, inside the embrace of the walls, and that is more than enough for happiness.

SOPHIE LEAVES BEFORE DAWN, off to Pisa in the dark, several flights and home to the West Coast. She also leaves a hole in my days, and it hits me quickly—I'm alone. What helps is this city, quick to come to life, a balm to strangers. Most of Lucca is the color of Tuscany, that sunflower yellow that looks so warm in the first and last hours of the day. I'm easily distracted on my slow walk to the Cathedral of San Martino. The labyrinth is at the western end, cut into a single stone on a prominent pillar.

Christian labyrinths came out of Greek mythology. A Latin inscription on the pillar explains that the design originated in Crete, a multi-chambered dungeon where King Minos disposed of his victims. It was overseen by his daughter, Ariadne, Goddess of the Labyrinth. No one who entered was ever able to get out; they were lost forever or mauled at the center by Minotaur, a half-man, half-bull. Every year, this king demanded fresh human sacrifices. Theseus volunteered. He was determined to kill the beast, even if it meant he would never be able to exit. Ariadne fell in love with the selfless boy. She offered him a spool of thick string, told him to unravel it as he went deep into the puzzle. He slayed Minotaur, freed those locked at the center, and found his way out by following the thread. He married Ariadne and sailed away to Athens.

This labyrinth once had an image of Theseus and Minotaur, but it grew faint with the rubbing of many fingers, until it disappeared entirely. While the mythic Greeks are gone, their message remains. You don't solve a labyrinth. You sacrifice for others. When you run your fingers over the grooves of pilgrims past, you're humbled by the not-knowing, the lack of direction. You need courage to enter and help to exit, though most Catholics would say once you're in, you never get out.

TWENTY-EIGHT

IN THE PATH OF THE LITTLE POOR MAN

The Franciscans opened the doors of their home on the rise above San Miniato some eight hundred years ago, a place of refuge and reflection through the centuries, no questions asked. You can see why someone would want to spend a life here, glazed by the Tuscan sun, high enough to catch the breeze in the afternoon and provide an unobstructed view of the fraternal luminaries of moon and stars at night. The lights of Florence, Pisa, and Lucca flicker in the distance. The monastery is redbrick and simple with a Romanesque façade, vaulted timbers inside, a lovely cloister. Saint Francis himself, Il Poverello, founded this abbey a decade or so before he died in rags and emaciation in the year 1226. But you won't get the lone priest who still greets Via Francigena pilgrims here to brag on this provenance. The staying power of Francis the mystic, Francis the lover of all living things, is humility. He and his followers were inferior to all, superior to none. He was the original holy fool. He danced. He sang. He laughed at his inadequacies. Shoeless and gaunt, he impressed the pope in Rome, won over the sultan in Egypt, gave comfort to the homeless in hovels. "Start by doing what is necessary," he said, "then do what is possible, and suddenly you are doing the impossible."

The impossible here is finding enough brothers to keep the monastery going through a ninth century. "We have only five friars left," said Father Alessandro Pretini, in announcing the end of Franciscan domain over this place, another sad mark in a church that cannot replenish the ranks of those who take holy orders. Worldwide, the number of Catholics has doubled in the last fifty years, yet there are fewer priests than in 1970. This place is run now by a group dedicated "to bringing joy to those who have lost hope," a lay charity, with a sole priest in residence.

The bones of Saint Francis are in Assisi, his hometown, in the basilica with the frescoes attributed to Giotto. The most dramatic scene shows him renouncing all material goods at the age of twenty-five. It's a moment that has never lost its hold on the world. Francis could have had it so easy: father a merchant laying out a path for the boy, business trips abroad, a villa with a view, his bride the best-looking woman around. He's beloved in his youth, a charming cutup, one of the town troubadours. He parties all night, sleeps until noon, commits "every kind of debauchery," his first biographer writes. His ambition is to be a knight, and for that he has to prove himself. He goes to war against the neighboring town of Perugia. He's knocked from his horse, cut and beaten, captured, cast into a rat-filled dungeon, released only because his father could afford the ransom. Back home, he's still determined to be a warrior with honor, but he's a wreck. War changes him. He's deeply depressed. Reluctantly, he outfits himself in armor, rides off to join crusading Christians sailing for the Holy Land. The pope has promised absolution for waging the latest in a century of intermittent war.

But during his first night on the road, he has a dream. It's stark and convincing, a call to a different life. In the morning, he can't shake it. He heads for a cave to think about what's happening to him. On the way home, he meets a leper, one of the castoffs living in the shadows of Umbria. He leaps from his horse and takes the man's hand, the skin mottled with scales and horrid black boils, soothes him. He kisses the leper on the lips. The touch changes his life. "What had seemed bitter to me was turned into sweetness of body and soul," he writes. In seclusion, he fasts and prays. And now another dream: Christ tells him to "repair my church." It's broken, corrupt, run by charlatans and hypocrites. The poor live shunned lives in sodden squalor, while bishops and other clerics reside in the opulent splendor of sun-washed hill towns. But what is he? Soon, just a half-starved man in a loincloth.

At home, he reveals his new life to his father. The patriarch is apoplectic. In public, Francis sheds his clothes, this at a time when the silks of nobles projected authority and status, and renounces any claim to family wealth. *That moment.* He wants to serve the poor, the passed over, beggars and sinners. His depression lifts. Into the wild he goes, singing. He seems . . . happy! What kind of lunatic is this prominent son of Assisi? He visits a priest living with a woman, an open scandal. Surely he'll scold the cleric or tell him to break it off and repent. Instead, he kisses the wayward father's hands. Soon, Francis is the talk of Umbria: they say he's crazy, wrong in the head. Robbers will get him if disease doesn't. He's mocked, taunted. But here's the thing his former friends don't understand: poverty is the ultimate freedom. You can't rob someone who has no possessions. You can't insult a person without pride.

He preaches to birds, tames a wolf, performs miracles, so they say. His philosophy is simple: all living things share a spirit. He's not a priest, has no standing in the church. He's not even an evangelist, for he says the only way to convince another of your faith is by wordless example. He begs for his meals, sleeps on a dirt floor. Still, he has the troubadour spirit. He likes to joke, to dance, to sing. "It is not fitting, when one is in God's service, to have a gloomy face or a chilling look," he says. His days of musical poetry serve him well when he writes his "Canticle of Brother Sun," said to be the first verse in the Italian language. When he goes to see the pope in Rome, the mighty Innocent III turns him away. He finds Francis repulsive, a wretch in a filthy tunic. The pope is busy ginning up fresh war with Islam, creating punishments for heretics, persecuting

Jews, tightening his grip over the Papal States, those territories in Italy under his direct sovereign rule. Innocent wants to conquer Jerusalem, to kill the Muslim infidels. His executions extend to Europe as well. In one day, on his watch, twenty thousand Christians of a different sort are slaughtered in southern France—murdered for heresy, three hundred years before the first Protestants were killed. "Go, brother," the most powerful pope of medieval times tells Francis. "Go to the pigs, to whom you are more fit to be compared than men, and roll with them."

When Francis returns from the sty, the pope relents, granting the persistent pauper a few minutes of his time. Francis proposes something bold. Instead of sending new armies to the Holy Land to fight and die, why not send him—a war veteran? It's an absurd idea. It takes seven years, and several aborted attempts, including a shipwreck, to pull it off. Francis walks much of the way through Egypt, at the cost of his health. He goes behind battle lines, which will surely get him killed. But nothing touches the man who has nothing. The mystic arrives bedraggled at the headquarters of the enemy. He's captured, but still gets his audience with the Sultan of Egypt, Malik al-Kamil. The holy man of Islam has grown tired of armed conflict. Francis himself is scarred by war, he explains.

"May the Lord give you peace," he says.

They argue about their respective Gods, built around two of the three religions connected to Abraham the patriarch and prophet, but move on, an attempt at ending further Crusades. The sultan admires some things about Christianity, and Francis is open to tenets of Islam. After he leaves, and for the rest of his life, Francis urges his followers to open their hearts to those that his pope wants to hate and kill.

Among the followers is Clare of Assisi, who enlists women to take up the way of Francis, to find redemption in helping the lowest among humans. For the last fourteen years of his life, she's a partner in poverty. But she is no supplicant. Born into one of the most important families in

Umbria, her father owned a palace in Assisi and a castle on the mountain above town. After hearing Francis speak, she leaves home as a teenager, exchanges her jewels and dresses for a rough robe and veil. She gives up all property, severs family ties, and lives in a shared community. She is the first woman to found a monastic order in Italy, known as the Poor Clares. The name is similar to the one Francis gives to his followers, Friars Minor.

Francis makes regular visits to a mountain outside Arezzo, La Verna, more than three thousand feet above the valley floor of the Arno. To get there, he hacks through woods and scrambles over rock to a knob of land donated to the Franciscans by a rich man. His health is failing. He contracted malaria while in North Africa. He also suffers from trachoma, an eye infection that makes him appear to be crying. He looks terrible. He seems to be withering before people's eyes, and yet, with each physical diminishment, his power grows. He sleeps in an open-air cave on the mountain, trying to get closer to God. Then it happens—a vision, an appearance, a jolt of transformation. He feels it instantly. The palms of his hands take on blood-hardened scars, as do his feet—as if a nail had been embedded in his skin. In his side is an open gash, similar to the one a Roman soldier delivered to Christ on the cross. He has the stigmata, the first person ever to claim the wounds of Jesus.

As he deteriorates over the last years of his life, he retreats to ever more austere conditions. Clare is with him, their souls fused in defiance of material comfort. Fire is a brother. So is the moon. So are the stars. So, in the end, is death. He still sleeps on a dirt floor, not unlike the dungeon in Perugia. When given a gift of food or a blanket, he passes it on to the poor. He has reached the state that he prayed for, when he asked God to "grant me the treasure of sublime poverty." He shows symptoms of leprosy, which he may have picked up from the sick that he would never turn away. What food he eats he can barely hold down. He dies in 1226 at the age of forty-five. Within ten years, there are five thousand Franciscans. His followers could have broken off, as did those inspired by Martin Luther three hundred years later. But they chose to stay with Rome, a counter to the overindulgent tendencies of other men of the cloth. Today, it's the largest religious order within the Catholic Church, still trying to live by the words of the mystic from Assisi. "Preach the Gospel at all times," he said. "When necessary use words."

I'm welcomed at the monastery with the traditional Franciscan greeting *"Pace e bene a tutti,"* and asked if I plan to stay the night. No, probably not. The road from Lucca was a mere twenty-five-mile drive. The day is young. My toes are healing nicely. I'll be back on the ground soon, ditching the car. A picture of Pope Francis is prominent here, as you would expect of the only pontiff to take the saint's name. He must know that he leads a church on the brink, in need of the kind of reawakening—or shove—that the Little Poor Man gave it eight hundred years ago.

Up north at La Verna, buses deliver thousands of people daily at the shrine where Francis received his stigmata. When I visited a few years ago, there was a long queue to see the rock where he knelt when given the wounds of the Lord. I hiked through a forest in the clouds above the parking lot, entered a monastery and church complex, where a placard warned: "Dear Pilgrim, do not write crosses on the wall. God bless you." The sanctuary was mobbed with all nationalities. The saint is a rock star. Long-robed and sandaled Franciscans roamed the byways, under *Silenzio* signs. I passed through a portico frescoed with the story of his life, opened a spiked metal door, and descended to a slab where Francis slept and was physically transformed, the open-air cave. The saint's relics—a bowl and drinking glass, his walking stick, a stain of his blood from a cloth he used to dab his stigmata—were inside a small chapel. In a huge, high-ceilinged dining hall, pilgrims ate pasta Bolognese and roasted chicken and drank wine crafted from vineyards below. It reminded me of a national park lodge.

I don't know if I believe in the stigmata. Whether it's true or not doesn't change my view of Francis. The silken and scented senior members of the Vatican curia couldn't wait for Francis to die. *He'll soon be gone*, they told themselves, *but we'll still be here*—the same thing they say about Pope Francis. But the Little Poor Man endures, the movies and biographies and buses climbing up the La Verna mountainside, because of that life story. At Stanford University's main library is a huge archive containing nothing but books, PhD theses, ephemera, and original writings from and about him. When I was there, I felt overwhelmed. You would think he was Cicero, Lincoln, or Napoleon. He had no army. He painted no masterpieces. He invented nothing. He ruled over nothing. He owned nothing. He was a waif from a dark and superstitious age.

So why do they need the miracle of the stigmata? Why did *he* need the open sores of an execution? I understand the desire to feel the pain of Christ, the ultimate way to submissiveness of self. But I also wonder if Francis would have the same hold on the material world had he not been linked to the miraculous—or for that matter, would Jesus? Leo Tolstoy, the mystic and Russian novelist, produced a literary experiment to test this premise. While in the midst of a profound spiritual crisis, Tolstoy tried to translate the four Gospels of the New Testament into a single story—minus the supernatural. His miracle-free gospel is a riveting story of a poor man who upends the planet with a message about loving other people. "In Christ's teaching," Tolstoy concluded, "lies the truth." It is enough for me to know that Francis spent a few nights in this aerie above San Miniato, shunning a bed for the floor.

In the Old World, the Roman Catholic Church is teetering—from secularism, from neglect, from the law, from its many self-inflicted blows, from an armament of secrecy. In the New World, it's deeply distressed. It grows, rapidly and vigorously and joyously, in places where people are hearing the stories of people like Saint Francis for the first time. As the Little Poor Man and his followers knew, arguments don't change minds; stories do. In looking for answers to its woes, a place for the church to start is what inspired the creation of this abbey, the lasting hold of one man's radical humility.

TWENTY-NINE

ALLEGORIES ON THE WALL

Out of a Tuscan dreamscape of cypress and silver-green olive trees, the towers of San Gimignano poke through the haze of autumn. A mere thirteen of the original seventy-two still stand. You see them from the valley, from nearby hill towns, from one-lane roads corkscrewing upward. If you'd been walking since Canterbury, this was the vision on the horizon long dreamed of. The medieval skyscrapers, built with the wealth of saffron dealers, were most welcoming, but also a warning. San G. lost two-thirds of its population to the Black Death, a reminder of how swiftly life could be taken in 1348. The sweep of sudden mortality focused your mind on what was beyond this life, as did the frescoed narratives inside the city.

Near the crest, shadowed by those towers, you would enter the Collegiata and look up. What you saw in the ceiling of that basilica was one of the most graphic depictions of evil anywhere in the Christian world— Taddeo di Bartolo's *Last Judgment*. The naked and the damned are stabbed and dismembered by oily-skinned, horn-headed demons. A grotesquely obese devil is literally eating humans. A man labeled a "sodomite" is tortured with a stake running up his ass and through his mouth.

At the table of those guilty of gluttony is food that can never be consumed by people bound in chains for eternity around its rim. All is terror and fear, designed to make you tremble. You are doomed. *Repent, pilgrim!*

Taddeo's gruesome scenes are rooted in the cryptic words of Christ. The version from Matthew's Gospel has him separating the good from the bad at the end of the world. How you spent your time on earth determined your sentence—that is, whether you passed the test when Jesus said, "I was hungry and you gave me food, I was thirsty and you gave me something to drink, I was a stranger and you welcomed me, I was naked and you gave me clothing, I was in prison and you visited me." The twist in this bedrock homily of the faith is that it wasn't Jesus in need of those charitable acts. It was "the least of my members," as he said at the end of his revelation. In his own words, that is the essence of Christianity.

Damnation meant being cast "away to the eternal fire." And though Taddeo's depiction leaves little to the imagination, the words of Christ invite a broad range of interpretations. Among them: Allegory or fate? Pope Francis tried to clarify this before an audience of children. A tearful little boy named Emanuele asked the pontiff if his deceased father, an atheist, was in heaven. The pope turned to the other kids to see if they thought God would abandon the child's father. "No!" came the shouted return. "There, Emanuele—that is the answer." He hugged the boy and whispered into his ear: "God has the heart of a father." Another time, as he sat with fifteen hundred homeless who'd been invited into the Vatican for a surprise meal, Francis offered this guidance on the hereafter: "In the poor, we find the presence of Jesus," he said. "They are our passport to paradise."

SAN GIMIGNANO NEVER FAILS to light a few candles of fresh insight, even though the town is overrun by selfie-stick-thick platoons in all seasons. When we lived in Italy, on the first warm day of spring, we pulled our kids out of school early and came to San G. I bought a cardboard half liter of wine, a loaf of rustic Tuscan bread, some cheese, prosciutto, and blood oranges from Sicily. I found a grassy seat with a view, just outside the city walls, took my shirt off, and reveled in the sun's warmth. A few weeks earlier, we had shivered through a rare snowstorm. Now, little yellow violets bloomed from notches in the towers. Noting the bread crumbs on my chest, my wife looked at me with a mix of disgust and bemusement.

"You're just one irrigation ditch short of a full Spokane."

We kept our kids from seeing the *Last Judgment* that day. It would have scared them, requiring an explanation that might prompt nightmares. We never did give them a tutorial on heaven and hell—two exclusive clubs, with too many requirements for membership. Living a good life is its own reward. You shouldn't have to be frightened into doing the right thing, or incentivized by a hereafter of bliss. Still, you never stop wondering about the tomorrow after death. In my mother's last hour, she faded in and out, wheezed a final gasp of incomprehension, and showed no sign that she was crossing over to a new realm. "I'm not afraid to die," she had said. "I have no regrets." Up until she got sick, the most important thing on her schedule was charity work at the Society of St. Vincent de Paul, taking food and clothes to those who lived at the margins. I know how she treated the least among us, and so I have no worries for her soul passing the threshold set by Christ. And I know she did it because her heart compelled her to service, not because of any calculation about the afterlife.

This time around, passing through San G. as a Via Francigena traveler, I feel lighter than I did at the start of this pilgrimage. I don't expect a miracle cure for my wife's cancer-tortured sister, but I've found that wishing for one is the most humbling form of prayer. I may never understand the randomness of cruelty, but it's futile to expect an ordered design to events. Not everything has a rational explanation. I may not get a moment with the pope. I may never forgive his church, and his church may never be mine again. Still, the closer I get to Rome, the less cluttered my thinking.

In town, I notice something encouraging. The contrast to the grim end-times fresco is a little side chapel in the Collegiata devoted to a sickly girl who died at the age of fifteen, in the year 1253—Saint Fina. Through the pain of what was likely a form of tuberculosis, through the loss of both parents, she remained remarkably cheerful, choosing to lie on a rough wood board rather than a bed. Upon her death, a profusion of yellow blossoms appeared, sprouting from nooks on the gray exterior walls of San Gimignano. What I saw on that spring day many years ago still blooms every March—the golden gillyflowers of Saint Fina. The oak plank, big pieces of which are preserved in the chapel, is a prompt for much giving to hospitals in the area. The chapel walls are plaster palettes for the emotional depth of Fina's story as painted by Ghirlandaio, the man who mentored Michelangelo. She lives—in those charitable acts in her name, in the two frescoes, in the explanation for why a riot of yellow flowers appears every year around the day she died, on March 12. Her little corner of the basilica is far more crowded with people than the floor beneath the *Last Judgment* ceiling. We're drawn to Fina.

You take Siena on its terms. Siena, by legend, is nearly as old as Rome. There's always someone else to come along. Residents couldn't care one way or the other, unless it concerns the greatest horse race on earth, the Palio. Having exhausted all clues about the afterlife from the ghastly depiction of it in San Gimignano, I need a whiff of secular stimulation to close out a long day. Inside the Palazzo Pubblico, off Siena's oddly shaped Campo, is a lesson in fourteenth-century color. In the hall where municipal rulers met, the walls are frescoed with a vast tale of two cities: *The Allegory of Good Government and Bad*, painted by Ambrogio Lorenzetti circa 1337. *Good Government* depicts prosperous and healthy citizens, shiny homes, and clean animals—a well-built and well-run city. *Bad Government*, on an opposite wall, is a nightmare of graft and grifters, the vile and the vainglorious. The city is in ruins, scorched of its vegetation and beauty, brutes roaming the street. At the center is a figure labeled Tyranny, with horns sprouting from his head, fangs protruding over his lips, his eyes narrowed in a stare not unlike the laser-hard gaze of Vladimir Putin. The Black Death swept through Siena not long after this brilliant fresco cycle was completed. It killed the artist in 1348 and dealt a staggering blow to Siena. The city would not regain its population until the twentieth century.

A former convent, Alma Domus, now run by the local archdiocese, will put me up for the night. After a brief interrogation—yes, I'm married, but traveling alone, on the old trail to Rome—I get a room with a view of Lorenzetti's city. How lucky am I to be seeing Siena fresh, through a pilgrim's-eye view. With a quick ceremony, I say goodbye to the shower shoes. My *figura* will now be *bella*. And, using the Wi-Fi of the old convent's common room, I fire off a nag note to the pope. I don't phrase it that way. More like an update: I'm getting closer, I've learned much, but the questions loom. From the pope's published schedule, I know he'll be home when I'm in Rome. *Francis, dear Francis—a pilgrim with a pen needs some clarity.* I'm beginning to wonder, with sadness of heart, if the pontiff has gone dark on me.

The next day, it's a two-minute walk to the residence of Catherine of Siena, the saint born during the plague, one of the most influential female diplomats of an age when women were treated like domestic servants. She is one of the few women Doctors of the Church, recognized for her theological insight. She was instrumental in bringing the papal seat back to Rome, from its relocation in Avignon during a prolonged dispute. Beginning in 1309, more than half a dozen popes, all of them French, cocooned in a palace in southern France while Rome fell apart. The cause of the breakup was a familiar one—to me, at least, after picking up so many nuggets of history left along the V.F. The church wanted more secular control, and secular potentates wanted more spiritual control. In Avignon, under a church-state marriage of convenience, medieval forces combined. Catherine's letters persuaded the papacy to return to Rome after sixty-seven years in Avignon. The source of her power was like that of Francis's: she was a mystic, not quite of this world, fasting to the point of starvation, while devoting her hours to helping the ravaged, the poor, and the dying. The city will never forget Catherine, not for a thousand years. How do I know this? Because it hasn't forgotten her yet. Italy is nothing if not loyal to its patron saints.

Five minutes the other way is the Campo. I've attended a Super Bowl, Game Seven of the World Series, an NBA final, but none of those came close to the blood rush of witnessing the Palio—the most adrenaline-filled seventy seconds in Europe. We saw it when we lived nearby. The main piazza, the racecourse, is wildly uneven, with wicked turns. I can still feel the rumble of horse hooves on dirt-covered stones, taking those narrow bends in a gallop, three laps guided by jockeys on barebacks. A horse does not need a rider to win; it just has to cross the finish line. Some are drugged. Some tumble and have to be put down. I knew that the Palio's origins dated to the thirteenth century, that it was a challenge between wards for bragging rights over the city, that the horses from the different *contrade* were paraded through churches and blessed, and that bribery was more responsible for victory than the speed of the mounted beast. But what I didn't know until I could understand Italian was what the cherubic-faced children in the stands shouted to rivals from other neighborhoods.

"Your mothers are whores!"

"Your sisters are sluts!"

"You sleep with dogs!"

"You eat shit for breakfast!"

And the Palio, of course, is held in honor of the Virgin Mary.

I STOP FOR CASH at the ATM of Monte dei Paschi di Siena, the oldest continuously operating bank in the world, founded in 1472. This institution practically invented banking. It was the pride of Siena, funding the Palio, and providing a way for pilgrims to use credit as they moved through a foreign land, a deterrence to robbers, offering loans to "poor or miserable or needy persons," as the charter read. Many thousands could never have made the spiritual trek to Rome without it. The Via Francigena owes a huge debt to the bank's early sense of duty. In this century, it gave out reckless loans, overpaid for rivals, splurged on hidden derivatives. It grew fat and corrupt, making money in the unregulated shadows of banking. The collapse was inevitable, the result of pride, greed, and scandal. Too big to fail, the bank had to be bailed out by the European Union, arousing the anger of populists, a voting mob that turned on those who governed them. For the cause of the crackup, look back inside the Palazzo Pubblico: they didn't heed their frescoes.

AT LEAST SIENA never went mad, unlike Florence, its longtime enemy. The best frescoes there are in San Marco, where you can see the Renaissance taking flight—its color and movement, its depth of field and appreciation for the human form, in the wall art of Fra Angelico. He painted scenes of miracles and wonder, with luminous Tuscan landscapes in the background, in forty-four of the dormitory cells of San Marco. Like Dom Pérignon, Fra Angelico was a monk who devoted his life to creating something beautiful and lasting in homage to God.

Not long after the brother of the brush died, Girolamo Savonarola settled in at San Marco as abbot. In just a few years, he turned his fellow friars into warriors, and the most cultured city in Europe into delirium. In profile, the best-known portrait of Savonarola shows a hooded, severe-looking man with a hawk's beak. If people start to look like their personalities as they age, that image is accurate. Savonarola first arrived in Florence in 1482, having denounced his family after taking vows as a Dominican monk—"You should consider me dead," he told them. He fasted and slept on a hard surface in a cold room. But his self-righteous sobriety would not be contained within the peaceful confines of San Marco.

He abhorred lusty art and literature at a time when Florence was enjoying both. Botticelli's *Primavera* and *The Birth of Venus* were sensual and exuberant, without any religious overtones, heralding the end of Gothic gloom. Here were half-clothed mythic figures in the prime of their lives, exuding joy. To Savonarola, it was "pagan art." He was obsessed with the darkest parts of the Book of Revelation: punishment for sinners on this earth, an even more barbarian torture after death. His world was apocalyptic. In his preaching at the Florence cathedral of Santa Maria del Fiore—under Brunelleschi's masterpiece, the largest dome in world at the time—he ranted against free expression. The people were wicked; God would soon punish them. "I am the hailstorm that shall smash the head of those who do not take cover," he thundered. He predicted deaths of public figures, movements of armies, Florence under siege. All came true in short time, giving power to a new prophet.

The church in Rome was at peak corruption, as Martin Luther proclaimed just a few years later. One pope, Innocent VIII, encouraged Torquemada's Inquisition and fathered sixteen children through several women. A second pope, Alexander VI, amassed an enormous personal fortune while cavorting with courtesans. It is said that Alexander, the most debauched of the Borgia pontiffs, even had an affair with one of his own daughters. Another pope contracted syphilis during his reign—a "disease very fond of priests, especially rich priests," as the Renaissance saying had it. That was Julius II, known as Il Papa Terribile. Simony, the selling of church positions, was rampant. All of this roused the justifiable ire of Savonarola. And when Alexander tried to buy off the monk with a cardinal's position, Savonarola said, "A red hat? I want a hat of blood."

At home, the violence was brutal and swift. Libertines were jailed, tortured, and executed. "The time for mercy is past," said Savonarola, urging his followers to "cut off the head" of those who opposed him. He denounced sodomites, gamblers, and blasphemers, as well as the Medici family, the wealthiest in Europe, enriched by a monopoly on the material used to dye clothes granted them by an earlier pope. After the Medici were forced to flee, the cleric from San Marco became de facto ruler. He wanted a "City of God" for the Republic of Florence. And in this city, at his request, a law was passed imposing the death penalty for sex between men. His youthful followers, thugs in service to a theocracy, went house to house, looking for perfume, art, poetry, chessboards, playing cards, mirrors, tapestries, musical instruments, books of poetry by Dante and Petrarch, statues, vases, portraits, fine clothes—anything of material beauty, anything that brought pleasure. Savonarola preached hatred and a vision of hell in Tuscany. "O, Italy, because of your lust, your avarice, your pride, your envy, your thieving, your extortion, you will suffer all manner of affliction and scourges."

A mob lit the Bonfire of the Vanities on February 7, 1497, in the Piazza della Signoria, the living room of Florence. The flames rose to sixty-five feet, a pyre consuming all the prideful objects that had been confiscated by Savonarola's brutes. From there, things got colder and crueler. The chill of winter lingered late into spring. Crops were thin, money disappeared from a city that had grown wealthy on free trade. Famine followed. The wicked pope excommunicated the entire city. The next year was so frigid that the River Arno froze, a crumbled ribbon of ice beneath the Ponte Vecchio. New mobs, formed in opposition to the monk, were known as the *arrabbiati*—hot and passionate, a name later attached to a spiced pasta. The accused turned on the accuser. How could a City of God be starving and freezing? Savonarola and his disciples in terror were arrested, thrown into a dungeon. They were tortured by rack, branding irons, and the *strappado*, a Florentine specialty—the hands of a victim tied behind the back, then the body strung up, snapping the shoulders. A court found him guilty of heresy, charlatanism, false prophecy. He was hanged, his body burned, and the ashes swept into the Arno. There would be no relics. Thus ended a five-year period when Florence was the living image of Bad Government.

TODAY, BUSES CIRCLE past San Marco and come to a stop at a café across the way from the monastery where Savonarola seethed. After nearly six hundred years of Dominican habitation, the last of San Marco's aging friars are leaving for good—just like at San Miniato. It's the end. "We are very few," said one old cleric, "increasingly fewer." An adjacent museum will take over operations. A painting of Savonarola's execution is on the walls inside, and a plaque marks the place where he was arrested in 1498. I used to wait outside the monastery for my bus back to the Chianti country, wondering at times how the tranquil enclosure of San Marco turned a monk into a madman. And then I heard a plausible explanation: Savonarola insisted on living in a cell without any art, not even Fra Angelico's frescoes. Our home was in the oldest officially designated wine-growing region in the world, dating to 1716, symbolized by the black rooster figure of Chianti Classico. In those hills between Florence and Siena, the *gallo nero* is now far more ubiquitous than the crucifix. You can see why, if faced with a choice between the dark and violent fundamentalism of Savonarola and the craft of turning sangiovese fruit into wine, people would lose themselves in the grape.

But it's more difficult to comprehend how someone who starts an honest search for the divine by stripping himself of goods and self-gratification ends up as a violent man, swollen with his own sense of pride and power. Savonarola and Francis of Assisi were not unsimilar. Both practiced self-denial. Both rejected the material gluttony of their spiritual overlords. Both sought a purified Christianity. But Francis was not afraid of poetry; he wrote some of the best verse in Europe. Francis did not turn against music, laughter, and art. He was a troubadour. Francis did not call for the execution of people deemed sinful; he befriended the shunned. The spirit in him had wings. In the dichotomy of these two men is the dichotomy of the Christian faith, one side struggling against the other, an open heart against a fist.

Seven years after the immolation of Florentine vanities, a seventeen-foot marble statue of the most perfect and unclothed human form was unveiled in the Piazza della Signoria. Michelangelo's *David* was deliberately placed in the very spot of the bonfire, the square D. H. Lawrence called "the center of the human world." The eyes of the young man who slayed the giant with his slingshot were cast in the direction of Rome, a clear warning. Not that Florence would ever abandon the Catholic Church. Indeed, the Medici would produce three popes, none of them living up to the first part of the title Holy Father. But sanity prevailed. And perhaps if Florence had something like Siena's Palio, an annual venting of the sacred and the profane, the city never would have gone insane. At times, history is the best hospice for a troubled time traveler, and this history is somewhat of a palliative, as with the story of Saint Fina in San Gimignano. We are drawn to light.

THIRTY

THE MIRACLE OF MONTEFIASCONE

Onward: to the Roman road connecting Siena to the Caput Mundi. This is it, the last stretch, the Via Cassia joined to the Via Francigena, one of the oldest byways in the world tangled with one of the loveliest. No more time for diversions. No more car, either. I've set my bearings to the pilgrim compass. The morning is dark and foreboding, a good day for rain, the Tuscans say. They need it. Some grapes have wrinkled into raisins, and sunflowers are head-down and seedy. The earth is hard, fields the color of cornbread, framed at the horizon by cypress trees in formation, the most faithful of flora. Every hilltop in the Val d'Orcia is topped by a castle or villa, most of them occupied over five centuries or more by a single family, for it's a social crime to sell land to which your name has long been attached.

Mysticism grows well in the southern sun. From here on, no village is without a shrine to the inexplicable. If England is the reason-based start of this Christian trail, and France the cynical center, Italy is soaked in the supernatural near the finish. I'm in Buonconvento, nineteen miles from Siena, on a Sunday, via the first train at dawn. The name means Happy Place in Latin. It's hard to tell what the predominant mood is, for

Buonconvento is inert today. After a pleasant circumambulation, I walk through Porta Siena, which is eight inches thick with iron fittings—a door built to deflect cannonballs and the flings of catapults. Like San Gimignano, this town prospered because of its prime location on the V.F. And it's flat, a reprieve from the hills, with a restorative fountain of pure drinking water. Near the church of San Pietro e Paolo is a hostel with a sign welcoming pilgrims. I wish I could stay. But I have to get to Monte-fiascone, hours away, by day's end. I'm meeting a woman. I've promised her magic, a mystery wine so good it killed a man who could not stop himself from drinking, and the Via Francigena at curtain time—the autumnal glow of the *tramonto*.

When I dropped the car in Siena, Avis showed some leniency; that is, I'm not in jail. I went in poker-faced, hedging somewhat, trying to frame *the thing* in the dispassionate, blameless way of fate. There'd been an *incidente, signore*, which left the car in less than perfect shape. What kind of *incidente*? Involving other people? Other cars or property? No, just a little hit to the vehicle's vanity. The clerk spent an hour making phone calls, sending forms back and forth, taking pictures and forwarding those to some unknowable place. At least he didn't call the Carabinieri. In the end, it was a thousand dollars, even though I'd taken all the insurance. That hurt. Was there a pilgrim discount?

"*Pellegrino?*"

"*Sì, sì.*"

"*Dove va?*"

"*A Roma.*"

"*Bravo, pellegrino.*"

"*Grazie.*"

"*Mi dispiace . . . ma senza sconto,*" said the clerk, shaking his head and handing me the full bill. Don't be so hard on yourself, he told me on the way out. There's not a vehicle in Italy that doesn't have a dent on it. As I walked back through Siena, I felt vulnerable without my wheels, but liberated as well.

———

AT THE EDGE of the largest volcanic lake in Europe, the caldera of Bolsena, the view of the expanse of wind-shredded water stops me in my tracks. It's an earthly convulsion settled for now, the islands holding out against geological inevitabilities. The storm is lurking. A line of sinister-looking clouds has moved in from the northwest, darkening the land. After using the limited regional train and bus combination to get here from Buonconvento, I'm out of public transportation options for the day. My feet must carry me all the way to Rome. Fresh blisters would kill me. A stabbing pain in the rehabbed quad could also bring an end to my camino. The immediate goal is Montefiascone. It's only ten miles, which I thought would be just the right distance to reacquaint my legs with the stones of the Via Francigena.

The archway into town proclaims Bolsena, the town on the shore, a place of miracles. One concerned Saint Christina, rising from the lake bottom after her father had her tied to a rock for refusing to renounce her faith. The other was with a doubting priest, who did not think a thin bread wafer at Mass could become the body of Christ. But when he held the host aloft in 1263, blood dripped down off his fingers. Those dried drops are here today, in a chapel, as is a stone with Christina's footprints embedded into it. Both stories sound suspect. I know, I know: it's late in the pilgrimage, and I still haven't found a way to keep my rational side in check. I'm trying. I have to think in another dimension, to remember Augustine's line about miracles not being contrary to nature, but only "contrary to what we know about nature." There is so much more to know, and anyone who doesn't believe that is bereft of imagination. The miracle I want to see, the one that I've been thinking about since France, is lying in a crypt in the basement of the tallest structure of Montefiascone. It's another woman, Saint Lucia Filippini, who died in 1732. She is one of the uncorrupted—her body preserved without embalming, as if she passed away a few days ago. I'm skeptical. But also intrigued by the do-it-yourself nature of the investigation. Any person of faith, or even those of little faith, can examine her corpse from a few feet outside its glass casket.

I hasten to the road, trying to beat the storm. The first three kilometers out of Bolsena are not designed for pedestrians. I'm walking against traffic, no room for a misstep. After an hour, the V.F. leaves the busy road for a tarmac, up a hill, then a long gradual descent before a stream, to a deserted-looking church with an overhang. I hear voices. An elderly couple, loaded down with lopsided backpacks, is taking a break from their camino. They introduce themselves; married for forty years, they tell me before even giving their names, hailing from the island of Sardinia. Did I say elderly? They seem so because they're fussing and passing half sentences back and forth like you would expect of a pair that's been together that long. But I'm sixty-two and age-phobic, so what do you call my reaction—projection?

The woman, Fulvia, is on the V.F. because she wants to be closer to God. And how's that going? I ask her. They just started a few days ago, in Acquapendente, twenty miles back. They're taking their time, doing about ten miles a day. Check with me in Rome, she says. Her husband, Sergio, is not interested in spiritual renewal. He thumps his chest. He wants to be *forte*, strong; walking the V.F. is a great way to get in shape. He can't wait to tell all his buddies in Speedos back at the bocce ball court in Sardinia that he walked the pilgrim's trail to Rome. The couple sets a rumpled cloth on a makeshift table and prepares a meal—slices of dried meat, an olive bruschetta spread of some sort over bread, grapes from a plastic container, and a little vino for each of them. They ask me to join. I'm not hungry. Watching the Sardinians, listening to them talk, seeing how gently they treat each other, I realize I was wrong about the fussing. This is love, refined.

When my mother was thirty years old, she decided she'd had enough of her marriage to my father. He was often on the road, with a foot-dragging sales job he took after his days as a delivery truck driver. All week he was gone, in Idaho and Montana, one dumpy town after another, trying to get miners and loggers to buy life insurance. You'd think it would be an easy sell. On Friday night, he'd tumble into his chair in our house, exhausted, draining a six-pack in two hours. When my mother talked about her week, he'd nod dutifully. But he was somewhere else. On rare occasions, she would tell him how much she was suffering inside, that life was slipping by, and there was so much she wanted to do. She was a caged bird. The babies kept coming. The money did not. They fell apart. They fought. My dad slept in a basement room. It was because of his snoring, he told us.

She met a man at the branch library where she loaded up on books every two weeks. He was a reader. He listened. He loved history, music, and art. He raved about her choice of novels and the way she wore her scarf. He suggested other titles, praised her for her intellect. And he was French, even wore a beret—the most exotic of creatures in the north end of Spokane, Washington. My mother started going to the library every few days. She began to fantasize about another life, somewhere, with this little foreign-accented bibliophile, a man *who gets her.* She withdrew even more from my dad. She thought about leaving. But she could not do it— not to us, not to him. It broke her up, this decision to stay; now she was trapped for life. But then . . . my dad improved in her eyes. As she observed the way he treated us, the tenderness, becoming the father he never had growing up on the South Side of Chicago, she fell in love with him—for the first time, actually. The kids had seen this side of him. I was flying a kite with him when I was six or seven, on a blustery spring day. A windstorm came out of nowhere. The string snapped; the kite spiraled down, crashed, and took off with the gust. He grabbed my hand and told me to run, to beat the squall. All the way home, he kept squeezing my hand. "Don't worry," he said, "I'll never let you go."

My dad would read only two books in his entire adult life, while she raced through that many in a week. He was asleep before eight p.m., while she was gearing up for *Masterpiece Theatre.* He could not complete three words on a Scrabble board, while she was maestro in our circle. But he was never mean. Never lost his temper. And she would never leave him. They made it to their fiftieth wedding anniversary, and then put five more on for good measure, before he died.

My mother revealed this story in her final days. What kept them together, she said, was not just her seeing my father in a different way, learning to love a companion who was less than ideal. But also, she was Catholic, as my mother explained, and a Catholic tries to stay in a marriage. She used to scoff at the guidance from the church on this. What did they know?

"They knew enough," she said. "And now you know."

I say goodbye to the Sardinians, just steps before the first thunderclap of the day. Back on the trail, through the woods I go. After the crossing, I'm on an empty road made of smooth flagstones, each fitting like a puzzle piece. It's the Via Cassia Antica, according to my guidebook, Roman footpath of legionaries and missionaries. The clouds collide and form an inky blot, the sky lowers and dumps its load. My raincoat is on, the pack protected as well. The torrent brings water pellets—*ping, ping, ping*— bouncing off the flagstones, slick and shiny. Rain is so restorative, but then I live in a place where water has been a benevolent master architect. Near town, I'm back on a road with traffic. Puddles have formed on the sides. When cars pass, even slow ones, they splash a heave of muddy water my way. My boots are drenched, so are my legs. I'm wearing shorts, so I don't care. I love it.

Another group of pilgrims, just starting to ascend the hill toward Montefiascone, welcomes me to join them. They are three women, all on the youngish side of middle-aged, all somewhat tall, all with wet hair, speaking German. I ask them about their journey so far. They started in Siena, headed for Rome. Any blisters yet? Biting dogs? Assholes in cars? Nothing. Not a single problem. Like most Germans, they speak impeccable English, and probably three other languages as well. I remember the line from *Casablanca*, when an officer of the occupying army, Major

Strasser, explained to the French police chief that "we Germans must get used to all climates." It's wonderful to replay the line without the Nazi edge. The Germans are a delight, and seem inordinately cheerful. They laugh at themselves in the rain. Every other sentence is punctuated by a guffaw. I'm also impressed by their pace. They're aggressive walkers, striding briskly. We march through the Porta del Borgo, the main entrance into town, soaked but triumphant. I hear a couple of bravos from people standing under protective doorways. Ahead a few blocks is an enormous archway of thick, finely cut stone blocks, a welcoming, over which is emblazoned:

VIA FRANCIGENA

100 KM ALLA TOMBA DI PIETRO

SHE LOOKS BEAUTIFUL. Fresh. Her eyes clear and blue. How does she do it? She crossed a continent and an ocean, three planes, a train, and walked the last half mile here with a loaded backpack in the rain. She doesn't complain. She never does. She sits on the edge of the bed in our little hotel overlooking the Corso Cavour, trying to smile between yawns. It's early morning in the time zone where she started her forty-hour day. She's ready to walk the last stretch of the Via Francigena, 100 kilometers to Rome.

"Hello, pilgrim."

"Ciao, bellissima."

My wife managed to break away from her cancer chores. It was not easy. She feels terrible leaving Margie. I'd assured her she could be in phone contact with her sister and the doctors. The latest news from Cancerworld is not good, but not bad either. The scans show spots, even after the fresh chemo, which is horrible. But not as many spots, which is somewhat encouraging. Her sister feels weak, and Joni worries about her not eating. Every new round of poison knocks her down again.

I'd promised Joni a *tramonto* for the ages: the sunset over Lake Bolsena below, with even more color bleeding into the distant Mediterranean to the west. But the sun will not be seen as it slips away today. We're in for the biggest storm in months. She's fine with that. She wants a quick nap. And in Italy, you're never more than a day or two from a theatrical sky at dusk.

I slip out into the rain and head for the largest structure in town, the hulk of the Cathedral of Santa Margherita. It's on high ground of this hill town, topped by the third largest dome in Italy—behind only St. Peter's in Rome and the Brunelleschi structure in Florence. You can see it for miles around. Normally, I'd be enthralled. But I skip the architectural masterpiece and head down side stairs, to the crypt of Saint Lucia Filippini, at the base of the cathedral. The door pushes open. I'm alone in an octagonal cellar. Alone, except for *her*. In the center, under lights, is a glass reliquary with a full body inside. It's just me and Lucy. She died in 1732, at the age of sixty. Her life work was building schools for girls and young women, to uplift their dignity, she said. If men were to be the rulers of the church, women would be the heart. Orphaned at the age of seven, she never forgot what it was like to be alone in the world. In helping girls find God, she tried to show a way to independence of mind and spirit. Every school was designed to send out graduates who would go forth and found other schools for women.

She is not known for doing anything miraculous, or for affecting some historic event. Rivers did not leap out of their channels at her command. Wolves did not lie down. She was not roasted at the stake, dropped into a lake, dismembered, or beheaded. She exuded goodness; she gave off an aura. In life, she was saintly—*that* was her miracle. And in death, something improbable happened: Lucy did not decay. Normally, a body swells, eyeballs turn to liquid, the skin goes green after it chills—the gruesome, inescapable process of decay, from dust to dust, as Scripture and science have it. None of this happened to her. After several years, Lucy was pronounced "incorruptible," an occurrence later certified by the church in the twentieth century, though incorruptibility is not by it-self a guarantee of sainthood. A pontifical commission relied on an ex-amination by pathologists for this classification.

I walk past a knee-high gate and inch my way toward the body. I expect something hideous. She is lying on her back, head turned to the side, wrapped in black. The face is visible, and though alabaster pale, it is clearly fleshy and not decayed. She's 285 years dead and she looks, well—extraordinary. The skin is not dark or mottled, but is somewhat smooth. Her eyes appear to be half open. *Half open.* I take another step and start to reel off a series of pictures. When I zoom in, I observe a slow but dis-cernible movement: the eyes are opening wider, to a half oval. *This can't be.* It jolts me. I feel a direct connection to the corpse, this saint, and maybe her link to God. For a long moment I'm frozen, and look around for other witnesses. I take dozens of pictures. I want proof. And then I back away, very slowly, behind the gate, out the door, hastening up the stairs, trotting back toward the hotel through the rain.

"You're saying she winked at you."

"She did, Jones. Maybe not a wink, or maybe not specifically directed at me. But I swear: there was movement in her eyes."

"You're crazy."

"Please don't doubt me."

"Maybe you saw what you wanted to believe."

"I don't think that's what happened. I didn't go in wanting to believe anything. Italy has so many mummies, you have to laugh at these displays of the dead. I went there like, 'O.K., what fresh *caca* is this?' But I saw it. Come with me tomorrow, I'll show you."

We're at dinner, in one of the few restaurants open in Montefiascone on a dark and miserable Sunday night. It's in an old cave that gives off an inviting glow. Over in a corner are the Germans. We heard them before we saw them—the laughter. I ask the women if they've been to the cathedral yet, which is just across the street, to the crypt, hoping to find a corroborating witness. No, they were busy drying their clothes, plotting tomorrow's route.

Joni thinks I've been too long on the pilgrim trail. She knows me for the skeptic I am. My bullshit detector is not flawless, but it's in fine working order. And here I am babbling about a centuries-old corpse who opened her eyes to me. It could be fraud, and woe to the Cathedral of Santa Margherita if they dare perpetuate such a thing. It's easy to make a doll's eyes open and shut. How hard would it be to do that to a mummy? As for the skin, maybe it was embalmed, or injected with some fluid, made to look fresh for the faithful. A good undertaker can do wonders for the departed. Again, if that's the case, eternal shame on the bishop of Montefiascone.

"Have some wine," says one of the Germans. "It's as good as the legend."

We toast to Joni's arrival, to being together again, to the wonders of the V.F., and to the Laughing Germans. We're drinking Est! Est!! Est!!! It's a *vino bianco*, the house wine in this little trattoria run by a couple and their grown son. When we lived in Italy, one floor above a man who made Chianti out of his four-hundred-year-old villa, I learned that nothing is worse than a wine without a story. The story of Est! Est!! Est!!! begins in the year 1107, with a German bishop making a pilgrimage to Rome, hoping to see the pope and get a promotion to cardinal. This man, Johann Fugger, was a bon vivant, Falstaffian in the telling, who made sure he always ate and drank well on his journey. To ensure that he was getting the best of the countryside, he sent his servant, Martin, ahead, with instructions to mark "Est" on the door of an inn with good vino. It was shorthand for the Latin *vinum est bonum*—the wine is good. In Montefiascone, the servant was so taken with the quality of a white wine that he scribbled *Est! Est!! Est!!!* on the door. When the bishop arrived and settled in to sample his servant's discovery, he was overwhelmed; until that moment, he'd never tasted the perfect expression of a grape. He ended his pilgrimage then and there, and spent the rest of his life in Montefiascone. He died, prematurely, from drinking Est to excess. And every August, the townspeople stage a parade to Bishop Fugger's tombstone and splash his favorite drink on the grave.

We eat focaccia fresh-baked over wood in the Etruscan style, tagliatelle with pecorino, and tiramisù for the caffeine and brandy laced throughout the sponge layers. It's biting when we step outside the warmth of the cave, the wind throwing rain at us. We link arms as we pass the cathedral where Lucy sleeps, and hurry down the *corso* past buildings of shuttered windows, where the lights are out and all of Montefiascone sleeps. We're the only guests in the chill of an old inn. It's too early for Italians to turn the heat on; most wait until October. We have a key to the thick wooden front door. We go up steps of worn marble, the click of our shoes on the stairs, to our tiny room, to our small world, to have and to hold in the cold as before, but fresh and familiar, the best of times.

THIRTY-ONE

THE WOMEN WHO LIVE FOREVER

Let's start by doing what is necessary, and then hope for the impossible. We need to see Lucy. For nine hours, Joni was lights out. I couldn't shut down my mind. I tried watching imaginary leaves falling in slow motion, my sheep-counting technique. I replayed tossing a fly-fishing line in the Kootenai River of Montana, the perfect cast, the slow three-count, the strike. Nothing worked. It was because of *her*, the 345-year-old woman in the crypt. I tried to give the ghosts along this trail a night off, but this one was too close. I went down a hallway to a den with books and Wi-Fi to read about Lucy, her good works, and her death—she was taken by cancer. It was in 1926 that her body was uncovered and found to be still undecayed, except for minor deterioration. I clicked through pictures I'd taken on my phone, zooming in on the image of her face. It was unclear, but through multiple frames there appeared to be movement of her eyelids. It made me tremble, staring at the ashen face of a corpse in the middle of the night in an empty hotel.

Breakfast is in a drafty room. Outside, it's grim and gray, the snarling tail of the storm moving through. We bundle up and walk the *corso*. I get my credential stamped, a very stylized print of a medieval V.F. wanderer inside "100 km to the Tomb of St. Pietro" letters. My pilgrim passport is nearly full: Canterbury, Dover, Calais, Saint-Omer, Arras, Laon, Reims, Épernay, Langres, Besançon, Lausanne, Montreux, Saint-Maurice, Vernayaz, Bourg-Saint-Pierre, Great Saint Bernard, Aosta, Ivrea, Pavia, Piacenza, Fidenza, Passo della Cisa, Pontremoli, Carrara, Lucca, San Miniato, San Gimignano, Siena, Buonconvento, Bolsena, Montefiascone. The names are transportive, each a memory capsule. I started as a hesitant wayfarer, afraid to tell anyone my true purpose. I was just a curious traveler, emotion in check, my soul in a jar. No more. I am the twenty-first-century version of the medieval man who adorns the signs along Sigeric's way. I want to finish and I want resolution, though I'm ready to accept neither.

At Santa Margherita, we descend the stairs to the basement, Lucy's lair. Joni is hesitant to move toward the casket. I shuffle closer and stare. The face still looks pliable and—yes, *incorruptible*. But the eyes are closed. Yesterday, they were half open. I'm sure of that. I show her my pictures. Joni shrugs.

"Inconclusive."

"What?"

"If you'd like me to believe you I will."

THREE MILES down the Roman road the rain stops. We shed our shells. We started on hard surface, two of us on a Monday morning, dodging puddles, waiting on a rainbow. No sign of the Laughing Germans or the Sardinians. Joni is ready to walk the full thirteen miles to the next town, Viterbo. She's been training. She's wearing turquoise running shoes, and her pack is fairly light. I'd advised her to be minimalist. We'll buy clothes in Rome. I sometimes stride a few steps ahead of her, which is rude. By midday, we need a siesta, but the ground is too wet for napping. We find a roadside bar and have double shots of espresso.

Joni has a question: Suppose Lucy did open her eyes for me. "What was the point?"

"To get me to believe."

"So you need a miracle to believe in God?"

"I looked this up last night: There are more than three hundred pre-served bodies on display in Italian churches. It seems like most of them are women."

"A lot of mummies."

"Saints, Jones. They're saints. And it's not the same as mummi-fication."

She has me thinking: What's the point of Lucy's incorruptibility? Miracles are an integral part of the faith of the Catholic Church. But miracles are also supposed to be rare, and put to maximum good use. So why the inexplicable in the cellar of Santa Margherita? It seems like a wasted miracle, a sideshow of the supernatural. Lucy is long gone to can-cer. My sister-in-law is alive, but dying, with hers. If anyone could use an intervention, it's that suffering member of our family. So I decide to bun-dle whatever happened in Montefiascone, whether gimmick or miracu-lous, into a prayer for Joni's sister. And when I tell her, she's grateful, but still doubting, and I press her:

"Don't Jews believe in miracles?"

WE PASS THE HOT SPRINGS of Bagnaccio, the thermal waters that drew wealthy Romans to build their villas here on the tufa rock plateau. The translation is "nasty old bath," a series of pools in an open field. Ba-gnaccio is one of the great body restoratives along the pilgrim route, a place to braise away the grime from months of travel. A muscle soak is tempting. But if we marinated in hot mineral water, we'd never get back on the trail again today. Is that German-accented laughter I hear behind a cloud of steam? Indeed, it's *them*. Most of the people lounging in these springs are unclothed. Germans have a reputation for being militantly nude, as one writer put it, and as we learned in spring months living in

Chianti. We keep walking. Better to remember those fellow pilgrims as high-spirited and fully clothed.

We push on, arriving in late afternoon in the stupendous maze of Viterbo, population almost seventy thousand. The streets are curled ribbons of cobblestone. I'm intrigued, at the open-air archaeological park, by a statue of the Goddess of Abundance, a dual-gendered figure with numerous breasts and testicles. Another statue is mighty Emperor Augustus, who hasn't lost a smidge of national esteem, situated in a grove of perfect pomegranates. The city's monuments to the embedded cultures here are mostly functioning. People live in homes built on foundations of Etruscan stone, draw water from the Empire's fountains, and pass under arches ordered up by the Vicars of Christ who lived here when Viterbo was called the City of Popes. As Rome crumbled, falling to thieves, rot, and civic unrest, Viterbo grew as a healthier home for the papal seat. At least nine popes lived here in the thirteenth century.

Just before dark, we take a room in a small hotel run by a woman of incandescent friendliness. She says we are lucky to be in town today. It's our great *buona fortuna*. And why is that?

"Funghi!" Her exclamation rattles the rafters. After the long dry summer, the storm has jolted the forest floor to life, delivering enough rain to bring forth an abundance of mushrooms. She scribbles the name of a restaurant and says we must eat there, but don't wait long to get going, every table will be taken. She starts in with the number of popes who lived just a few blocks away, her civic duty. I politely cut her off. She also talks up Saint Rose of Viterbo, another incorruptible, who died just before her seventeenth birthday in 1251, a story that I encourage. I no longer care much about dead popes—the crooked, the corpulent, the ass-grabby conjugal. But I'm obsessed with well-preserved dead women. Am I the worst pilgrim on the Via Francigena?

Rose was a teenager who came from the poorest of the poor and spent her short life trying to help those like her. She owns Viterbo. Every year in her honor, people parade a ninety-foot portable tower through the streets, held aloft by the strongest men. Her preserved body follows. Rose's heart, kept in a separate reliquary, was autopsied a few years ago by a team of doctors, who wrote up the report in *Lancet*. It's not clear to me, nor was it to them, what they were looking for in an eight-hundred-year-old organ. "We have to ask: Does this answer any burning questions in medicine or history?" said one of the authorities. "I'm not sure this does."

Still, I know what it's like to hold on to a loved one who dies young. When I was twenty-two, my two best friends were killed—a few months apart, in separate, violent auto accidents. My friend Dick, who always said you should never hold back when you see something wrong, was hit head-on by a drunk driver. My other friend Bob was a runner, much faster than me, and quiet. He fell asleep at the wheel, after driving through a long night on the interstate, and flipped his car. I'd never known death of any kind; suddenly, two guys I loved as brothers were gone at the dawn of their adult lives. I would not let them go. For a time, we talked in dreams, and they were the same as they'd been in life—funny, daring, full of insight and comfort. These visits were random, something I could not affect, and I always felt renewed by them. Yet something was missing: never, in life or after death, did I get to say goodbye, for you can't control a conversation in a dream. As the years passed, the appearances became rare, until sometime after my thirtieth birthday, when my friends left me for good. They would always be twenty-two. I would have memory, the part of me shaped by those lost lives, and a resolve not to put off the things that need to be said until later, because later may never come.

The restaurant is full. We beg, cajole, and charm while sniffing the steam from passing plates of mushroom-laden magnificence. The owner gives in, allowing us to sit at a small table by the door. It's drafty and chilly every time someone exits or enters, but we don't care, for it's also cozy and romantic. We begin with a mushroom bruschetta, follow that with a divine soup made with *funghi*, and land the 'shroom trifecta with *pappardelle con porcini freschi.* After an hour, I feel like the Viterbo pope known as Martin the Glutton, but we have one more dish still to come: a slow-cooked rabbit quarter, with a sauce of what-else.

I mention a story about an island in Lake Bolsena. At one time, instead of having to stop in at the seven major churches of Rome, a pilgrim could get a plenary indulgence from the pope by praying at each of the seven chapels on the island.

"A . . . plenary . . . indulgence?" says Joni, drawing the words out. "And this will keep you out of hell? Or get you into heaven?"

"You don't have to worry, Jones, since Jews don't believe in life after death."

"That's not entirely true. By my training, we don't believe in such specific places."

"So what happens?"

"Do you think you know?"

"I don't."

"Does anybody?"

"Not with certainty."

"In the Jewish tradition, the afterlife can take many forms. You can live on through others who were affected by you. If you were a decent human being, kind, sharing, charitable, and loving, you're remembered."

"I like that."

"Yeah?"

"But just in case, I'll hold you a place."

"And what about Lucy? She's in heaven. That comes with being a saint?"

"That's the rule."

"She's a miracle on earth, but if she were alive today, she couldn't say Mass. She couldn't be a priest."

"True."

"At least among Reform Jews, women are rabbis."

"Progress."

It's my Jewish wife who encouraged me to see the pope the first time we were in Rome, years ago. I wanted to go for a run. It's my Jewish wife from Squirrel Hill in Pittsburgh who urged me to take this pilgrimage. It's my Jewish wife who loves the Christmas season—her father was in retail and would have gone under without it. It's my Jewish wife who reminded me, when my views of the Vatican were at low ebb, that Pope Francis went to Auschwitz, spending a day there in silent prayer. I often tell her she missed the boat, that Jesus was not a minor prophet. When I say she should consider how the short life of a poor man in a distant land changed the world—a Jew, at that—she reminds me of the awful things people do in this man's name. So it goes, back and forth, each chiseling away at the other's theological foundations, but each adding to them as well—ultimately creating something new between us. We will never settle it; life would be boring if we did.

I'm going to miss the City of Popes. Not for the papal detritus, but for the many curiosities. You could traipse around Viterbo for days with only a vague knowledge of the civilizations cake-layered into it, and still want more. They haven't messed with it. They haven't tarted up their past or packaged it into a marketable narrative. *Arrivederci, Viterbo.* Stay real for the next pilgrim.

Into the olive tree jungle we go, among the arboreal elderly. Some years ago, a killer freeze snuffed out many thousands of acres of these living ambassadors of Italy. It was worse than a wildfire, and left landowners in mourning. A lethal blight, passed by spittlebugs, took out others. Leaves went brown and stiff, skeletal limbs clacked in the wind. The trees died of thirst, their water passage lanes choked off. Those that survived are centuries old, the *ulivi secolari*, and exude a pride of place, their trunks as thick-wrinkled as elephant skin. Farmers will soon have their nets on the ground to pick up the shakedown of the harvest, and then the fruit goes under the great stone presses, those cranks and wheels. The

November extra virgin oil—boldly aromatic, nutty, deep green—is the heart of the Mediterranean diet. First taste, after first press, is a stop-the-world moment. And unlike wine, every day that passes thereafter takes something away from the oil.

The trail gets tricky in parts. We come to a locked gate, with no indication of which way to go. Ah—here are footprints over muddy grass, a diversion blazed by morning pilgrims, perhaps the Laughing Germans. Water flows, a freshet from the rain, that grows to a creek and expands to a stream the longer we follow. Then it's onto private land, between the rails of fences, still guided by markers, through straight rows of hazelnut trees, past twenty-foot-tall Roman funerary towers conquered by creeping vines. The ground is covered with nuts. We're walking on mahogany ball bearings in the heart of hazelnut country. Italy produces more than any country but one, and a third of all the nuts are grown in Lazio. Joni scoops up a single *nocciola* and hands it to me.

"Bring it home. We'll remember this day."

We're trying to get to Vetralla, a long day's walk through a section of the V.F. where trees are revered—and not just the ones that produce oil or protein for candied confections. The people of Lazio have long known that trees have feelings. Recent studies suggest that many species experience pain, communicate with one another, send out distress signals, and lead complicated sex lives. None of this is a surprise to the forest dwellers of Etruria. Every May, a Wedding of the Trees takes place atop nearby Mount Fogliano in front of thousands of dancing women and men. Two sturdy hardwoods, chosen for outward virility, are draped in ribbons and garlands, and sealed for life by a priest. The marriage is notarized, a way to ensure leafy fidelity through troubled years ahead. The union is pagan in origin, though that hasn't kept the monks who live in a local nearby monastery from blessing the entire event.

Hiking during the last part of the day is brutal. Everything hurts. We're both dragging, not saying anything, lost in our thoughts. It's warm and sticky, in the mid-70s. Our water is gone. Vetralla is on a hill that appears when the forest clears, and disappears when we're back in the woods. I try to think of this aching ambulation as a duty, like the labors of monks in the scriptorium at Saint-Omer, or the hike of hermits to that cliffside dwelling at Saint-Maurice. But it's an imperfect comparison. This is low-level pain. And yet it's not tedious if you put it to good use. A friend in Seattle, Ron Sims, gave me some advice after he walked the Camino de Santiago. Sims and I both grew up in Spokane. But he came from one of the few African American families in our overwhelmingly white hometown; barely a day went by, he told me, when someone didn't cruelly remind him of his race. By the time he got to college, he was full of rage. By the time he was the highest elected official in King County, which covers the heart of the Seattle metro area, race was always in the room with him whenever he spoke. And by the time he walked toward God in Spain in his late sixties, he found a way to let it go—all the petty, bigoted assholes. "One by one, I got rid of them along the trail," he said. "By the end of my camino, this baggage was gone. I was free of them. I wondered why I even let these people stay in my head for so long."

At day's end, Joni looks flushed. She sits on a chair in our room inside the family-run *agriturismo* in a valley at the base of Vetralla. She stares at the wall, blank-faced. She doesn't unstrap her pack.

"Are you O.K.?"

"I can't move."

"Let's take your pack off. Get a shower and rest."

"No, just let me be still for a while."

She sits, sphinxlike, for half an hour. Then she finally removes her weight, changes, cleans up, and shows signs of renewal. We're famished. The two women who run this little inn say that dinner will not be ready for hours. We can hike up the hill to Vetralla, which sits on the lower slope of Mount Fogliano, where the trees were married, and get something to eat. We've already done fifteen miles, counting two wrong-way diversions. The twilight should provide enough illumination to find our way. So we hit the road again, a slog over pavement with no shoulder, an encounter with an unleashed dog, an alley that dead-ends, a full hour to get to the crest of Vetralla. The story here is that Noah ran the Ark aground on these heights during the epic flood. While repairing his vessel, he became a fan of the local wines and stocked the Ark accordingly. Sure, *what else you got, Vetralla?* The town was given to the English, to Henry VIII, by Pope Julius II. This was before the big monarch went rogue, founding his own branch of Christianity. The Brits held on to Vetralla for hundreds of years, one of two towns in Italy under protection of the Crown. Well then, perhaps we'll find bangers and mash in a pub full of lit-up soccer hooligans. No such luck. Vetralla is not open for business this evening. In the dark, using our cell phone flashlights, we retrace the tortured route back—all told, an additional three miles after we'd dropped packs at the *agriturismo*. Ron Sims told me one other thing before I left: a pilgrimage, he said, is doing something you don't think you can do, which Joni proves tonight. Dinner at the farmhouse, cooked by the mother and served by her daughter, is *pasta arrabbiata* and a pork loin buried under *funghi* and oil from the olive trees we passed this morning. It's heaven.

"Since when do you eat pork?"

"Since walking twenty miles in a day."

THIRTY-TWO

COMPANIONS OF THE CAMINO

Breakfast of ibuprofen. Walking over a blanket of mist-covered hazelnuts before dawn's first light, *crunch, crunch, crunch*. Up the hill, past the same unleashed dog to Vetralla again, and now the town is awake. In a bar, we devour pastries just removed from the *forno*, cappuccini, and catch the news on an overhead television screen. We hike almost nine miles before our next stop, which is in Capranica. Feet fine. Backs holding up. And a reward: lasagna in the Roman style—without the béchamel or the meat ragù, heavy on cheese and tomato ricotta sauce. On most Italian days, you walk so you can eat, especially when the fuel is this good. Afterward, we light out beyond the hazelnut groves through a thick forest of chestnuts ablaze with color. The trail cuts through stone of hardened volcanic sponge, and deeper into the woods. We cross a waterfall on a rickety wood-poled bridge and into nature's hushed tones, away from any urban noise, then on mud and a slippery path next to the stream banks. It feels primeval. I would hate to be alone. The drop from the cliffs is precipitous. We have to concentrate. Some trees are down, blocking the path in places, felled by the storm. Time slows. We're lost, and will be stuck in this jungle of wet woods. It's my fault. I stopped following the guidebook.

But at a low point we find voices and a welcome trio of pilgrims. They are led by a woman from Lucca, a paramedic named Monica. She projects an imperious optimism that is much needed this late in the day, when gloom is at our heels. We stay with them for the last two miles, listening to their stories. They love the Via Francigena for the variety of terrain and the history, and their journey is an effort to raise money for emergency medical services inside the walls of their hometown. They heard about us from the Sardinians. *Us?* They laugh when they say this. What's so funny? *Americans! Walking!* Monica likes to sing as she strolls. Her voice carries us along until we emerge from the colors of fall to an open vista. There on a rise of tufa is Sutri, a place first settled during the middle of the Bronze Age, about 2,800 years ago. We part, the *lucchesi* off to stay at a convent, we to another family farm at the edge of town.

Sutri wears its Etruscan years with elegance, in the ancestral center of a civilization that lost its freedom more than four hundred years before the birth of Christ to expansion-minded Romans. After conquest, an amphitheater a third the size of the Colosseum rose near the town center. We're also in the heart of the old Papal States, the Vatican-ruled kingdom in central Italy. But the Etruscan dead predominate, with their vast necropolis at ground level, more than sixty tombs in the rock, and shrines to their gods. Our knowledge of them is almost entirely from objects left behind—murals and sarcophagi ornamented with lively figures. From these, we can guess that they were fun-loving, fond of large banquets, dancing, music, and sport. Their funerals were not unlike Irish wakes, sending the dead off on a wave of good cheer and well-told stories. They built sewage lines under roads and were likely responsible for introducing wine to the peninsula, sometime in the ninth century BC. Many deities of both sexes were worshipped, among them a goddess of wisdom, of night, of fire and of gold, and male gods of sun, storms, and the underworld. The afterlife, by all appearances, was a drinking party, for no Etruscan went to the great beyond without being prepared for a bacchanal.

What stands out among this glorious litter of antiquity is Santa Maria del Parto, a church built into the enormous rock foundation of a Mithraeum, dedicated to a cryptic Roman cult. Unable to completely banish the old gods, Christians incorporated them, as the Italians have done all along the Via Francigena—but here, to a fine blend. Greeks shaped the Etruscans, the Etruscans melded the Romans, and the church built on the teachings of Jesus Christ is a descendant of those cultures, along with its significant Jewish influence. You can't fully understand Christianity's hold on Italians without some knowledge of the ruins all over this part of the pilgrim trail. At this temple that became a church is an inscription, some words that people of any faith can follow: Pray or pass on. We do both, fifty kilometers from Rome.

The next day starts on the wrong road, miles from the trail. I was feeling so good about cajoling a ride from a middle-aged man staying at the same place as us. Last night over dinner he showed off his pictures of the pope from St. Peter's Square. He got very close and something clicked inside him; it deeply affected him. He wants to go back soon. He drove us to what I thought was a shortcut. The day is supposed to be only twelve miles, though much of it will be uphill. We follow red-and-black notches on telephone poles, which I mistake for V.F. signs. They're utility markers. We backtrack all the way to Sutri, and begin there, an hour before noon. But the day is cloudless, we're blister-free, and within Rome's magnetic pull.

Our destination, the town of Campagnano di Roma, is another jewel atop a hill, a mélange of faded pastel. This follows the pattern, going back to the middle of France. At the end of every day on the V.F. is an Old World town placed in the windblown heights, the highest perch around. They look lovely from afar, these summit towns, and they're magical once you get inside the walls. But you have to work for the payoff, at a time of the day when you're spent. We link up again with Monica and friends at the base of the final ascent. She's in desperate need of a beer. I try to engage her in some tales from her camino, wondering in particular if she saw Lucy. But she says they're pounding down the miles, with little time for sites. When we start the push up the hill, she breaks into what is almost a trot, and begins to chant:

"*Birra! Birra! Birra!*"

Campagnano di Roma is worth the climb. I feel light-headed and happy, or is that the endorphins? As soon as we walk under the portal, I fall for this place, which dates to 1500 BC. After shedding packs, I'm back out walking the length of Campagnano—twice. It has the same amenities as any other lost Italian small town: the fruit vendor and the butcher, the flowers in terra-cotta and those that drip from arched entrances, the well-dressed little children licking cones beneath the counter of a *gelateria*, protected by their *nonne*, the polished shoes of elderly men who sit outside in the last light. But in Campagnano things look like they fit, and always have, an organic whole, with no need to mourn a gloried past or pine for something more modern. The man who runs the restaurant in the place where we bed down for the night is of the same breezy self-confidence. He tells us precisely what to eat—*minestra*, a soup made of eight vegetables, the gnocchi with pesto and cherry tomatoes, a veal *limone* with the brightest zest of local citrus. I ask him if he makes everything in house, *fatto a mano*. He laughs and pats his sizable gut. "And I eat everything I make, even if you don't."

Being this close to Rome has a way of concentrating the senses. The nearer we get, the more we accept the immutable, but also the more palpable the joy. The two exist together, oddly without dissonance. We know we're going to get lost again today and tomorrow. We understand that physical pain is part of the package. We recognize that there will come a time in the afternoon when we say *basta*, we can't make it any farther, and start to cramp and feel a bit of self-pity. I will go into a church and come out with a head full of questions and exclamations. Joni will put up with me. We will have the same conversation, with minor changes, based on what she heard from her sister that morning. She calls Margie just as she goes to bed in Los Angeles. Joni is walking with sorrow, but she also is walking for something more. What, I can't tell. The glimpse into another's interior life is not enough to know the whole, even in a spouse.

I leave her at a café the next day in Formello, a few hours south of Campagnano, to climb a bell tower dedicated to V.F. pilgrims. There are sixteen glass steps. On every tread is the name of another stop along the camino from Canterbury. I take them slowly, with my pack on, pausing to remember something from each of the places. I can't imagine much has changed in the months since I set out. Pilgrims still flock to the altar where Thomas Becket was hacked to death. The lost voices from the scriptorium of Saint-Omer remain overlooked. Champagne bottles get turned, one eighth at a time. The first snow of the dark season is piling up on the pass at Great Saint Bernard, though the doors of the refuge will never be locked. Augustine's bones draw Augustine acolytes. Lucca's walls are not coming down. What changes are the people who take the journey. What was dead to one is alive to another.

The stairs top out with a view over the sienna-colored roofs of Lazio. Retracing my steps, down to the base of the tower, I stop at a large metal bowl filled with assorted talismans. A pilgrim is advised to unload something that was carried along the way. I leave behind the little stone I picked up on the beach in Dover. My friend Sam says I have too many chips on my shoulder—about the Brits and the Irish, about the monopoly that Harvard and Yale have on the Supreme Court, about the way the East Coast still condescends to the West—all the things I couldn't shake at the start of this pilgrimage, when I tried to lighten the load. My little grudges are nothing, a hill of beans when you think in Etruscan time. With the clink of an English pebble in an Italian kettle, it's goodbye to all that.

ODE TO A MEGALITHIC ARCH: each stone weighs half a ton or more. Each was cut by hand into a block. There's no mortar. No cement. No rebar. Gravity and the compression of the years hold it all together. The curved span frames a small cutout of sky. Why don't the center stones, the ones directly over my head, fall to the ground? In America, we build our arches for show, as in the Gateway structure in St. Louis, more than six hundred feet of stainless steel overlooking the Mississippi. But will a pilgrim walk under it two thousand years from now?

A complaint: Why do Italians dump their trash in the most beautiful places? We walk through Veio *"parco naturale,"* a wonderland of pines, verdant canyons, and waterfalls just outside the last towns along the V.F. But there's nothing natural about the things that have been thrown to the ground in this open country before Rome. At the bottom of one ravine is a clutter of rusted appliances, televisions, mattresses, and other crap from people's homes. A long stretch of fence holds the tumbleweeds of plastic bags. It's not just unsightly and unhealthy, but unbecoming a people who know better than almost any other how to make the beautiful out of the ordinary. They shame themselves with these small acts of civic vandalism.

A discovery: at the end of today's walk, outside the last town where we will sleep before Rome, is a church dedicated to Saint Pancras. *Him!* The headless boy saint whose name was given to my first stop on the Tube in London is a bookend at Rome's edge. And just as we lounge against a fountain wall, tanking up on cold water, a wedding party arrives for a rehearsal at the church of Saint Pancras—bride, groom, best friends, kids, priest, musicians. How renewing.

Another discovery: Carlo the London blogger, in person. We had dropped packs at a little hotel named for Apollo—unfit for a god, fine for a pilgrim—and walked along the spine of La Storta looking for a final meal matching the culinary grandeur of the V.F. Sigeric the Serious spent two nights here. It's odd that he stayed that long, for he was so close to getting his pallium from the pope—the woolen cloak and object of his pilgrimage. We'd been given three suggestions for dinner. The first place was closed. The second was booked for eternity. In search of the third, I got distracted trying to find the chapel where Saint Ignatius of Loyola received his vision from God in 1537. It's in a busy traffic circle named for the appearance, the Piazza della Visione. The tiny space where the founder of the Jesuits saw his apparition is faded pink with grime on the outside, a homeless man sleeping on a bench. It was open, but I was the only visitor. The detour cost us seats at the last restaurant. The owner said it was impossible—no openings until tomorrow. From the back of the room, someone shouted at me.

"Timo—vieni qui!"

It's Monica, urging us to come forward. She summons the owner. We are her friends, she explains; it would be an insult for the restaurateur not to find a place for us. Bring chairs. As we walk inside, I hear guffawing from another part of the room, the Laughing Germans. They wave. At Monica's table of ten people, we also find the Sardinian couple, beaming. Everyone is here. We meet the Englishman Carlo Laurenzi, who—it turns out—has a son now living near Seattle. Of course I recognize the name.

"Carlo from London?"

"Yes."

"Carlo who was given horse piss to drink in France?"

"You remembered."

"Carlo who almost didn't make it?"

"I may not still. I've lost almost two stone."

That's about twenty-eight pounds. He looks sinewy. His bald head is bronzed. He introduces us to a man he's been traveling with of late, a stringy-lean Russian with wild, bone-colored hair and a patchy beard, who speaks very little English. The man was a nuclear physicist and knows many secrets from the Soviet era. He's walking the V.F. to atone for some connection to the Chernobyl nuclear disaster of 1986, which killed hundreds of people through radiation exposure.

We share many courses, many stories, many discoveries, many explanations, many glasses of wine. The Italians are as appalled by the litter along the trail as we are. It's because of the Mafia, Sergio, the Sardinian man, explains—they control the trash business. And also, blame it on pride, on trying to maintain a *bella figura*. How so? Nobody wants to be associated with a urine-stained mattress outside your home awaiting garbage pickup. Better to throw it in a ravine at night.

Carlo says he lost all that weight despite eating more than 3,000 calories a day. It's because he pushed the pace, trying to do twenty-five kilometers every leg. I ask him if he's independently wealthy. He laughs.

"I'm independently poor," he says. He sold his flat in London and cashed out part of his pension to make this pilgrimage. What he will do after seeing the pope, he does not know. He has no plans. But he's no longer an atheist.

"I gave up on the concept of God at the age of fourteen or fifteen. I brought up two boys as atheists. For most of my life, I've worn my atheism like a safety blanket."

"So now you believe?"

"I'm still skeptical about the gods of the main religions, Judaism, Christianity, Islam, but I believe." His two goals of the trek to Rome—to reflect on his late parents, and to consider the nature of God—have been met. But nothing is finished. "My sense today is that something sentient exists, separate from us, but I can't tell you what." I wondered if he prayed along the way.

"What is prayer?"

"I've asked myself the same question."

"Maybe it's just the process of quieting a busy brain. That's what's so great about the Via Francigena. I love the opportunity to think."

He mentions the baffling things that happened to him when he was younger, the accidents that should have killed him, the driving source of his spiritual curiosity.

"It could be a statistical anomaly. I don't know. Why didn't I die?"

We linger; nobody wants to leave. More wine is passed. More stories told. After tomorrow, we'll be part of the masses mobbing St. Peter's Square, no longer pilgrims. The plotting of a day's route, the anxious scanning of the sky, the concerns about water and food, shouldering a pack—all will be replaced by the ordinary.

I tell Carlo about Saint Lucia the incorruptible, looking for a second opinion from a seasoned skeptic. He didn't go to the crypt in Monte-fiascone. Can't help me. But his companion, the Russian nuclear scientist, saw something similar to my experience. *The eyes*, he told Carlo. Great. So my corroborating witness will have to be a man who knows too much and can't say anything.

IN THE MORNING, my legs refuse to move; they're unresponsive. I cannot get out of bed. It's a strange and horrifying paralysis, without cause, with Rome so close. I start to sweat, overcome by a wave of panic. After all these months, I'm not going to make it. But . . . it's only a dream, a classic anxiety projection. I open my eyes in murky light and pull back the blinds.

We're hoofing it down the traffic-clogged Via Cassia part of the trail, past old suburbs that merge with even older ones, dodging cars, scooters, and the exhaust flatulence of gasping buses. It's an urban route now, the spill of Rome all around. Blank walls and signs are graffiti-covered, trash cans are stuffed to overflowing. Joni has settled into a good rhythm; she's found her pace. She's wearing a dress, very practical, which also means she'll be making a *bella figura* upon our entrance into the city. We keep our eyes straight ahead, on the prize, moving with urgency. The forecast is not good: a nasty thunderstorm is supposed to roll through sometime in the afternoon. The route takes us to Monte Mario park, a big rock promontory in the city's outer limits, remarkably litter-free. We stroll by autumn-painted trees, track upward to a clearing 456 feet above the city, the highest natural perch over Rome. And there it is: the dome of St. Peter's Basilica. Michelangelo's design, which he conceived in old age and oversaw until his death at eighty-eight, rises from a thicket of apartments and red-roofed buildings, umbrella pines and the hidden bend of the Tiber. To his final day, Michelangelo tried to live up to his life motto: the greatest danger, he said, "is not that we aim too high and miss it, but that we aim too low and reach it." The sky darkens and broods; birds screech by. The first thunderclap rattles overhead. We'll need to take cover very soon. But for now, in a Roman moment for today and many tomorrows, we aren't going anywhere.

"Stop," I say. "Take it in." *Kairos* time.

THIRTY-THREE

PILGRIM'S PROGRESS

Dutifully, I tried to visit the tombs of Peter and Paul; a pair of thorns that crowned the head of Christ; the wood fragments from the cross to which he was hammered. All of them are here, their authenticity backed by varying degrees of certitude, at the final stops in Rome that a pilgrim is supposed to visit. You cross the finish line when you link your tenuous existence to that perpetual past. We started in Saint John Lateran, the first major church of Catholicism, built on the site of a fourth-century foundation from a time when the scattering of Christians worshipped in meeting houses. For more than a thousand years, the Lateran was home to every pope. Inside, it's all hard edges and glittering surfaces, mosaics, and frescoes, with too much empty space between ceiling and floor. The skulls of Peter and Paul, the two Christian founders, one crucified upside down, the other beheaded, are in a raised reliquary over the main altar. So say the guidebooks, relying on tradition.

The palace that housed the successors to Saint Peter was also where the Lateran Treaty was signed in 1929. It was a shameful pact from a shameful period. The thug, the narcissist, the father of Fascism, Benito Mussolini, traded signatures with Pope Pius XI here, sealing an authoritarian state to the ancient faith of this land. Had not the results of melding crown with cross, of armies marching off to war behind *God Is on Our Side* banners—all the serviceable lessons from eras gone—meant anything? The twentieth century would usher in the greatest wave of horror ever seen. And the signing of the Lateran Treaty signaled that the leaders of the largest religion in the world, nearly one-in-three people on the planet in 1930, would be largely passive as dictators prepared to slaughter millions.

What Pius XI got in return was sovereignty, a 109-acre compound—his kingdom for a piece of paper. Mussolini reigned by terror and theater of the dark arts. In his formative years, he hated Christianity, asserting that "God does not exist" in one missive. He was known as a *mangiaprete*—priest-eater—and his gangster followers beat up clerics with a political conscience. But his murderous cult of personality would be fragile without the church. "In youth, give your flesh to the devil," he said. "In old age give your bones to the Lord." In return for autonomy, Catholic authority would look the other way while Mussolini built a police state and allied himself with Hitler. Il Duce was hailed by the pope as "a man sent by Providence." When Mussolini gassed thousands of people in Ethiopia, the church did not protest. He never made it to the stage of holy benevolence. While trying to flee Italy in 1945, he and his mistress were shot by partisans at Lake Como. Their bodies were spat and urinated upon, then strung upside down from a rusty beam next to a petrol station in Milan. Providence didn't save him.

Out front, facing this colossus of church-state ostentation, just beyond the monstrosities in marbles, the gold-barreled ceilings, the bronze door from the old Roman Senate, the tombs of many popes, is a large statue of Saint Francis of Assisi. He's holding his arms out, as if in disgust, as if to say, *"Basta!"*

A better moment, not so clouded with corruption and compromise, would be found at Santa Croce in Gerusalemme. So we hoped. Here are two pieces from the Crown of Thorns, a sliver of the cross from the good thief who died alongside Jesus, a finger from Thomas the doubting apostle. The main attraction is the Titulus Crucis, the sign that hung over the slain Christ's head. The world-class relics came from Helena, mother of Constantine, as part of the haul she brought back from the Holy Land in 326. Christians were heartened when a panel of experts assembled in 1997 to gauge the authenticity of the board of walnut wood said it was indeed possible that Titulus came from the time of Christ. But later radiocarbon dating, peer-reviewed by experts, placed it sometime between 980 and 1146. Most likely, it's a medieval forgery.

On another day we went to visit the tomb of Saint Paul. Though his skull is in the Lateran, the rest of his remains are below an altar in the Basilica of Saint Paul Outside the Walls. It was built over the site where Paul was executed during the reign of Nero, not long after Rome burned. The ruler blamed the great fire on Christians, but he likely started it himself. Emperor at sixteen, Nero murdered his mother and at least one of his many wives, then killed himself as the Empire turned on him. He never played the fiddle, not while Rome burned or at any other time; it didn't exist until ten centuries after his death. I got very close to what is left of Paul, author of nearly half the books of the New Testament, written on perishable papyrus. This vast basilica, one of the ten largest churches in the world, was oddly empty on a weekday but for a guard manning a metal detector. When Joni stepped outside, I lingered; for a good ten minutes, it was just Paul and myself. I tried to refrain from engaging the crypt in argument over the subjects I'd tossed around on the Via Francigena. As these things go, I found Lucy's company in Montefiascone more stimulating.

At least no church in Rome claims the Holy Prepuce, the foreskin snipped from the penis of the baby Jesus. It was well traveled, from an old Hebrew woman who put it in an alabaster box after the circumcision, to the treasury chest of Charlemagne, who gifted it to Pope Leo III on Christmas Day 800, to sanctuaries all over medieval Europe, to its last known home in the closet of a parish priest in Calcata, thirty miles north of Rome. The priest reported it stolen in 1983. Relic hunters say the trail has gone cold since.

None of it matters, not to me. The sacred scraps prove nothing, for the proof of a faith is not found in bits of bone or chips of wood or flakes of skin. The body parts are evidence of only one thing: the certainty of death. The Catholic Church tries too hard. Christ said many good things. Those many good things have held up far longer than any physical object, and will outlive any treaty with a tyrant made in his name. He was nailed to a cross by Romans—that is not disputed. He rose from the dead—that is. I believe in the Resurrection, and I owe this sentiment to the Via Francigena. I'd been moving in this direction for a month or so, even as I grew more disgusted with the powerful custodian of this life-affirming event. The evidence from the first century, the many people who swore they had seen the risen Christ and chose death rather than recanting, is a compelling argument—for who would die for a fraud? But what cinched it for me was something the young Lutheran minister in Geneva, Andy Willis, said about the message of Easter from Jesus, something that echoes Jewish sentiment on what happens after death: "Nothing can keep my love in a grave."

It was with this realization—and after that third day in Rome—that I knew I'd had enough. I was done with relics, done with the remnants of the sacred dead, done with calling out to place and time. And though I still would need to get my Testimonium certified at the Vatican, though I awaited final word on an audience with the pope, I was done being a pilgrim. You lose something—a great deal, actually—when you give up your peregrination. For months, every step taken was in the direction of Rome, the complexity of life simplified to a journey, one of the oldest of human callings. Each dawn promised something new or startling in a wondrous part of the Old World. Each day brought some twist from nature, some quizzical artifact from the past, a small personal challenge. Each dusk allowed time for rumination about the verities of a trail compressed by the patter of 150 generations, my footsteps now added to theirs. I wasn't ready to be just another tourist waiting in line to see a Caravaggio. But I had to bring things to a close. Millions who came before me believed they'd been given absolution for their sins, and went home with a clean soul. They got their passage to eternity. My return ticket is not such an easy one-way. I've resolved some things, but other matters will have to remain irresolvable. At the least, I know this: What I discovered was not served in a stiff shot. A stiff shot doesn't last.

No longer obligated to follow someone else's path, we have a few days to let the Eternal City reveal itself. We stand now before the hooded figure of Giordano Bruno in the Campo de' Fiori. The statue of Bruno dominates this piazza, his face barely visible behind a cowl. He's manacled and holding a book—about to go to his death. A former Dominican priest, this philosopher, writer, teacher, poet, and polymath was burned naked on this spot in 1600, a papal jubilee year, executed under orders of Pope Clement VIII and the Inquisition. Like Servetus, he was killed for thinking on his own, his arguments backed by new theories that would become old science known by every third-grader in the years to come. Specifically, his capital crime was espousing a belief that the earth was not the center of the universe. Bruno was no cosmologist, and certainly no atheist. He picked up his planetary notions from Copernicus, the Polish astronomer. Bruno believed that life was made up of an infinitesimal number of tiny particles, and God was present in all of them. The statue was unveiled in 1889 by some of the leading thinkers of Europe. At the base are these words: To Bruno, from the generation that he foresaw.

We find a seat in the late-lingering sunlight. At this hour, the square belongs to the languorous. Bruno is staring at the Vatican, barely a mile away. This may sound like a heretical thought while in the aura of this convicted heretic, but today "the generation that he foresaw" would have to include the pope just across the river, the man who tells Christians that they must "never fear the truth." My literary trail-mate Christopher

Hitchens said faith cannot stand up to reason. "We no longer have any need of a god to explain what is no longer mysterious," he wrote. Yet each mystery explained, Pope Francis would say, builds the case *for* God, which is a reason he welcomed Stephen Hawking into the Vatican. He encourages us to consider what it means that our galaxy is but a speck, one of more than 200 billion in the universe, and that we are part of a whole made up of particles. Francis celebrates what Bruno was killed for.

But Francis will *soon be gone*, and the church that he tried to make more humane and reasonable and just in the name of a Nazarene pauper is sure to be dragged down, yet again, by the weight of its history. The durability of those dark centuries past is not reassuring—not to me— even if the durability of the pauper's words is.

Nine years after Bruno's execution, Galileo invented the telescope, a portal to scientific truths that reduced the biblical interpretation of creation to a fable. For these discoveries, he was condemned, forced to recant, and spent the last eight years of his life under house arrest. He barely escaped being tied to a pyre. And 350 years after Galileo's persecution, following thirteen years of study by Vatican theologians, Pope John Paul II in 1992 issued a formal acknowledgment of the church's error. Galileo was right, he said. The church was wrong. Science is not the enemy. Today, astronomy students train at the Vatican Observatory—two words that could not be joined without threat of undermining what prior popes preached for eighteen centuries. Bruno still awaits his vindication. The closest he got was in 2000, again from John Paul II, who made a general apology and begged for a pardon for "the sins of yesterday's Christians" and "for the violence that some have used in the service of the truth." Does that settle it?

For seven years, Bruno was a prisoner in Castel Sant'Angelo, in the dungeon of that cylindrical fortress on the banks of the Tiber. Prompted by the life and death of the heretic, we cross the pedestrian bridge to the place of his incarceration. It's the most indestructible rock pile in Rome and once its tallest structure, built as a mausoleum for Emperor Hadrian, who died in AD 138. Deep inside, we walk up the spiral ramp. The lower level of the castle, where Bruno was held, is dark and dank; you can almost feel the mildew creeping in from the malarial, garbage-choked Tiber of four hundred years ago. On another floor is the Passetto di Borgo, the half-mile-long fortified escape route between the Vatican and this fort. At one terrace is a catapult that looks to be in working order, and cannons next to iron balls stacked in pyramids. Up higher are light-filled and well-tended papal apartments—used as a refuge when the Vatican was under siege—with portraits on the wall. Through the window are some of the best views of St. Peter's Basilica. It's so close, but I'm not ready for the pope, not just yet. I study the painting of a man with a labyrinth sewn into his vest—a final maze at Via Francigena's end. The subject looks becalmed, fingering the puzzle on his chest. On his hat is a motto inspired by Petrarch: "Hope guides me."

Hadrian's ashes are in a vault with his wife. Having reigned for twenty-one years, building the wall in his name that straddled the northern edge of the Empire in Britain, remaking the Pantheon after it was nearly destroyed by fire, he hoped to live on in the most fortified mausoleum in the Mediterranean. *To live on*—who doesn't want that? Hadrian's fear was that the afterlife would be "bare and ghastly and without grace." As he lay dying, he wrote a touching bit of verse, a send-off to the realm of the unknown:

> *Little lost and gentle soul,*
> *Companion and guest of this body,*
> *Get ready now to go down into*
> *Colorless, arduous and bare places*
> *Where you will no longer have the usual entertainments.*

The emperor's tomb is cold and final, matching his fear of where he would end up, that sad place devoid of "the usual entertainments." He died at age sixty-two. The number glares back at me—*sixty-two*, this look in the mirror of my own death. Hadrian stayed in the grave. But this finality doesn't have to be a portent. Death is not an eternal sleep. The Via Francigena has taught me otherwise.

IN OUR LAST DAYS, the light is soft and forgiving of Rome's age, a gauze on the great monuments. We are still without schedule or pressure, but I feel a pull nonetheless, moving toward St. Peter's Square several times, and then backing off. This afternoon we lean against the sun-warmed exterior of the Gesù, the massive mother church of the Jesuits. We wait until a small side door opens at four p.m., the entrance to the last home of Saint Ignatius of Loyola. His apartment is upstairs. Up the steps we go to the living quarters of the founder of the Jesuits.

Like Francis of Assisi, Ignatius lived a turbulent life. One of thirteen children born into a Spanish Basque family, he dreamed of conquest, wealth, and women. He killed people in war and relished the blood he shed. In 1521, he was badly wounded when a cannonball from the French crushed his legs. After he was put back together—the legs broken and reassembled in primitive surgery—he would always walk with a limp, one leg shorter than the other. While in recovery, he read philosophy and history and felt drawn to another kind of quest. His pilgrimage lasted a lifetime. As a mystic, Ignatius attracted the attention of the Inquisition, and he may have been executed but for his rhetorical dexterity. The vision he experienced in La Storta, where I stopped before dinner on my last night on the Via Francigena, led him to Rome. There, he founded an order designed as an intellectual counter to the Reformation—the Society of Jesus, eventually producing the first Jesuit pope, Francis, in 2013. Ignatius wrote a manual, *Spiritual Exercises*, still widely used, though it's a rigorous triathlon for the soul.

I do not feel the presence of Ignatius in this darkened apartment until we turn a corner and find his shoes on a display ledge—worn and shapeless slippers of five-hundred-year-old leather, the heels collapsed, frayed at the front where toes would rub. There's no ankle support and very little left of the soles. I take a picture for my Jesuit friend, Father Steve. For years, popes paraded around in red shoes of status, and it was customary for a pilgrim greeting the pontiff to kneel and kiss the scarlet feet in submission. Pope Francis eschewed the gleaming leather for simple loafers. *He* would kiss the feet of the homeless, criminals, and nonbelievers; no one was expected to do the same for him. Footwear always tells a small part of a story, as I learned in my own walk to Rome. In this coda to the Jesuit shadings of the Via Francigena, Ignatius is unlocked from his own grave.

At dusk we're at the Spanish Steps, the best staircase in Italy. The fountain of the half-sinking boat is at the base, the church at the top, and in between is a rise of seats where you can sense the labored pulse of a tired city. We sit until the sky darkens and the mood of Rome pivots, and then move toward music in the piazza nearby. We are enchanted now by a beautiful woman in a black dress with an open umbrella at her feet. She is seated at a piano near a café. She has rolled the piano out from somewhere and started to play. Her music fills the square and rivets the crowd, stopping strollers in their tracks; she's that good. People dining al fresco put aside their conversations to listen. We are spellbound as her fingers glide over keys of ebony and ivory. I shiver, for I know now, though I don't say anything, that Margie will soon depart from this earth. She would love the moment; in her world, music was the highest form of prayer. The miracle I'd begged for in Laon, and dropped into the current of continuous pleading in Saint-Maurice, and attached to my experience with the incorruptible corpse of Saint Lucia, is not to be. I know the cancer will kill her. I feel her passing. But she will never be stuck like Hadrian, her love in a grave. She is with us now.

In midmorning the next day, we walk on a little path of crushed rock to a Renaissance villa, built for Pope Julius III in 1555. It's a fine house, mustard-colored on the outside, with perfect proportions throughout. It went from the hands of the church to the city in the nineteenth century.

They smartly dedicated this home to the original Italians, a museum for the Etruscans. We glide past the funerary objects to a room that holds a married couple behind glass, a masterpiece from 2,600 years ago. It's the only thing I want to see. I first heard about this man and woman years ago, when we lived in the Chianti country. The winemaker who lived below us had kicked up a small, chipped artifact of some sort from the Etruscan era; it had been buried in the hard dirt where he grew his sangiovese grapes. To me, the object was full of mystery. To the Chianti farmer, it was a trifle. If you want to know something about these ancients, he said, go to Rome and see the Sarcophagus of the Spouses.

So here we are before a bride and groom in their prime, full-figured and life-sized in painted terra-cotta, reclining affectionately in the afterlife. Of all the monuments to the dead along the Via Francigena, all the reliquaries and raised tombs and glass crypts, this one is the most exuberant. It represents the Etruscan view of the hereafter. The man embraces his wife. This is what Diderot wanted with his lover, what he could not square with his atheism—"to combine myself with you when we are no longer here." The hair is braided, the eyes are almond-shaped. They're radiant, presiding over a banquet, in keeping with the Etruscan idea of what follows this life. In a way, it's very much the story of the Resurrection. They're both smiling, like the angel in the cathedral of Reims. Here is more of the small proof I need, another affirmation of the joyful defiance of linear time: their love is free of the grave, passed on every time someone like us returns the smile.

At last—time with the pope. I got tickets the night before, but was uncertain, until this morning, whether I would go. Joni pushed me. I will not get my chance to ask Francis questions I've been thinking about since Canterbury. And yet, I don't feel slighted or incomplete, my pilgrimage stunted. Just the opposite. The day is cloudless and warm as we cross into the world's smallest sovereign state, a mere two-tenths of a square mile. Vatican City has its own post office, long the most efficient in Italy, and an ATM machine with instructions in Latin, and a labyrinth of boxwood hedges where the pontiff can lose himself in thought. We check into a small room just off the main square. I unfold a frayed pilgrim passport, four stapled pages inked with stamps from the stops of the Via Francigena. The medieval pilgrimage from Canterbury was made in the spring and usually took ten weeks. I also started in the blush of the year's seasonal renewal, and it took me about the same time, discounting days of deliberate diversion. After looking briefly at marks of my destinations, a clerk presents me with a certificate with my name, signed by a Vatican official, *Testimonium Peregrinationis Peractae ad Limina Petri*. It's official. I know how the Scarecrow felt when he got his brain.

We pass through metal detectors, walk by frowning and brow-furrowed Swiss Guards in frilly uniforms and black berets. In the pool of people in the piazza outside St. Peter's, there's a buzz, a shared sense of anticipation. Nobody pushes or shoves. Some of those who are lucky to have seats offer them to the elderly or the frail. I'm happy to be here, my selfish concerns subsumed by the hopes of the whole. For the most part, it's a surprisingly young crowd, with many people of color, and more women than men—the future of the church, if it can keep from betraying them. Some Catholics want a museum for a religion, the centuries-old still life of sanctity, doctrine mortared to the statues. What I see today is very much a vibrant faith, people moved not so much by grandeur—though that's certainly a part of it—but by something else.

The pope arrives by a vehicle just larger than a golf cart, doing a couple of laps as the crowd rushes forward. I can't help thinking of the first time I saw the Rolling Stones, or *Bruuuuuce*. I get within ten yards or so for a good view of an octogenarian with a glow and a lovely smile, a whirl of billowy white. I shout out a salutation—the prayer message I said I would deliver for the woman from the mountains near Aosta. It feels good to keep that promise, which I'd nearly forgotten about. Bernini's masterpiece—the colonnades, the piazza in the form of an ellipse—

is civic architecture with a beating heart, not unlike the church that presents itself with this crowd. In the portico are statues of Constantine and Charlemagne, fronting the basilica built with riches from the sales of indulgences. Inside is the tomb holding the rest of Saint Peter, the man who disowned Christ before the rooster crowed on the day of his crucifixion. Also inside, crowded into the last available niche in the basilica's nave, is a relatively recent statue of my friend Saint Lucia Filippini. Though I can't see her from our position in the piazza, I return her wink from two weeks ago.

The Holy Father settles into a chair and offers a greeting to pilgrims in many languages. The wind nearly knocks off his skullcap. He speaks softly, mostly in comfortable Italian cadence, occasionally using his hands. My mind drifts, for the day is so glorious, but a few of his words land on me as a tap on the shoulder. "Never yield to negativity." And "Keep your eyes open to the beauty all around you." And "If you are sitting, get up and go. If boredom paralyzes you, fill your life with good works." And finally, this, repeating something he has said many times: "You must always forgive." Forgive? He's been meeting regularly with victims of sexual abuse, asking us to judge him by his actions, as his church works its way through reconciliation with "the greatest desolation," as he calls it. On impulse, I offer up my absolution to the faith for the crimes against my family, riding a Roman breeze. I'm swayed by the words of someone I'd read about one night on the V.F., that man who chose to forgive as a way to free himself from the chain that bound him to his tormentor. I can't speak for my brother.

The Via Francigena is a trail of ideas, and it helps to walk with eyes open—otherwise you miss the bread crumbs of epiphany along the way. There's no Testimonium for the memories I'm loaded down with here at the pathway's end, but my passport is full. I will not soon forget dawn at the mountain monastery at Great Saint Bernard, still turning over the words of Father John of Flavigny. I will remember French children singing in a square where Christians were once hectored into going to war.

And I will go to my grave trying to find a place within my fortress of reason for the living face of a long-dead saint in the crypt at Montefiascone. I will not look at a thunderstorm in the same way after watching the many moods of the sky over the Marne. Nor will I belittle a given day, no matter how boring or wasted. I will never hike without blister medication or take another shortcut. These are aspirations, mind you, so I expect to come up short. Beyond that is a conviction, this pilgrim's progress: There is no way. The way is made by walking. I first heard that in Calais, words attributed to a homeless man, the patron saint of wanderers. I didn't understand it until Rome.

ACKNOWLEDGMENTS

A journey of a thousand miles began, and was sustained by many a writer's friend. In Seattle, I'm indebted to Father Stephen Sundborg, S.J., the president of Seattle University, a brilliant Jesuit theologian whom I've been lucky to know since high school. He used his mysterious influence to open doors in the mysterious Vatican; more important, he was a friend and encouraging voice along the way. Another theologian, a half century younger than Father Steve, Sam Rennebohm, was kind enough to read an early draft and help me with my thinking, all while pursuing his PhD in psychology and raising a baby boy with his wife, Annie.

On the trail, I'm grateful to Julia Peters of Canterbury, for sharing insights from her own camino to Rome earlier, and to Carlo Laurenzi of London, a gifted Italian-Brit. In France, Rémy Cordonnier opened the magnificent library of Saint-Omer to me on short notice, and the Franciscan brother Alexis Mensah offered his time in a town obsessed with time. Father John of Flavigny took a break from his retreat in the Alps to share thoughts that guided me through the Italian part of the trail. Thanks to my son, Casey, and my daughter, Sophie, for joining me along parts of the Via Francigena, and challenging some of my comfortable conclusions on matters of the soul, while finding memorable places to end a long day. My wife, Joni Balter, was a hill-charging companion at the end of the camino, and kept me from foolishness in the writing. We mourn the loss of her sister, Margie.

Every writer should have as good a vetting circle as I have. Combing through the manuscript were Vashon Island friends John McCoy and his wife, Karen Chesledon. John is a world-class editor, writer, and Roman Catholic bon vivant; Karen is a spiritual seeker more dutiful than I. Another couple, my friends Sam Howe Verhovek and his wife, Lisa, were honest, unsparing, and right in their remarks. The great ally of authors Steven Barclay was encouraging on the French part of the pilgrimage and gave wind to my sails afterward. If America were a better country, or had a better president, he would be ambassador to France now.

In New York, my friend Carol Mann put me together once again with perfect publishing partners, and read the draft as well. At Viking, my new home, thanks to Trent Duffy and Anna Jardine for extraordinary copyediting and fact-checking, to Carolyn Coleburn for getting this book out the door, and to Emily Neuberger for handling all the messy details. I'm deeply grateful to be working again with Andrea Schulz, who was flat-out brilliant with suggestions that this writer, by reflex, usually rejects. Thanks to all. If I'm lucky, you'll be called on again.

SOURCES

1. London Falling

Sigeric the Serious, brief history, from Confraternity of Pilgrims to Rome, www
.pilgrimstorome.org.uk.

Total number of Catholics as 1.3 billion, from Vatican, http://www.fides.org/en/news
/64944-VATICAN_CATHOLIC_CHURCH_STATISTICS_2018.

Pancras, www.catholic.org/saints, though they stress the biography is less than reliable.

Shakespeare quote, from *King Richard II*, Act II, Scene 1.

Loss of religion. The numbers are from the British Social Attitudes Survey, updated to
the most recent, http://www.bsa.natcen.ac.uk/latest-report/british-social-attitudes-28
/religion.aspx.

Loss of religion fallout, *The Spectator*, June 13, 2015.

Rise of the "Nones" in the United States, http://www.pewresearch.org/fact-tank/2018/04
/25/key-findings-about-americans-belief-in-god.

Number of churches closed since 1980, *The Economist*, https://www.economist.com
/news/britain/21704836-britain-unusually-irreligious-and-becoming-more-so
-calls-national-debate.

Worldwide religious growth: http://www.pewforum.org/2012/12/18/global-religious
-landscape-exec.

Church of England criticism, from the bishop of Buckingham's blog, http://bishopalan
.blogspot.com/2012/03/time-for-reboot-not-bailout.html.

Half of American Catholics lapsed, from Pew survey, as reported in a story at https://www
.smithsonianmag.com/smart-news/half-american-catholics-have-lapsed-180956662/.

Quote by Saint Augustine, from *Confessions*, Penguin Books, 1961.

200 million pilgrims a year, from information about the PBS series *Sacred Journeys with
Bruce Feiler*, https://www.pbs.org/wgbh/sacredjourneys/content/about/.

Reasons to walk the V.F., https://www.viefrancigene.org/en/resource/news/chi-si-mette
-cammino-sulla-francigena-analisi-e-ri.

2. *A Canterbury Tale*

Cathedral details from a tour by author, and from website, www.canterbury
-cathedral.org.

Story of the killing, from *Saint Thomas Becket*, by Christopher Harper-Bill, Scala
Publishing, the official version sold at Canterbury Cathedral, no publication date.

Becket's place, from *A History of Christianity*, by Paul Johnson, Atheneum, 1976.

"What is the point," from *Daily Mail*, October 12, 2017.

Archbishop's power and monarch, from *New York Times*, January 15, 2018.

Welby childhood, early atheism, from a profile of him in *The Telegraph*, July 12, 2013.

Death of Welby child, from *The Telegraph*, December 21, 2014.

Welby's depression, from *Christianity Today*, October 12, 2017.

Britain names minister for loneliness, from *New York Times*, January 17, 2018.

Welby's Jewish background, from *The Times of Israel*, June 18, 2013.

Expulsion of Jews, from *The Murder of William of Norwich*, by E. M. Rose, Oxford
University Press, 2016.

Welby on power of narrative, from Anglican News Service, http://www.anglicannews.org
/news/2016/04/archbishop-justin-welbys-sermon-at-the-acc-16-opening-eucharist.aspx.

Welby on "understanding the world," from his website list of sermons, http://www
.archbishopofcanterbury.org.

Conversion of the British Isles and Saint Patrick, from *How the Irish Saved Civilization*,
by Thomas Cahill, Doubleday, 1995.

History of Augustine's landing, from "St. Martin's Church: The Early History," a
pamphlet handed out by the church.

More on how the English converted, from Bede's eighth-century history, https://
sourcebooks.fordham.edu/halsall/basis/bede-book1.asp.

Quote, "How these Christians love . . . ," from Johnson, *A History of Christianity*.

Christ, ". . . good news," Luke 4:18.

Becket quote on clerical rule, from Johnson, *A History of Christianity*.

Queen Mary and Queen Elizabeth persecutions, from "Elizabeth I's War with English
Catholics," *BBC History Magazine*, May 2014.

Pope visits Canterbury, from BBC, http://news.bbc.co.uk/onthisday/hi/dates/stories/may/29/newsid_4171000/4171657.stm.

Return of Becket's elbow, from *The Guardian*, May 27, 2016.

Cult of relics, from *The Age of the Pilgrimage: The Medieval Journey to God*, by Jonathan Sumption, HiddenSprings/Paulist Press, 2003.

First sign, from the guidebook *Via Francigena: Pilgrim Trail Canterbury to Rome*, by Alison Raju, Cicerone, 2011. Note: Not always 100 percent reliable on the route-finding, as other pilgrims have testified as well.

Quote on Christian influence, from Johnson, *A History of Christianity*.

Women as majority of Anglican ministers, from *The Guardian*, April 16, 2012.

Revelation of Welby's parents, from *The Independent*, April 9, 2016.

Welby's mother's statement, issued April 7, 2016.

Welby's statement on revelation, issued April 8, 2016.

3. At the Cliff of the Kingdom

Christopher Hitchens, from *God Is Not Great: How Religion Poisons Everything*, Twelve/Grand Central Publishing, 2007.

Carlo Laurenzi, from author interviews with him, and from his blog, https://viafrancigena2017.wordpress.com/blog.

Pope quote on atheism, from CNN, February 23, 2017.

Pope quote, "it's this or nothing," from *America: The Jesuit Review*, June 9, 2016.

Atheists in Sweden, from Reuters, October 27, 2016.

Pope quote, "people of pilgrims," from *National Catholic Register*, October 24, 2016.

Abandoned church on trail to Dover, and Julia Peters, from author correspondence with Ms. Peters, who lives in Canterbury.

Medieval medicine, http://www.historylearningsite.co.uk/medieval-england/health-and-medicine-in-medieval-england.

Medieval diet, from author visit to Dover Castle.

Roland the Farter, from *1215: The Year of Magna Carta*, by Danny Danziger and John Gillingham, Touchstone, 2003.

"The English drink no water," quoted in *A World Lit Only by Fire*, by William Manchester, Back Bay, 1992.

Background on Pope Francis's first two years, from *The Francis Miracle: Inside the Transformation of the Pope and the Church*, by John L. Allen Jr., Time Books, 2015.

Pope on proselytizing, https://www.lifesitenews.com/news/pope-very-grave-sin-for-catholics-to-try-to-convert-orthodox.

Church history and heretics, from Johnson, *A History of Christianity*.

Pope Pius XII silent on Holocaust, ibid. More on Pius XII and Holocaust, from *Jerusalem Post*, March 27, 2010.

Pope Francis on mortality, Catholic News Service, https://www.catholicnews.com /services/englishnews/2017/pope-gives-youths-three-missions-before-synod-world -youth-day.cfm.

4. Besieged at Calais

The Jungle razed, from *New York Times*, October 25, 2016.

Sunni vs. Shiite fight over successor to Muhammad, *New York Times*, January 4, 2016.

Oscar Wilde pardoned, *The Irish Post*, February 2, 2017.

Quotes from Wilde, from *Oscar Wilde: The Unrepentant Years*, by Nicholas Frankel, Harvard University Press, 2016.

Economic despair in Calais, from *New York Times*, April 29, 2017.

"We don't want them," reported in *Sydney Morning Herald*, October 26, 2016.

Bernard of Clairvaux, from the Medieval Sourcebook: St. Bernard, a collection of public domain texts circulated by Fordham University, https://sourcebooks.fordham.edu /sbook.asp.

Bernard responsible for Second Crusade, from *The Decline and Fall of the Roman Empire*, by Edward Gibbon, published 1776 through 1789. I relied on the 1983 Penguin edition.

Saint Labre and Amettes, from author visit to town and his shrine, and from *LightFoot Companion to the Via Francigena—Canterbury to Rome*, by Babette Gallard, Pilgrimage Publications, 2014.

Ethelred the Unready, https://www.britroyals.com/kings.asp?id=ethelred2.

Sigeric and Ethelred, from *The Anglo-Saxon Age*, by Martin Wall, Amberley Publishing, 2015.

5. The Lost City of Saint-Omer

Information on monks and prayer at Saint-Omer, from author interview with Rémy Cordonnier, director of ancient collections, Bibliothèque de Saint-Omer.

Quote on humane Christians, from Johnson, *A History of Christianity*.

History of library, number of books, from Patrimoines de Saint-Omer, http://www .patrimoines-saint-omer.fr/uk/Les-ressources/Les-partenaires/La-bibliotheque- d-agglomeration-de-Saint-Omer.

Monasteries' growth throughout Europe, from Cahill, *How the Irish Saved Civilization*.

Victor Hugo quote on ruins, from *The Memoirs of Victor Hugo*, by Victor Hugo, Serenity Publishers, 2011.

How books were written in Middle Ages, from *Books Before Gutenberg*, a publication of the Harry Ransom Center, University of Texas at Austin, http://www.hrc.utexas.edu.

History of writing, from *Guns, Germs and Steel*, by Jared Diamond, Norton, 1997.

Limits on mental capacity, from Johnson, *A History of Christianity*.

Gutenberg history, from *New York Times*, January 27, 2001. And from Diamond, *Guns, Germs and Steel*. More Gutenberg, http://www.gutenberg-bible.com/history.html.

SOURCES

Finding the Shakespeare, from author interview with Mr. Cordonnier.

Number of Catholics in France, from the journal *LaCroix*, January 12, 2017, from a study commissioned by Bayard Presse.

Hitchens on miracles, from his book *God Is Not Great*.

Victor Hugo quote, from http://freethoughtalmanac.com/?tag=freethinker.

6. A Night at the Monastery

Reference to guidebook, Raju, *Via Francigena*.

Early Christians, from the Book of Acts.

Gospel admonition to austerity, from Matthew 19:21.

Ulfilas in Germany and Martin in Gaul, from "Jesus and the Origins of Christianity," a *National Geographic* special publication, reissued edition, December 2018.

Ulfilas and Martin, and conversion in fourth century, from "Ulfilas, Bishop of the Goths," *Encyclopædia Britannica*, https://www.britannica.com/biography/Ulfilas.

Benedictine order, life of Benedict, from *Encyclopædia Britannica*, https://www.britannica.com/biography/Saint-Benedict-of-Nursia.

Quote on fornicating monks, from Manchester, *A World Lit Only by Fire*.

History of monks, from Johnson, *A History of Christianity*.

Story of Skellig Michael and Viking conversion, from author visit to Skellig Michael, County Kerry, Ireland.

History of Abbey of Saint Paul, from Traditional Vocations Blog, September 11, 2015, http://tradvocations.blogspot.com/2015/09/abbaye-saint-paul-de-wisques.html.

Typical day at the monastery, from schedule posted at the abbey. Also, "A Day in the Life of a Monk," from https://www.quarrabbey.org/site.php?menuaccess=27.

Killing of Father Jacques Hamel, from *The Guardian*, July 26, 2016.

7. War and Peace on the Western Front

Treaty of London details, from "An Early Nonaggression Pact," by Garrett Mattingly, *Journal of Modern History*, March 1938.

"Great seminal catastrophe," George Kennan description, as quoted by Geoffrey Wheatcroft, *The Nation*, October 5, 2017.

Jefferson quote, from letter of Thomas Jefferson to John Adams, April 11, 1823.

Scottish casualties in Battle of Arras, from BBC, April 9, 2017.

Tuchman quote, from *The Guns of August*, by Barbara Tuchman, Ballantine, 1994.

War widows, from *The First World War*, by John Keegan, Vintage, 2000.

More World War I casualty figures, and details on prosthetics, from Museum of the Great War, Péronne, France, author visit.

Poem, "In Flanders Fields," by John McCrae.

8. The Miracles of Laon

Laon cable car, from a plaque on display at the foothill of the old lift.

Seven Wonders of Laon, from a handout at the Laon tourist office.

Saint Augustine on miracles, from *Confessions*.

Scientific examination of miracle cures at Lourdes, https://www.ncbi.nlm.nih.gov/pmc/articles/PMC3854941.

Number of miracles recorded in Bible, from *The Good News Bible*, American Bible Society, 1966, a "translation which seeks to state clearly and accurately the meaning of the original texts in words and forms that are widely accepted by people who use English."

Paul's conversion from Acts of the Apostles 9:3–17.

Paul a Pharisee, Acts 23:6, "I am a Pharisee, the son of Pharisees."

Paul approving of murder of Saint Stephen, Acts 8:1.

Paul's appearance, from Johnson, *A History of Christianity*.

Population of Christians and people in Roman Empire. There is no consensus among scholars on these numbers, but I relied on a well-documented recent book, *The Triumph of Christianity: How a Forbidden Religion Swept the World*, by Bart D. Ehrman, Simon & Schuster, 2018.

Conversion of Constantine, ibid.

Conversion of Clovis, from *A History of the Franks*, by Gregory of Tours, Penguin Classics, 1976.

Miracles requirements and sainthood, from website of American canon lawyer Cathy Caridi, http://canonlawmadeeasy.com/2013/07/18/how-many-miracles-are-required-to-canonize-a-saint/#forward.

Miracle mummies, from *The Incorruptibles: A Study of the Incorruption in the Bodies of Various Saints*, by Joan Carroll Cruz, Tan Books, 1997.

Michael O'Neill, Stanford graduate, on miracles, from his book *Exploring the Miraculous*, Our Sunday Visitor Publishing, 2015. And from his website, http://www.miraclehunter.com.

9. Sluts and Saints Along the Chemin des Dames

Joan of Arc in Corbény, from a plaque in the town.

Joan burned twice over after her death, from *The Independent*, October 11, 2012.

More Joan biography, from *Joan of Arc: A History*, by Helen Castor, HarperCollins, 2015.

Quote of officer on seeing Joan sleeping in the hay, from *Joan: The Mysterious Life of the Heretic Who Became a Saint*, by Donald Spoto, HarperSanFrancisco, 2007.

King Solomon's wives, from 1 Kings 11:3.

Jesus on sex, and the Old Testament on sex, from *Unprotected Texts: The Bible's Surprising Contradictions About Sex and Desire*, by Jennifer Wright Knust, HarperCollins, 2011.

Mary's life, possible siblings of Jesus, from *National Geographic*, November 8, 2015, cover story on the life of Mary.

Jesus's response, after woman praises his mother, from Luke 11:27.

Jesus had a brother, mentioned in Mark 6:3. Slightly different versions elsewhere, but Good News Bible contains this sentence: "Isn't he the carpenter, the son of Mary, and the brother of James . . . ," which is nearly identical to Matthew 13:55.

Jesus had a brother "virtually indisputable," from *Zealot: The Life and Times of Jesus of Nazareth*, by Reza Aslan, Random House, 2013.

Gnostic Gospels, discovery, meaning, and quotes from *The Gnostic Gospels*, by Elaine Pagels, Vintage, 1979.

Mary Magdalene, from *The Resurrection of Mary Magdalene*, by Jane Schaberg, Bloomsbury, 2004. Note that the Gospels are in conflict whether Mary was the first person to see the resurrected Christ or merely one of the first. John says she was the first, in John 20:11–18.

Gospel of Mary, from the Gnostic Society Library, http://gnosis.org/library/marygosp .htm. See also "Who Framed Mary Magdalene?," by Heidi Schlumpf, *U.S. Catholic*, April 2000.

Christ appearing to Mary Magdalene, and her thinking he was the gardener, from John 20:15.

Woman wins argument with Christ, Mark 7:24, and Matthew 15:21, and thanks to Nicholas Kristof for alerting me to this.

Paul on sex, from 1 Corinthians 7:1; on marriage, 7:8–9; on no direct command from God on his view, 7:25.

Charlemagne forbidding his daughters from marrying, from *La Belle France*, by Alistair Horne, Vintage, 2006.

Jerome, from Johnson, *A History of Christianity*.

Jerome's possible affair with Paula, which he denied in Epistle 45, https://epistolae.ctl .columbia.edu/woman/34.html.

Quote on Jerome's influence on Bible, from https://www.franciscanmedia.org /saint-jerome-the-bible-translator.

Lucretius, from *The Swerve: How the World Became Modern*, by Stephen Greenblatt, Norton, 2011.

Augustine, from his *Confessions*.

Augustine's influence, from "The Invention of Sex," by Stephen Greenblatt, *The New Yorker*, June 19, 2017.

Pope Gregory recasting Mary Magdalene, from Homily 33, http://magdalhnh.blogspot .com/2009/01/homily-33.html.

Early church appealing to women, from *The Rise of Christianity*, by Rodney Stark, HarperCollins, 1997.

Brigid, from Cahill, *How the Irish Saved Civilization*.

Brigid of Ireland praying for ugliness, from *Irish America*, February/March 2018.

Twain quote on Joan, from *Personal Recollections of Joan of Arc*, by Mark Twain, Harper and Brothers, 1896.

Joan biography, from *The Life of Joan of Arc*, vol. 1, by Anatole France, John Lane, 1908.

Joan's trial, from Spoto, *Joan*.

Joan judged by forty-two male clerics, from Horne, *La Belle France*.

Total number of priests and nuns, from http://www.fides.org/en/news/64944 -VATICAN_CATHOLIC_CHURCH_STATISTICS_2018.

Half of clerics had wives in the Middle Ages, from Johnson, *A History of Christianity*.

Martin Luther quote on masturbation, from Helen L. Owen, "When Did the Catholic Church Decide Priests Should Be Celibate?," History News Network, October 2001.

Pope Francis on priestly celibacy, as reported on CNN, February 23, 2017.

Pope on priests, men, and disciples, as reported on NPR, November 1, 2016.

10. When God Anointed Kings

William of Saint-Thierry, from *On the Nature and Dignity of Love*, Cistercian Publications, 1981.

Belloc, his book on the walk to Rome, *The Path to Rome*, by Hilaire Belloc, first published 1902. I relied on the 2015 Wallachia Publishers edition.

Europe a "heathen continent," from *Christianity Today*, April 18, 2016.

Clovis's place in French history, from Horne, *La Belle France*.

Number of Christians martyred by Rome, from Stark, *The Rise of Christianity*.

More Christian deaths from fellow Christians than Roman persecution, from Manchester, *A World Lit Only by Fire*.

Destruction by Christians of classical statues, temples, etc., from *The Darkening Age: The Christian Destruction of the Classical World*, by Catherine Nixey, Houghton Mifflin Harcourt, 2018.

Roma locuta est saying, from Johnson, *A History of Christianity*.

Total number of Christians, as percentage of Empire, from Stark, *The Rise of Christianity*.

Julian's complaint about corpses, as quoted in *Rome: A History in Seven Sackings*, by Matthew Kneale, Simon & Schuster, 2018.

Durant quote, from *The Story of Civilization*, vol. 3, by Will Durant, Simon & Schuster, 1944.

Conventional view of fall of Rome, from Gibbon, *The Decline and Fall of the Roman Empire*.

Story of Romulus Augustulus, in part, from *The Last Roman: Romulus Augustulus and the Decline of the West*, by Adrian Murdoch, Stroud, 2006.

Gibbon quote, from *The Decline and Fall of the Roman Empire*.

Prohibitions against the Jews, from Danziger and Gillingham, *1215*.

Jews killed in Spain and Portugal, from Manchester, *A World Lit Only by Fire*.

King's oath to "extirpate heretics," from *Citizens: A Chronicle of the French Revolution*, by Simon Schama, Vintage, 1990.

Inquisition in Spain, including quote from papal delegation, from Johnson, *A History of Christianity*.

Story of the Holy Ampulla, from *The Legend of the Ste. Ampoule*, by Sir Francis Oppenheimer, Faber & Faber, 1953.

Smiling Angel, from the official cathedral brochure. Additional information from *New York Times*, December 4, 2015.

11. The Highest Use of Monks

Moët & Chandon, from author visit and tour at winery in Épernay.

Churchill and champagne, from NPR, April 1, 2016, https://www.npr.org/sections/thesalt/2016/04/01/472459579/hitler-couldnt-defeat-churchill-but-champagne-nearly-did.

Bottles of champagne consumed by Churchill, https://www.telegraph.co.uk/food-and-drink/drinks/the-day-i-tried-to-match-churchill-drink-for-drink.

William of Newburgh quote, from Danziger and Gillingham, *1215*.

Hautvillers, from author visit to Dom Pérignon's tomb.

12. Napoleon Was Bullied Here

Pope on heaven being boring, from *National Catholic Register*, April 27, 2018.

Pope Francis, "Allow yourself to be amazed," as reported in *Crux*, October 15, 2017.

Châlons-en-Champagne observations, including information on the Via Agrippa, from author visit.

Roman roads quote, from Manchester, *A World Lit Only by Fire*.

Napoleon's life at the military school of Brienne-le-Château, from a brochure at the Museum of Napoleon in Brienne, author visit.

Napoleon early years, family, from *Napoleon: A Life*, by Andrew Roberts, Penguin, 2014.

Napoleon resistance to teachers, from *In the Footsteps of Napoleon*, by James Morgan, Macmillan, 1915.

Napoleon's mother, from Shannon Salin, author and historian of Napoleon's family, from her website, https://shannonselin.com/2014/03/napoleons-mother-letizia-bonaparte.

Joan Egan's story of miscarriage, bishop, and hysterectomy, from recorded interviews with her in 2014.

Napoleon's term for Holy Roman Empire, from Roberts, *Napoleon*.

Napoleon quote on how Brienne shaped him, and the million francs left to the town in his will, from Museum of Napoleon.

13. Wars of Religion

Scenes in Wassy, from author visit.

Descriptions of the massacre, from an account posted outside the Musée Protestant de la Grange de Wassy.

Crusades, Pope Urban, and Saint Bernard, from Sumption, *The Age of the Pilgrimage*.

Number killed in Crusades, including massacres of Jews, from *Washington Post* fact-check, February 16, 2015.

Bernard's apology, from "Apologia for the Second Crusade," courtesy Fordham University, Medieval Sourcebook, https://sourcebooks.fordham.edu/source/bernard-apol.asp.

Erasmus, from Johnson, *A History of Christianity*.

More on Erasmus's philosophy and Martin Luther, from *Fatal Discord: Erasmus, Luther, and the Fight for the Western Mind*, by Michael Massing, HarperCollins, 2018.

Killing of first Protestant heretic, from *Heresy and Orthodoxy in Sixteenth-Century Paris: François Le Picart and the Beginnings of the Catholic Reformation*, by Larissa Juliet Taylor, Brill, 1999.

Huguenots' suffering, from *The Huguenots: A Biography of a Minority*, by George A. Rothrock, Rowman and Littlefield, 1979.

Saint Bartholomew's Day Massacre, and details of other Wars of Religion, from the Virtual Museum of Protestantism, https://www.museeprotestant.org/en.

"Kill them all," from Horne, *La Belle France*.

Wars of Religion details, from *The French Religion Wars—1562–98*, by Robert J. Knecht, Osprey Publishing, 2002.

Total number killed, 15 percent of France, from Knecht, *The French Religion Wars*.

Casualties compared with American Civil War, https://www.battlefields.org/learn/articles/civil-war-facts.

Casualties during the Thirty Years War, from "What Happened in the Thirty Years War?," by P.C., *The Economist*, January 17, 2016.

Casualties compared with Napoleonic Wars, from *The Napoleonic Wars, 1803–1815*, by David Gates, Pimlico, 2003.

Casualties compared with World War I, from Massing, *Fatal Discord*.

Church issues apology, from "Pope Says Sorry for Sins of Church," by Rory Carroll, *The Guardian*, March 13, 2000.

14. Wanderings

Where to stay, from tourist office in Brienne-le-Château, and *mairie* of Châteauvillain.

Clairvaux Abbey, from fact sheet given by tour guide. Additional information from "Clairvaux Abbey, France: Tales of the Unexpected," by Kathy Arnold, *The Telegraph*, March 8, 2014.

Dovecotes, from "Pigeon Towers: The Rise and Fall of a 17th-Century Status Symbol," *Atlas Obscura*, April 17, 2015, https://www.atlasobscura.com/articles/dovecotes.

15. The Hollowed House of Light

Diderot's life, from *Diderot: A Critical Biography*, by P. N. Furbank, Knopf, 1992.

Additional Diderot bio, from *The Embattled Philosopher*, by Lester G. Crocker, Michigan State College Press, 1954.

Diderot details in Langres, from author visit.

Diderot quote on banishing God, from his book *Philosophical Thoughts*, first published in 1746. I relied on a Kindle edition, translated by Kirk Watson.

Diderot inventions, books, the *Encyclopédie*, from author visit to the Maison des Lumières in Langres.

American founding fathers as deists, http://nationalhumanitiescenter.org/tserve/eighteen/ekeyinfo/deism.htm.

Jefferson on clerics and witches, from *The God Delusion*, by Richard Dawkins, Mariner Books, 2008.

Other authors on Index of Prohibited Books, http://www.uscatholic.org/church/2010/08/does-church-still-ban-books.

Rights of Man, from The Declaration of the Rights of Man and of the Citizen.

French Revolution, Cult of Reason details, from *The Oxford History of the French Revolution*, by William Doyle, Clarendon Press, 1999.

French literacy rates higher than in modern United States, Schama, *Citizens*. And from http://www.nobility.org/2011/08/22/astonishing-adult-literacy-rates.

Pope Francis on science and truth, from *USA Today*, May 12, 2017.

Rousseau's falling-out with Diderot, change of heart on secularism, from *The New Yorker*, August 2, 2016.

Ayn Rand, as quoted in *New York Times*, July 14, 2017.

Diderot letter to his lover, as quoted in *The New Yorker*, March 4, 2019.

Religion of Humanity, from *New York Times Magazine*, January 1, 2017.

16. United Europe's Ticking Clock

Besançon, town details, from author visit and interview at tourism office.

Watches and time, influence on other watchmakers, from *New York Times*, January 15, 2018.

Details on Besançon's relationship to time, from author visit to Musée du Temps, Besançon.

Hugo biographical details, from *Victor Hugo: A Biography*, by Graham Robb, Norton, 1998.

Hugo speech on future of Europe, https://www.ellopos.net/politics/hugo-addresses-europe.asp.

European Union teetering, in part from *New York Times*, March 25, 2017.

Richard Dawkins comment, from *The Independent*, July 18, 2018.

Pope quote "vacuum of values," from *The Independent*, March 24, 2017.

Franciscans, from author interview by email with Brother Alexis Mensah.

"Who of you by worrying . . . ," from Luke 12:25.

17. The Betrayal

Personal recollections of the parish and Father Patrick G. O'Donnell, from interviews with my brother, mother, and other family members.

Suicide story of brother's best friend, from "Sins of the Father," *Inlander*, January 22, 2004. More details of suicide and aftermath, from *National Catholic Register*, November 10, 2006.

Rita Flynn details, from her obituary, *Spokesman Review*, September 17, 2011, http://www.legacy.com/obituaries/spokesman/obituary.aspx?page=lifestory&pid=153661024.

O'Donnell apologizes, admits number of victims, from *Spokesman Review*, November 13, 2008, http://www.spokesman.com/stories/2008/nov/13/former-priest-settles-lawsuit.

YouTube video of O'Donnell admitting to past abuse, and apologizing, at https://www.youtube.com/watch?v=a1l4IjLWHo4.

Story of Spokane archdiocese, http://www.natcath.org/NCR_Online/archives2/2006d/111006/111006a.php.

Papal apology, from *New York Times*, June 10, 2015, https://www.nytimes.com/2015/06/11/world/europe/papal-responses-to-sexual-abuse-in-the-church.html.

18. Refuge and Reform

Certificate of an indulgence on display at the International Museum of the Reformation, Geneva, Switzerland, author visit.

Metal lockbox with slogan, from NPR, October 20, 2016.

Details on types of indulgences, birth of the Reformation, from author interview with Gabriel de Montmollin, director of the International Museum of the Reformation.

Luther and church response to his 95 theses, from *Martin Luther: The Man Who Rediscovered God and Changed the World*, by Eric Metaxas, Viking, 2018.

Additional Luther, from *Martin Luther: A Life*, by Martin E. Marty, Penguin, 2004.

Settlers through the years at Lausanne, from Gallard, *LightFoot Companion to the Via Francigena*.

Hidden Bibles, Bible print run, from the International Museum of the Reformation.

Gutenberg got his start selling mirrors, https://www.themorgan.org/collections/works/gutenberg/who-was-gutenberg.

Luther wrote a third of all books in German, from *The New Yorker*, October 30, 2017.

Attacking the pope, from Metaxas, *Martin Luther*.

Luther's marriage, kids, home, ibid.

Number of Lutherans worldwide, from global Lutheran headquarters, https://www.lutheranworld.org/sites/default/files/LWI-Statistics-2013-EN.pdf.

Luther quote on peasants, from his pamphlet "Against the Murdering and Thieving Hordes of Peasants," as quoted in Metaxas, *Martin Luther.*

Anti-Semitic remarks, from Luther's pamphlet "On the Jews and Their Lies," Liberty Bell Publications, 2004.

More anti-Semitic words, summarized here, https://www.jewishvirtuallibrary.org /martin-luther-quot-the-jews-and-their-lies-quot.

Nazis blame Luther, a reference to testimony of Julius Streicher at Nuremberg trials, from *The New Yorker*, October 30, 2017.

Pope praises Reformation, from *The Economist*, November 2, 2016.

Pope quote on good of Reformation, *New York Times*, October 31, 2016.

19. A Theocracy on the Lake

City of Refuge, a bas-relief sculpture in the city.

Servetus, from *Hunted Heretic: The Life and Death of Michael Servetus*, by Roland H. Bainton, Blackstone Editions, 2003.

Four of the most expensive cities in the world in Switzerland, https://www.eca-international .com/news/june-2015/hong-kong-now-more-expensive-than-tokyo-for-expatr.

Jeremy England's theory of origin of life, https://www.salon.com/2015/01/03/god_is_on _the_ropes_the_brilliant_new_science_that_has_creationists_and_the_christian _right_terrified.

Religious police in Geneva, and torture of dissidents, from Manchester, *A World Lit Only by Fire.*

Calvin quote, "sure truth," ibid.

Number of executions in Calvin's Geneva, from *Reformations: The Early Modern World, 1450–1650*, by Carlos M. N. Eire, Yale University Press, 2018.

Calvin and suicidal man, from a sworn statement by Calvin, dated January 23, 1545, in the archives at the International Museum of the Reformation.

Servetus's heretical theology while on the run, from *On the Errors of the Trinity*, by Michael Servetus, Harvard University Press, 1932.

Calvin early life, from *Calvin*, by Bruce Gordon, Yale University Press, 2009.

Calvin in Geneva, from *Calvin's Geneva*, by E. William Monter, John Wiley & Sons, 1967.

Calvin on threat to Servetus, from Bainton, *Hunted Heretic.*

Calvin quote on Servetus, from *Letters of John Calvin*, edited by Jules Bonnet, 2009, first published in 1923.

Description of the burning at the stake, from *Out of the Flames*, by Lawrence Goldstone and Nancy Goldstone, Crown, 2008.

Bainton quote on "singular distinction," from Bainton, *Hunted Heretic.*

Religious affiliation in modern Switzerland, from Swiss Federal Statistical Office, https://www.bfs.admin.ch/bfs/en/home/search.html#religious%20affiliation.

20. The Permanent Prayer of Saint-Maurice

Size and peculiarities of the Lausanne Cathedral, from author interview with Anna Decoro, church docent, and from https://www.lausanne-tourisme.ch/en/Z5081.

Cathedral largest in Switzerland, https://www.myswitzerland.com/en-us/cathedrale-de-notre-dame-cathedral-of-our-lady-lausanne.html.

Napoleon logistics, from Roberts, *Napoleon*.

Napoleon's two tons of cheese, from Gallard, *LightFoot Companion to the Via Francigena*.

Abbey of Saint-Maurice details, from a guide at the site, a brochure on the history, and its website, http://www.abbaye-stmaurice.ch/page.php?label=home-en#content.

Sigismund, from author interview with guide at Saint-Maurice.

Sigismund as a saint, from https://saintsandblesseds.wordpress.com/2009/05/06/st-sigismund-of-burgundy.

Biography of Saint Maurice, in part, from *National Catholic Reporter*, https://www.ncronline.org/blogs/ncr-today/black-saints-maurice.

More on Maurice, from "Who Was the First Black Saint?," by Henry Louis Gates Jr., from *The Root*, https://www.theroot.com/who-was-the-first-black-saint-1790893913.

More Catholics in Africa than Europe within twenty years, from *The New Republic*, February 13, 2013.

Town, churches named for Maurice, and his lasting influence, from *The Continuing Witness of St. Maurice*, by William B. Sweetser Jr., from research done for a dissertation and reprinted here: http://fatherdavidbirdosb.blogspot.com/2015/09/father-nicolas-buttet-catholic-founder.html.

Nicolas Buttet, from http://fatherdavidbirdosb.blogspot.com/2015/09/father-nicolas-buttet-catholic-founder.html.

Guidebook quote on "the worst section," from Raju, *Via Francigena*.

21. A Pilgrim over the Alps

Heat wave, in part from *New York Times*, August 6, 2017.

Napoleon on a mule, from https://www.napoleon.org, history website of the Fondation Napoléon.

Napoleon on avalanches, as quoted in Roberts, *Napoleon*.

Napoleon's bill at Bourg-Saint-Pierre, from Gallard, *LightFoot Companion to the Via Francigena*.

Story of Gonzaga, https://www.franciscanmedia.org/saint-aloysius-gonzaga.

22. Monastery in the Sky

Napoleon greeted at Saint Bernard, from Fondation Napoléon, https://www.napoleon.org.

Background on Saint Bernard dogs, from the museum at Great Saint Bernard Pass.

Saint Bernard's story, from "St. Bernard of Menthon," *The Catholic Encyclopedia*, first published 1907, and also from the museum.

Pope Francis sees a shrink, from Associated Press, "Pope Saw Female, Jewish Psychoanalyst Weekly at 42 to 'Clarify Some Things,'" September 1, 2017, https://talkingpointsmemo.com/world-news/pope-francis-psychoanalyst-weekly-sessions.

Father John of Flavigny, from author interview with him at Great Saint Bernard Hospice.

The Ignatian Method, further explained in *The Jesuit* Ratio Studiorum: *400th Anniversary Perspectives*, edited by Vincent J. Duminuco, Fordham University Press, 2000.

23. Mountain Myths

Oscar Wilde poem, "Sonnet on Approaching Italy," 1881, from Bartleby.com, and thanks to Gallard, *LightFoot Companion to the Via Francigena*, for flagging this.

Wilde in Rome, from Frankel, *Oscar Wilde*.

Quotes from Wilde in Rome from "Purple Hours: Oscar Wilde in Rome," from www .padraigrooney.com.

Vatican embraces Wilde, from *The Independent*, July 16, 2009.

Church position on gays, from *Catechism of the Catholic Church*, 2357–2359.

Letter on gays, from the Congregation for the Doctrine of the Faith, October 1, 1986.

Pope tells gay man God loves you, from *New York Times*, May 21, 2018, https://www .nytimes.com/2018/05/21/world/europe/pope-francis-gays-god-made-you-this -way-.html.

Alps and sanatoriums and playgrounds, Mont Blanc first scaled, from *The Economist*, January 27, 2018.

Brief history of the House of Savoy, from *Encyclopædia Britannica*, https://www .britannica.com/topic/House-of-Savoy.

Saint Grat's story, as told in several church depictions in Val d'Aosta.

Myth and the Cognitive Revolution, from *Sapiens: A Brief History of Humankind*, by Yuval Noah Harari, Harper Perennial, 2015.

Joseph Campbell on myth, from *Bill Moyers on Faith and Reason*, PBS series, http://www .pbs.org/moyers/faithandreason/perspectives1.html.

Aosta arch, and details of the town, from author visit, and information from Aosta tourist information office.

Story of Augustus, from *The First Emperor: Caesar Augustus and the Triumph of Rome*, by Anthony Everitt, Random House, 2006.

Pantheon transition, from http://romeonsegway.com/10-facts-about-the -pantheon.

24. Proving the Existence of God

Anselmo's biography, from *Encyclopædia Britannica*, https://www.britannica.com
/biography/Saint-Anselm-of-Canterbury.

Anselmo's argument, from Fordham University, "Anselm on God's Existence," https://
sourcebooks.fordham.edu/source/anselm.asp.

Anselmo quote on existence of God, from *Proslogion*, as presented ibid.

Thomas Aquinas, proof, from his *Summa Theologica*, written 1265–1274, as summarized
by Fordham University, https://sourcebooks.fordham.edu/source/aquinas3.asp.

Stephen Hawking quotes, from his *Brief Answers to the Big Questions*, Bantam, 2018.

Napoleon in Italy, theological debate, from Roberts, *Napoleon*.

"Pascal's Wager," from *Pascal's Pensées*, E. P. Dutton, 1958; the *Pensées* were first
published in 1620.

Essence of Anselmo's argument, more bio, from Stanford Encyclopedia of Philosophy,
https://plato.stanford.edu/entries/anselm.

Pope and "powerful magic wand," from NPR, September 22, 2015.

25. A Farewell to Augustine

Roman legionnaires, twenty-two miles a day, from *The Fall of the Roman Empire:
A New History of Rome and the Barbarians*, by Peter Heather, Oxford University
Press, 2007.

Battle of the Oranges, brochure from tourist information office in Ivrea, and https://
www.atlasobscura.com/places/battle-of-the-oranges.

Augustine early life, from his *Confessions*.

Augustine on choice and origin of evil, from "On Free Will," Cambridge Texts on the
History of Philosophy, 2010.

Comparative discussion on free will and predestination, thanks to the paper "Augustine:
Advocate of Free Will, Defender of Predestination," by Brandon Peterson, http://sites
.nd.edu/ujournal/files/2014/07/Peterson_05-06.pdf.

Augustine on God's test, from *Confessions*.

Italy's record low birthrate, from Reuters, March 6, 2017, https://www.reuters.com
/article/us-italy-birthrate/births-in-italy-hit-record-low-in-2016-population-ages
-idUSKBN16D28U.

26. A Series of Unfortunate Events in a Small Car

Brief history of Piacenza, from tourist information office.

More than thirty hostels, from Raju, *Via Francigena*.

Fascist attitude toward slippers, from Kneale, *Rome: A History in Seven Sackings*.

Story of Eataly, from its homepage, https://www.eataly.com/us_en/magazine/eataly
-stories/story-of-eataly.

Pope Francis on pilgrims, from June 9, 2015, Tektron Ministries, https://www
.tektonministries.org/catholic-pope-francis-pilgrimage-is-a-symbol-of-life.

Francis letter to bishops on sex abuse, December 28, 2016, https://w2.vatican.va/content
/francesco/en/letters/2016/documents/papa-francesco_20161228_santi-innocenti.html.

Pope on abuse, from *The Guardian*, August 17, 2017, https://www.theguardian.com
/world/2017/aug/17/pope-francis-sexual-abuse-priests-absolute-monstrosity-terrible-sin.

Daniel Pittet forgives abuser, https://www.catholicnewsagency.com/news
/pope-lauds-courageous-witness-of-abuse-victim-who-chose-to-forgive-80070.

Story of Fidenza's statuary, from author tour of the church.

Half the pilgrims of the year 1300 robbed or killed, from Sumption, *The Age of the
Pilgrimage.*

Robbers in the Apennines, forest cut to protect them, from Raju,
Via Francigena.

27. The Way out of a Labyrinth

Background on ancient Etruscan statues, from author visit to the Pontremoli Museum of
the Stele Statues.

Frederick II, from *Frederick II: A Medieval Emperor,* by David Abulafia, Oxford
Paperbacks, 1992.

More Frederick, from Fordham University Medieval Sourcebook, https://sourcebooks
.fordham.edu/source/salimbene1.asp.

History of testaroli, from *Rustico: Regional Italian Country Cooking*, by Micol Negrin,
Clarkson Potter, 2002.

New interest in testaroli, *Wall Street Journal*, March 5, 2006.

Story of the Abbey of San Caprasio, from a plaque on the wall in the abbey.

Carrara marble and Michelangelo, from author visit to the Civic Museum of Marble in
Carrara. Quote from there as well.

The *Pietà*'s origin, quote from Michelangelo, from *The Atlantic*, August 3, 2017.

The *Pietà* as only signed piece by Michelangelo, from http://www.italianrenaissance.org
/michelangelos-pieta.

Quote on wandering Irish, from Sumption, *The Age of Pilgrimage.*

Greek mythology and the labyrinth, from "Labyrinth from the Cathedral of San
Martino in Lucca, Italy," Loyola University of Chicago, Medieval Studies, https://
www.luc.edu/medieval/labyrinths/lucca.shtml.

Further explanation of the labyrinth, from "The Mystery of the Great Labyrinth,"
by John James, *Studies in Comparative Religion* 11, no. 2 (Spring 1977).

28. In the Path of the Little Poor Man

History of the Convent of San Francisco, from author visit and interview.

The basic outline of the story of Francis, from www.catholic.org/saints.

Franciscans leave San Miniato, from "Few Friars, the Franciscans Leave the Convent," December 7, 2015, from "Our News," https://www.cuoio.it.

Number of priests since 1970, from *New York Times*, September 26, 2018.

Young life of Francis from *The New Yorker*, January 14, 2013, https://www.newyorker.com/magazine/2013/01/14/rich-man-poor-man.

Francis on kissing a leper, from his words, collected in *The Writings of St. Francis of Assisi*, Franciscan Publications, 2011.

Francis's trip to Egypt, from *The Saint and the Sultan*, by Paul Moses, Doubleday Religion, 2009.

Clare of Assisi, from Catholic Encyclopedia Online, http://www.newadvent.org/cathen/04004a.htm.

The stigmata, from "The Mystery of the Five Wounds," https://www.smithsonianmag.com/history/the-mystery-of-the-five-wounds-361799.

More stigmata, from author visit to the Franciscan sanctuary at La Verna. See also preceding note.

Tolstoy's gospel, from *The Gospel in Brief*, by Leo Tolstoy, Dover Publications, 2008, first published in 1893.

29. Allegories on the Wall

Number of towers still standing, from history of San Gimignano, at http://www.sangimignano.com/en/art-and-culture/town-history.asp.

Black Death and other historical information about San Gimignano, ibid.

Last judgment, from Matthew 25:31–46.

Pope's response to child on atheist dad, from *Parenting*, April 17, 2018.

Pope on the poor, as reported by the Catholic News Agency, November 19, 2017.

Saint Fina, from a brochure inside the Collegiata in San Gimignano, next to her relics, telling her story.

Siena nearly as old as Rome, from http://www.aboutsiena.com/history-of-Siena.html.

Explanation of *The Allegory of Good Government and Bad*, from description inside the Palazzo Pubblico in Siena, and from "Art in Tuscany," http://www.travelingintuscany.com/art/ambrogiolorenzetti/goodandbadovernment.htm.

Siena after the Black Death, from "The Lasting Consequences of Plague in Siena," by Ryan S. Davis, http://www.montana.edu/historybug/yersiniaessays/davis.html.

Catherine of Siena and Avignon's papacy, from Johnson, *A History of Christianity*, and from *National Catholic Register*, April 27, 2013.

Palio details, from *New York Times*, April 22, 2018, and from author witness of the race.

Bank of Monte dei Paschi, history, from *The Guardian*, December 22, 2016, https://www.theguardian.com/business/2016/dec/22/monte-dei-paschi-the-history-of-the-worlds-oldest-bank.

Bank collapses, from *New York Times*, June 1, 2017, https://www.nytimes.com/2017/06/01/business/dealbook/italy-bank-mps-debt.html.

Fra Angelico's San Marco frescoes, from "Art in Tuscany," http://www.travelingintuscany.com/art/fraangelico/conventodisanmarco.htm.

Quotes from Savonarola and details of his reign of terror, from *Death in Florence: The Medici, Savonarola and the Battle for the Soul of a Renaissance City*, by Paul Strathern, Pegasus, 2015.

Quote "We are very few," from *New York Times*, September 26, 2018.

D. H. Lawrence quote on the piazza, from *Italian Days*, by Barbara Grizzuti Harrison, Ticknor & Fields, 1989.

30. The Miracle of Montefiascone

Buonconvento, from author visit to the town.

Story of Saint Christina, from visit to her shrine in Bolsena and in part from https://www.catholic.org/saints/saint.php?saint_id=148.

Cathedral in Montefiascone third-largest dome in Italy, from Raju, *Via Francigena*.

Story of Saint Lucia Filippini, from *National Catholic Weekly*, March 22, 2016.

Background on incorruptibles, from *Christian Mummification*, by Ken Jeremiah, McFarland & Co., 2012.

Est! Est!! Est!!! I heard the story in Montefiascone, but for scholarly backup relied on "Tales of the Vine," from https://bubblyprofessor.com/2011/01/20/est-est-est.

31. The Women Who Live Forever

More than three hundred preserved bodies in Italy, from Jeremiah, *Christian Mummification*.

Roman Goddess of Abundance, from author visit to Museo del Colle del Duomo, Viterbo.

Popes and Viterbo, from http://www.etruscanlife.com/en/art-history/perche-viterbo-viene-chiamata-citta-dei-papi.

The heart of Saint Rose, from Associated Press, June 10, 2010, http://www.foxnews.com/world/2010/06/10/experts-examine-mummy-th-century-saint-say-died-heart-defect.html.

The seven chapels on the island of Lake Bolsena, from Gallard, *LightFoot Companion to the Via Francigena*.

Pope at Auschwitz, from *Jerusalem Post*, February 12, 2017.

Death of Italy's olive trees, from *National Geographic*, August 10, 2018, https://www.nationalgeographic.com/science/2018/08/italy-olive-trees-dying-xylella.

Trees and feelings, from *The Secret Life of Trees*, by Peter Wohlleben, Greystone Books, 2016.

32. Companions of the Camino

Story of Sutri and the Etruscans, from author visit to Sutri archaeological park, including catacombs and amphitheater, and from visit to Santa Maria del Parto.

Etruscan life, from *The Etruscans*, by Graeme Barker and Tom Rasmussen, Blackwell, 1998.

Ignatius in La Storta, from author visit to Piazza della Visione, and from Faber Centre of Ignatian Spirituality, https://www.faberspirituality.org.au/vision-at-la-storta.

Carlo Laurenzi, author interview in La Storta, and follow-up interview in Seattle.

Dome of St. Peter's Basilica, Michelangelo's role, http://www.vaticanstate.va/content /vaticanstate/en/monumenti/basilica-di-s-pietro/cupola.html.

33. Pilgrim's Progress

Heads of Saints Peter and Paul, Saint John Lateran, http://www.sacred-destinations .com/italy/rome-san-giovanni-laterano. Saint John Lateran website doesn't acknowledge the heads of Peter and Paul, http://www.vatican.va/various/basiliche/san _giovanni/index_it.htm.

Shameful history of Lateran Treaty, from *The Pope and Mussolini: The Secret History of Pius XI and the Rise of Fascism in Europe*, by David I. Kertzer, Random House, 2014.

Most popular religion worldwide at start of twentieth century, as percentage of global population, http://christianityinview.com/religion-statistics.html.

Saint Paul's remains, from official Vatican City website, http://www.vatican.va/various /basiliche/san_paolo/en/basilica/tomba.htm.

Life and death of Nero, https://www.livescience.com/40277-emperor-nero -facts.html.

Holy Prepuce, from *Slate*, December 19, 2006, http://www.slate.com/articles/life /faithbased/2006/12/fore_shame.html. More on foreskin, from National Geographic documentary *The Quest of the Holy Foreskin*, 2103.

Bruno biography, beliefs, and death, from *Giordano Bruno: Philosopher/Heretic*, by Ingrid Rowland, University of Chicago Press, 2009.

Additional Bruno from *The New Yorker*, August 25, 2008.

Hitchens quote, from his *God Is Not Great*.

Vatican recants on Galileo, from *New York Times*, October 31, 1992.

Pope John Paul II acknowledges errors, https://w2.vatican.va/content/john-paul-ii/en /homilies/2000/documents/hf_jp-ii_hom_20000312_pardon.html.

Life of Hadrian, from *Historia Augusta*, published online in Loeb Classical Library, http://penelope.uchicago.edu/Thayer/E/home.html.

Quote from Hadrian's poem, as translated and presented by the museum that runs Castel Sant'Angelo, though there are other translations that differ slightly.

Jesuits and Ignatius, from author visit to home of Ignatius in the church of the Gesù, Rome.

Ignatius's life and teachings, from *Spiritual Exercises of Ignatius of Loyola*, originally published in 1548. I relied on the Loyola Press version, 1992.

Etruscans, from author visit; additional information from museum website, http://www.villagiulia.beniculturali.it.

Size of the Vatican, from official Vatican City website, http://www.vaticanstate.va/content/vaticanstate/en.html.

INDEX

Page numbers in italics refer to illustrations.